Kim Dickson
403-945-0623

For Shane—
Love. Love. Love.

R.I.P. Max
January 15, 2001—June 3, 2009

She's just fourteen
Little movie star queen
There isn't much
She hasn't seen
She's ridden in limousine cars
Dated pop stars with rainbow hair
She says that's nowhere
She always says
I'm just a sexy trashcan
But she's just a little girl
Who thinks like a man
Sometimes her daddy spoiled her
Sometimes he treated her rough
Sometimes she's gentle
Sometimes that chick she's tough

But she's always too nice to the driver
She says, James have you had your supper?
She's always too high on arrival
She runs on her high platform heels
She falls flat on her face
She knows how life feels
And she's just fourteen

—From "She's Just 14" by John Phillips

INTRODUCTION

PHILLIPS, LAURA MACKENZIE

In the mideighties, when I was on tour with the New Mamas & the Papas, a porter brought two packages up to my hotel room. One contained a book, my father's newly published memoir, but I was more interested in the other package—a flat FedEx letter containing an eighth of an ounce of cocaine.

The band, a reconstituted version of the Mamas & the Papas, included my father, Denny Doherty, Spanky McFarlane, and me. We were on an extended tour, performing in city after city for more than 250 days of the year. In each city, a FedEx like the one I was holding awaited me, and I spent all day every day in my hotel room, shooting up coke, coming out only to appear onstage for the nightly gig. Then I'd return to my hotel and do more coke. I was twenty-six years old.

I put Dad's book aside, opened the FedEx, and prepared a shot. Using a scarf, I tied off my arm. As I looked for a vein, I felt the familiar rush that accompanied the ritual itself. I knew what was coming. I pushed the needle in. As the coke entered my bloodstream I felt a euphoric onrush of sensation. I was back where I wanted to be.

Only then did I pick up my father's book. *Papa John: A Music Legend's Shattering Journey Through Sex, Drugs, and Rock 'n' Roll* was a brick of a book with the title faux spray-painted on the jacket in neon colors. I turned it over in my hands to look at the photo of my father on the back. He was clean-shaven and smiling a newscaster smile, the sanitized, post-rehab version of my father. He didn't look remotely like his hipster self.

Then I flipped to the index and looked to see if I was in it. There I was: "Phillips, Laura Mackenzie." Under my name was a list of subheadings and page numbers. I scanned down the entries:

Phillips, Laura Mackenzie
acting career of . . .
arrested on drug charges . . .
attempts to clean out . . .
in California . . .
childhood of . . .
drug use by . . .
early childhood of . . .
at finishing school in Switzerland . . .
Jeff Sessler and . . .
marriage to Jeff Sessler . . .
Peter Asher and . . .
rape . . .
shipboard romance on QE 2 *. . .*

There it was, my life to date, with highlights selected, cross-referenced, and alphabetized. I had been organized and reduced to a list of sensational and mostly regrettable and/or humiliating anecdotes. Being indexed, particularly under such dubious headings, gave me a weird feeling that definitely wasn't pride. I felt like I wasn't a real person, just a list of incidents and accidents. Whoever compiled that index—I'm pretty sure my father wasn't up to such a mundane and detailed task—was just doing his or her job, but it was cruelly reductive.

Decades passed before I thought about that index again. In 2008, now nearly fifty years old, I found myself in a police station in the San Fernando Valley in Los Angeles. I was sitting in a hallway on a bench. My hands were cuffed and the handcuffs were hooked to the bench. All the cops were staring at me: the middle-aged lady, the former child star, who had just been busted at the airport for heroin possession. A low, low moment.

How had I gotten myself here? Was this happening? The best and worst moments of my life have always felt surreal, as if the events were just another entry in that foreign index someone else created. But the cuffs cut into my hands with the cold rigidity of reality. I'd been addicted to drugs before, and I'd overcome my addiction. That was fifteen years ago, so many long, mostly happy, entirely drug-free years. I never thought I would relapse. I'd been clean for so long that I thought I was fixed. But if the addiction was a cancer that had been carefully excised, well, I'd missed a spot. It had grown back, all the more fierce and malignant. Here I was again. Back at the bottom, caught in the arms of a bad-news lover I thought I had dumped for good. I could envision the new entry in the index, typed in the same font. Chronologically, it belonged right below "happy working mother." It would say, "second arrest on drug charges," a one-line condemnation that only hinted at everything that had led me to that bench.

All my life I've been a person who starts things and can't finish them. As a junkie, as an actress and musician, as a mother—it's been hard for me to complete even the simplest cycles of action. Like using one tube of toothpaste from beginning to end before buying the next. I'd inevitably leave it in a hotel, or lose track of it for long enough that I'd have to open another tube, then rediscover the original—half the time, at best. Sitting on that bench, looking ahead, I knew that in some way I had to go back. I had to go back fifteen years, to all the work I'd done when I got sober, to the surgery that had sent me into remission for so long. I had to see what was left unfinished.

In a way, the surreal feeling is a shield. I have demons, haunted parts of my life and myself that are painful and scary. Facing them, revealing them, makes them too real. But I think about the index of my father's book, and how it reduced me to highlights and lowlights. I think about my mug shot in the tabloids. And I think of all that happened before, between, and after. The rest of the story. It is time to sort out a life that too often I left blurry, unprocessed, unreal, hoping that in doing so I would be leaving it behind me forever. It is time for me to return to that life, to face it, explain it, accept it, and let it rest as the insane, fun, ridiculous, terrifying, and true sequence that led a bright, goofy, famous little girl to a bleak jail bench, and I want to do it right, so that it is real and whole, and I in turn become real and whole.

I'm nearly twice as old as I was when my father's book came out, and though this is my story, not my father's, my relationship with him is undeniably central to my life. Dad was the great and terrible sun around which his children, wives, girlfriends, fellow musicians, and drug dealers orbited, relentlessly drawn to his fierce, inspiring, damaging light. The alternate solar system my dad drew me into had hilarious moments—like sliding down the banisters of my dad's Malibu mansion with Donovan—and portentous scenes, like when I tried cocaine for the first time at the age of eleven. There are happy memories of the stable work and family I found on *One Day at a Time*. There are loving and painful memories of the fucked-up family I wouldn't trade for the world. There are lost memories—conversations and chronologies I wish I could remember—and events I know my whole being wants to erase forever. There was a father-daughter relationship that crossed the boundaries of love to break many taboos, as my father was wont to do. My life was one of a kind—not everyone has a rock-star father, childhood stardom, and enough money and fame before the age of sixteen to last a lifetime. I have had more than my share of highs and lows. But all of it happened, it's real, and it's who I am.

PART ONE

LAURA PHILLIPS

1

Our condo: a perfectly nice place to live. My mother kept an orderly, clean house. She drove us to school every day and cooked dinner every night. She was a proper lady, the kind of woman who never wore white after Labor Day, crossed her legs at the ankle, and expected her children to be well mannered and respectful. We said please and thank you. We never let the screen door slam. We knew how to set a dinner table. My mother was sweet and warm, and she knew how to make life fun for my brother Jeffrey and me even if there wasn't much money. She'd buy a bunch of beads and we'd sit by the fire making necklaces. We'd cover the kitchen table with newspaper and have crab legs like we used to when we lived in Virginia. There was laughing, singing, dancing, and playing dress-up. At bedtime, she cuddled me, held me, called me Laurabelle, my little snowflake, my baby girl. These are the things that a mother does, and we expected them. Five days a week. But when Friday rolled around, everything changed.

Weekends, we entered another world. My dad, John Phillips, was a rock star, the leader and songwriter of the Mamas & the Papas. The Mamas & the Papas were huge in 1966. Their first album had just come out, and it was the number one album on the Billboard 200. Money poured in from hits like "Monday, Monday" and "California Dreamin'." Dad was fabulously rich and famous.

After school on Friday, a cavernous Fleetwood limo would glide down our street in Tarzana, a suburban neighborhood in

L.A.'s San Fernando Valley. The limo would roll to a stop in front of our condo complex. I was six years old and my brother was seven. The neighborhood children would make thrones out of their hands and carry us to the car. As we climbed in, the kids would peer in the windows, hoping to get a glimpse of our father. He was never in the car. The engine purred, and we slid out of reality. The limo would transport us to either Dad's mansion in Bel Air or his mansion in the Malibu Colony, where our relatively stable childhood veered down a psychopharma rabbit hole.

I was conceived during a short reconciliation between my parents. As a little girl I hardly lived with my father. My dad had ditched my mother for a sixteen-year-old girl named Michelle when I was two, maybe younger. In the next few years Mom began to work at the Pentagon to support the three of us—herself, my brother, and me. There wasn't a lot of money, we lived in a small apartment in Alexandria, Virginia, and my mom dated a lot. Every Sunday we had dinner, either at my grandmother Dini's or at my aunt Rosie's. Meanwhile, Dad and his new wife, Michelle Phillips, became famous with the Mamas & the Papas practically overnight and lived a recklessly extravagant life.

Dad and Michelle made their home in Los Angeles, and eventually my mother moved there too, so now my parents were living in the same city, but in different worlds. Dad and Michelle's life felt like a fairy tale. She was beautiful and so young, the quintessential California girl. Dad was almost six foot six and dressed in handmade floor-length caftans and the like. He looked . . . like Jesus in tie-dye. On weekends Michelle took me clothes shopping at Bambola in Beverly Hills. She bought me tiny kid gloves in all different colors, dresses with matching coats, ankle socks, and Mary Janes. This alone was enough to make a princess out of me, but the dichotomy between my parents' lives was far bigger than being spoiled with clothes by Michelle. As soon as we drove through the massive wrought-iron gate of Bel Air, the contrast was mind-boggling. We were special. We were royalty.

My father was always surrounded by a noisy, outrageous, wild party. Rock 'n' roll stars, aristocracy, and Hollywood trash streamed in and out of his homes. He lived beyond his means. There were eight Rolls-Royces in the driveway and two Ferraris. The house was full of priceless antiques, but if something broke, it never got fixed. The housekeeper hadn't been paid, or she was fucking my father. There was a cook, but nobody shopped for food. The house was complete chaos, a bizarre mix of excess and oblivion, luxury and incompetence. I swam naked at midnight in the pool or the ocean and scrounged for dinner. I chased the pet peacocks around the estate grounds and had no idea what I might hear or see on any given night.

At the house in Bel Air my brother and I shared a room with twin beds. One night we awoke to hear Dad and Michelle making some kind of ruckus. It surpassed the everyday level of ruckus, so we sat up in bed and started calling for them, "Hey! What's going on?"

Michelle came into the room. She said, "Don't worry, your father and I were just playing." She was carrying a long stick with metal stubs poking out of it. Jeffrey and I looked at each other. This was no innocent game of Monopoly. Years later I channel-surfed past a show about cowboys and recognized the weird stick Michelle had been holding that night. It was a cattle prod. They were chasing each other around with a cattle prod. That may have been an isolated bizarre incident. But life then seemed to be nothing but a long, continuous series of isolated bizarre incidents, so much weirdness every day that the weirdness became everyday.

The Mamas & the Papas played the Hollywood Bowl, a famous amphitheater smack in the middle of Hollywood. It was the Mamas & the Papas' first formal live gig. Michelle decided to commemorate the event by piercing my ears. I was seven years old, compliant—a perfect dress-up doll for Michelle. She sat me on the bedroom floor and gathered a sewing needle, pink thread, ice, and a wine cork. Holding the wine cork behind my ear to protect my neck, she forced the threaded needle through my ear, and then tied little peacock feathers (from the pet peacocks) to the ends of the pink threads. Michelle had assembled her tools so thoughtfully and executed the procedure so calmly—which was even more impressive when I later found out she was on acid at the time.

Barry McGuire, who sang "Eve of Destruction," was coming with us to the Bowl. He was dressed in a cream-colored suit, but he couldn't find his shoes, so he painted his feet green. If I'd been a few years older I certainly would have figured out that they were all either on acid or, like me, following the lead of those who were.

The Hollywood Bowl show is fuzzy. I was really young. I remember screaming, "Dad! Dad!" from the audience. Later, backstage, I met Jimi Hendrix. Jimi Hendrix didn't mean much to me—he had not yet ignited his guitar onstage at the Monterey Pop Festival, which my father would organize. A giant purple velvet hat floats in my consciousness, attached to the name Hendrix, a vague visual footnote, my own purple haze.

My mother flipped out when she saw that my virgin earlobes had been violated. Pearl studs at eighteen was more her cup of tea. Plus, the threads weren't big enough for earrings and I had to have my ears repierced, and the holes were completely crooked and have been my whole life. For all the asymmetry of my childhood, I'm still disproportionately pissed off about that.

It was a double life: doing what was expected at my mother's, and not answering to anyone at my dad's. I always was aware of the effect my father had on my mom. Even in my seven-year-old brain, I was aware that she was envious, angry, and sad. Often sad. I worried as much as a child can, but the fun at my dad's was irresistible. There was music, guitars, parties, rock stars, and the very seductive attitude of "We're all kids here." I'd ask my dad, "Can I go play on the beach?" and he'd say, "Whatever turns you on, kid." So I'd burst out the back door, free, a crazy kid chasing the dogs on the beach until we were all worn out. Occasionally the cook would attempt to impose a modicum of order. She'd say, "Now, young lady, you clean your room. Your dad's going to be mad," and I'd say, "No, he's not." How could he when he lived so wild? Meanwhile, in Tarzana, my mom was watching me walk down the street, yelling after me to tuck in my shirt. She was trying her best to raise her kids, but we were being shown another kind of life, and it was no competition. Would you rather live at Disneyland or in a condo in Tarzana? Being at Dad's was like riding the Matterhorn all day long, and the weekends, by moment and memory, dominated the school week.

My dad's friends never treated me like a child, not exactly. I was more like an accessory, a cute little prop who might amuse or entertain. One weekend before we'd moved to Los Angeles from Virginia—I must have been five or six—we were with Dad in L.A. for a visit. His fellow band member Cass Eliot (the other "Mama") had a party at her house in Laurel Canyon. We walked into Cass's house and there were Paul McCartney and George Harrison.

When I saw Paul McCartney I glommed on to him like a baby groupie. He kept saying, "Go on, love, get up and dance." In a rare moment of shyness, I demurred. I was afraid people would laugh at me. He insisted. I refused. This exchange circled, a teasing game between a little kid and a world-famous musician.

Finally I broke down and started dancing. The adults began to point and laugh at the little five-year-old dancing for the rock star. I turned bright red and burst into tears, but then Paul McCartney started consoling me. I was no dummy. I liked being consoled by Paul McCartney. The more he comforted, the more tears I summoned. Finally he picked me up and carried me into a hammock that was suspended in the middle of Cass's dining room on a pulley. Someone hoisted us up, up, up. The ceilings were two stories tall and we were suspended fifteen feet in the air. I was still snuffling. Paul snuggled up with me until I finally calmed down and eventually fell asleep. The two of us napped together in that hammock, suspended high above the party. You could say I got high and slept with Paul McCartney.

There was something about my father. He was a cool, countercultural guy who attracted some of the most creative people of his time: Mick Jagger, Keith Richards, Gram Parsons, Warren Beatty, Jane Fonda, Jack Nicholson, Candy Bergen. Most of his friends did drugs, didn't sleep much, and made lots of money: Excellent role models all. What was it that made my father so compelling? People were so drawn to him—musicians, thinkers, beautiful women. He was tall and cool and always fabulously dressed. He drove fancy cars and threw outrageous parties. He was just as much a master of play as he was a master of music. The world was his drug-rock playground, and everyone wanted a turn on the slide. As his daughter, his light was magnified for me. I always wanted to be closer, brighter, warmer. What was fun and games for his friends would develop into a too-powerful life force for me.

At the time I was still just a kid with a lot of energy. But Dad wasn't exactly organizing softball games. The adults at the beach house, and the beach house after that, and the one after that, were always stoned, laughing, and playing guitars. My whole life I've been surrounded by men with guitars. Friends, boyfriends, husbands, son. They sit around, jamming, writing, and talking. That's where the men-with-guitars theme began, in my dad's beach houses.

Gram Parsons was a good friend of my dad's. I didn't know who he was—as far as I was concerned he was just a gentle, quiet man who was at Dad's house all the time and could play the piano like nobody's business. Dad had a baby-blue baby grand in his bedroom in Bel Air. I'd sit there on the piano bench listening to Gram Parsons play for hours. Chuck Barris was often there too. I recognized him as the host of *The Gong Show*. He'd sit on the couch in a big fur coat, not saying much, not gonging Gram Parsons, just hanging out. But as I look back it's hard to believe that Barris's claims to have worked for the CIA were true. I was only a kid, but I was pretty sure he was stoned.

Stoner hangs weren't very kid-friendly. I got bored. Sometimes I found ways to entertain myself. I would walk to the market with money my dad gave me, buy seeds, and plant a wildflower garden. Or I'd climb into my dad's beautiful old Rolls-Royce Silver Cloud. I'd drag the neighborhood beach cat into the backseat with me and pretend we were having tea. There was a big phone in that car; I have no idea how they managed to put a phone in a car in the seventies, but mine was not to question the technology—which I was explicitly *not* to use. The backseat had mahogany tray tables. I'd pull one down, lean against it, and chat with my friends for fifty dollars a minute. That car phone was the most expensive babysitter in history.

One time when the limo dropped me off in Malibu, I walked in to find a completely empty house. This was not wholly unusual; I was expected to fend for myself. So I was chilling, wondering if anyone would show up, waiting for my father as I often did, when Donovan Leitch walked in the door. "What's going on, kid?"

In "Mellow Yellow" Donovan sings, "I'm just mad about Fourteen / She's just mad about me," a lyric that aroused suspicion of pedophilia. But I was only ten—still safely *under* underage. He chatted with me, goofing with the kid who happened to be home, and we decided to make something to eat. We discovered brownie mix in the kitchen and we agreed that brownies would make an excellent lunch. Donovan found a bowl, I got a spoon, we added eggs, we took turns stirring, all the while happily chatting about how yummy they would be. We dug up a pan we were pretty sure would do the trick and put the brownies in the oven. They were cooking; they smelled delicious; and then, out of the blue, Donovan said, "You can't have any." This had to be a cruel joke.

"Why not?" I asked.

"These are special grown-up brownies," Donovan said. It

turns out Donovan had found my dad's pot and added it to the mix. Well, that was just plain mean. When he went into the other room, I looked at the brownies. They didn't look different from any other brownies. They sure smelled like regular brownies. I was hungry. And besides, I was in my dad's house. There were no rules here. I helped myself to a brownie. And another. Next thing I knew everything was funny and Donovan and I were sliding down the banister over and over again. If you don't count my hammock suspension with Paul McCartney, *that* was the first time I got high. I was ten.

Two days later I was playing Barbies by the pool in Tarzana with my best friend, Julie, to all eyes looking like a kid who comfortably straddled two worlds. But the Barbies masked what was really going on. At Dad's I was a weird little savage on the periphery, tap-dancing and singing, eager for any kind of attention. I'd transform over the weekend into an out-of-control little maniac, and when I came home to Mom's, she'd spend all week retraining me in manners and etiquette. How hard it must have been for my mother, watching us go off every Friday and knowing that the kids who came home weren't going to be the same. In Tarzana I wanted to fit in too—I faked failing an eye test to get glasses and fashioned a retainer out of paper clips so I could look like the other kids—but between the controlled order of my mother's home and the wild freedom of my father's decadence, I already knew which I'd choose. I was my father's daughter.

2

My father wanted me to live and learn as he did, through experience and experimentation, so he sent me to Summerhill, a "free" school, which meant that going to classes was optional. The teachers were hippies and the kids were rich and undisciplined. Our class was called the Electric Bananas—from the Donovan song "Mellow Yellow." People generally thought that line referred to smoking banana peels to get high, but Donovan ultimately revealed that it wasn't anything so unseemly—he was only referring to a yellow vibrator. Either way, as a name for a school class it set a clear tone. Ollie, the headmaster, took us dumpster diving. Smoking was permitted. I picked up the habit in fifth grade. Sex ed was our favorite course—the teachers drew diagrams in the dirt with sticks, caveman style. You know, life lessons.

When we opted not to go to classes, which was most of the time, there were horses and chickens and lots of land to get lost in. We pretended to be Jesse James or cowboys and Indians on real horses. And deep in the woods we played kissing games, the standard "doctor" scenarios but amped up by the hippie culture. Jefferson Burstyn, Ellen Burstyn's adorable son, was my sweetheart. In the shade of the trees we climbed under a blanket, took our pants off, and thought we had sex. Those stick drawings left a lot to the imagination.

For a while California had brought out some of the hippie in my mother, but as soon as she got involved with Lenny, a big Jewish businessman who wore slacks, button-down shirts, loafers, and a belt with a gold buckle, she shaped herself to his ideal, acting the role of a proper wife. The other Summerhill parents had beat-up VW buses, braids, and fringed boots. They lived in Topanga Canyon or Laurel Canyon, Bohemian enclaves. Meanwhile, Lenny would drop me off at school in his Cadillac. Once I got out of that car, I was in my father's world. Poor Mom, she must have seen that her hold on me was slipping. I was a person with no boundaries going to a school with no boundaries.

To celebrate my tenth birthday, Dad threw a party at the Bel Air house. All the kids from school were there. I met Dad's new girlfriend, Genevieve Waite, that night. She was eighteen, a South African model, singer, and actor. Also there was my now-ex-stepmother Michelle's daughter, Chynna, my new little sister, who was only a year old, so it couldn't have been an easy time for them, but as far as I was concerned the shift was subtle. I watched my father's lovers and wives crisscross paths: involved, broken up, jealous, mellow. As far as I knew, love and lust ebbed and flowed and my parents and their lovers were just splinters of driftwood bobbing along with the tide. Michelle and Chynna were still always around the house, so I never felt like I lost them. Half the time I wanted to play with Chynna—she was like a little doll—and the rest of the time I wanted to strangle her for dethroning me as Daddy's little princess.

For the birthday party, my father screened *Dumbo* on his movie projector, though at ten we were too old for it. It was probably a stoner favorite. Then, oddly, he screened the Monterey Pop Festival. I guess he was showing off. Dad was proud of having organized the festival and introducing not just Hendrix but the Who, Janis Joplin, and Otis Redding to the American public.

Not long after that party I started hitting puberty. My dad and his friends were sitting around rolling joints on a Saturday morning when, in front of ten adults, my father said, "Look at my little girl. She's poppin' tits." It was the kind of thing that some men of that time used to say—"Look, she's becoming a woman"—not lascivious, just oblivious to how sensitive a young girl is about her development. I felt horribly exposed. I wanted to disappear. To this day the word "tits" creeps me out.

Anyway, maybe it hooked into my father's head that I was getting older, because later that day he gave me a new, adult responsibility. That afternoon his friends were . . . still sitting around rolling joints. I was bored and bouncing off the walls: "What can I do?" "I want to plant flowers." "Can we go get seashells?" "Can we go to the store?"

At loose ends, I tried to find ways to occupy myself, but you can only make so many sand castles or expensive covert phone calls. So on this particular day—the same day he outed my blossoming womanhood—Dad said, "I'm going to give you a project." Dad had a job for me! This was exciting. I was in. He took the top of a shoe box and put a bunch of Thai sticks in it. Then he tore off the stiff cardboard top of a rolling paper pack. He showed me how to scrunch up the dried buds into pieces, shuffling the leaves with the cardboard so the seeds fell to the bottom. Once the pot was clean, he showed me how to attach two papers to make a fat joint. I had ten-year-old fingers, but in short order I got really good at rolling joints. I was the official joint-roller for all the adults. Sort of a rite of passage to go along with puberty, I guess.

Parents have certain responsibilities. Most have an innate sense of what might be good for their kids, and what might be bad for them. They make choices based on those beliefs. They shelter their children from activities and influences that might harm them or lead them in the wrong direction. That feeling of protection hit me the instant I saw my newborn son, and it was so powerful and intertwined with love that I can't imagine separating the two. My father was different. He loved me, but under ordinary circumstances he didn't see himself as my protector and guide. He saw himself as a very cool person who loved to hang out with other cool people, including his own cool children.

And so it was that my father and Genevieve, while hanging out in their new part-time digs—the penthouse suite at the Chateau Marmont—had no qualms about dipping into a cereal bowl filled to the brim with white powder and inhaling it in front of me and my brother. We watched them, fascinated, until they went to "take a nap," which seems an unlikely thing to do after snorting massive quantities of cocaine, but whatever. They stowed the bowl of coke in the cabinet under the TV. After they left the room Jeffrey said, "Let's try it." It wasn't his first time. He was twelve, after all. I asked him what it felt like. He handed me a vibrator—because such things were occasionally randomly accessible (though not, in this case, yellow like Donovan's legendary dildo)—and told me to put it between my teeth. That, he said, was what cocaine felt like.

I didn't snort enough to feel a physical response, but the ritual of it was fun, and it made me feel bigger and older and grown-up. Because, as most parents realize, *children want to grow up to be just like their parents.* The following weekend I found a silver box that had a little spoon attached on a chain. I filled it with my dad's coke and took it to school.

I was now enrolled in Highland Hall, a Waldorf school. We read Tolstoy in fifth grade and studied Greek, Spanish, and German, each once a week. My friend Lisa, who'd moved from Summerhill at the same time, was my best friend at school.

I brought my secret stash of coke to our seats near the back of the class. Lisa was a funky girl who always carried a briefcase, and now she opened it up on the desk to shield me from the teacher's view. I took out the coke, but just as I was about to snort my first spoonful I accidentally dropped the silver box and coke spilled all over the floor. The teacher said, "What's going on back there?"

I replied, "It's only baby powder for gym class." The teacher let it slide. I guess the notion that sixth graders would be snorting coke in the middle of math class didn't occur to him. I didn't care so much about the lost drugs—the point was to break the rules and get away with it, and we did. The next weekend when I walked into the beach house, Genevieve said, "Oh, here comes the little drug thief." I was worried that my dad would be pissed—he really didn't like me dipping into his supply. But that was the last I heard about it.

The 1971 San Fernando earthquake happened exactly at six in the morning. In my bedroom at my mom's I had one of those pre-LCD digital clocks where the numbers flip by and I remember waking up, seeing the clock turn from 5:59 to 6:00, and feeling the whole place go bananas. We kids were oblivious to the lives lost and damage done and thought the earthquake and its aftermath were great fun. School was canceled. The sidewalks were all buckled and broken up, so roller skating, which was one of our favorite pastimes, became an obstacle course. With a pack of the neighborhood kids, I went skating for hours. Those post-earthquake days were unexpectedly special for me. For that moment in time, having good, clean, post-disaster fun, I felt the rare sensation of being a normal kid, just like the other kids. We were all in something together. I was oblivious to the deeper meaning then, but later I would collect and cherish memories of feeling like I was part of a community instead of an oddly privileged outsider.

Our double life affected both me and my brother, but whereas I was willful and mischievous, my brother was downright bad. It was the usual stuff between him and my mom: *clean your room—you live like a pig; do your homework; don't give me any lip, young man; stop playing your saxophone—it's midnight!* But it always escalated to a screaming match, and there were times when it almost got violent. Dad didn't help matters, of course. He bought Jeffrey a BB gun, and my brother promptly shot out all the lights around my grandma's pool. Jeffrey always had a sweet heart, but in those days he was a volcano, ready to erupt.

Unlike Jeffrey, I tried not to ruffle my mother's feathers. I wanted everything to go smoothly. I tweaked my attitude and style to fit in with different friends, the chameleon act that I was mastering with my parents. With my Highland Hall friends it was all about dropping acid most days, wandering around the hills, wondering at the flora and fauna. The kids I knew from Tarzana—the Valley—were a different scene. There was a huge group of really rich kids who lived in very fancy houses in the hills. In the daytime the Laundromat in the nearby strip mall was our hang. We'd drink beer and lounge on the warm dryers for hours. At night I'd crawl out onto the ledge outside my bedroom window. My Valley friends would wait for me below. I'd climb down the fire escape, jump to the ground, and be free.

My friend Julie and I would drop acid, "borrow" her sister's car, and meet up with friends. Julie was a much better underage driver than I was. The only time I tried to drive I ran straight into a mailbox. One night we went to a party somewhere in the hills. I was wearing what hipster kids wore in those days: a polyester button-down shirt tucked into high-waisted baby blue bellbottom corduroys, and a sparkly belt. My hair was cut in a shag. I had a shag for years.

The party was in one of those big ranch-style Encino homes with a terraced backyard and pool. Gwen, who straightened her hair with an iron, then rolled it in soda cans with setting lotion to get it even straighter, lived here. There was a huge open floor plan. The living room furniture had plastic covers and the white carpeting had plastic runners to preserve their purity. But now kids were everywhere. Gwen's parents were obviously out of town. Gwen said, "Everyone stay out of the living room or my parents will know for sure I had a party." Good luck with that, Gwen.

I had some rum punch and a few drags off a joint. I had a thing for this kid Henry. I was gangly, with big teeth and a big smile, kinda goofy-looking, but Henry was one of the cool guys. He took me into a closet, a big walk-in closet. We started making out. Then we had sex. It was my first real time, unless you count playing doctor at Summerhill, which I don't. So we had sex, then Henry walked out of the closet and never spoke to me again.

When it came down to sex in the closet, my reaction was: *What's all the fanfare about? That wasn't very much fun.* The act itself was insignificant, but I didn't have huge expectations for sex. I had never been told that it was deeply meaningful, or romantic, or something that a girl might wait to do. But I did want that boy to like me, and the way he walked away was devastating.

I played it up for my girlfriends, but I don't have a good poker face. If I'm hurt you can see it. I felt like a piece of meat. We busted out of the party. On our way out I saw the party damage. The white rug was trashed. The living room was a war zone. Poor Gwen. She would be grounded for a month.

Back at the condo complex the morning sun cast a golden mirror on my third-floor window. My friends formed a pyramid and I climbed up to reach the fire escape. I caught the bottom rung of the ladder and swung myself up, as I'd done so many times before. I crawled into my bedroom window and sobbed into my pillow, mourning not something I'd lost, but something I'd never had.

3

My mother was frantically in love with my father. They had been high school sweethearts and jitterbug champions. Her parents—my grandparents—were none too pleased with the match. They were eastern seaboard aristocracy—my grandfather, James Frederick Adams Jr., was a descendant of the president John Adams. After my mother finished high school, my grandmother sent her off to finishing school to get her away from Dad, whom she called a "half-breed" because his mother was Cherokee. But my parents didn't let go of each other easily. Mom came back from finishing school, found herself pregnant, and married my dad. I'm sure she thought that kind of love would last forever. For her it did.

I can only guess what promises Dad made to lure Mom from Alexandria, Virginia, to Los Angeles with two small children. My dad could talk anyone into anything. I'm sure he wanted us near him, and she may have hoped for a reconciliation—another reconciliation, those doomed reconciliations that were par for the course for my dad and his lovers.

It was the early sixties, when being a single mom with two kids wasn't exactly socially accepted, on top of everything else that made it difficult. So my mom left her job at the Pentagon, where she was assistant to Robert S. McNamara, secretary of defense, probably still vying for the marriage she expected and couldn't imagine life without. She followed my dad—her first love, the man who broke her heart by rote, but most of all by throwing her under the bus for a sixteen-year-old when she had two small children—she followed him across the country.

In Virginia, my father had paid sporadic child support and sometimes dinner was ketchup and saltines. In Los Angeles, nothing changed. Dad bought us a condo but soon stopped making the payments. An eviction notice appeared on the front door and my mother sued my father for back alimony and won.

For all his irresponsibility, Mom never stopped loving Dad. She wasn't built that way. But when Lenny, the guy who drove us to Summerhill in his Cadillac, came along, I'm sure she welcomed the notion of a financially stable, traditional man who would support her and take care of her.

Jeffrey and I were excited about Lenny too. Mom had been a serial dater and we liked the idea of her in a stable relationship. When they got married—I was nine or ten—Jeffrey and I cooked them a celebratory wedding dinner. We decorated the table with cake toppers and baby's breath from a craft store down the street and made an elaborate fondue dinner. We had high hopes. But Lenny was bad news. He married my mother and proceeded to beat the crap out of her on a regular basis.

My brother had been causing trouble for a while, but when Mom got married Jeffrey got worse. He enraged Lenny, who turned scary, looming, loud. Our family was emotional—I've always been one to wail at the drop of a hat. Even a McDonald's commercial can make me tear up. But Lenny's emotions were big and violent. He was angry in a way that was completely foreign to me. He was the antithesis of everything we knew.

Finally, Lenny and my mom sent Jeffrey away to the Bar 717 Ranch, a "clean up your act" school for kids in a national forest near Hayfork, in Northern California. It was one of those places where delinquent kids mucked out horse stalls in order to learn how to obey their parents. Dad taught us to question authority and Mom sent Jeffrey to a school for kids with authority problems. No wonder we were fucked up.

I could barely stand the thought of a day in that condo without my big brother. He and I had matching blankets with flowered patterns on them. Mine was reddish pink and his was blue.

When Jeffrey left I got his blanket out of his room and slept with it every night. I'd hold the blanket and keen, *Jeffrey, Jeffrey.*

After a year at school Jeffrey came home, but not much had changed. My mother held our household together as best she could. She made cookies at Christmas, we decorated the tree every year, we watched the ball drop in Times Square on New Year's Eve. But she was still reeling from my hurricane father, who was riding in limos and living in mansions and married to one woman, then the next, and her despair must have numbed her to Lenny's battery. He broke her mastoid bone. He broke her wrist. When she and I did a teens-and-their-mothers shoot for the magazine *Tiger Beat,* she hid the broken wrist and wore makeup to disguise two black eyes.

Mom was our structure and stability. When we lost faith in her, Jeffrey and I ran wild. We drank, smoked pot, dropped acid, stayed up late, went to parties, cut school. In front of our condo were beautiful olive trees that dropped purple-brown olives. When I came home from school my mother would say, "Your eyes are red." I'd say, "I know. I'm so allergic to those olive trees," but I'm pretty sure we both knew that I'd been smoking pot on the walk home. My mom never busted me sneaking out or taking acid. But she now had two out-of-control children. She yelled at us, blaming my father for the drugs, but my mother wasn't exactly a model of purity. She was drinking more and more. Then something happened that convinced me once and for all that she was a hypocrite. A few hours after a big argument about pot, or whatever, Mom was downstairs with Lenny and some other people. On my way to the bathroom I walked past the top of the stairs and heard my mother say something, then inhale. It sounded like she was smoking a joint. Then I heard her say, "Ooh, the roach is the best part." After all the crap talk she gave us about drugs! Her credibility went up in smoke, so to speak.

Jeffrey bore the brunt of Lenny's violence. One night I heard a knock and saw Jeffrey standing on the ledge outside my window. He had his sax around his neck and his albums under his arm. He said, "I'm running away."

I said, "You cannot leave me here." Being alone had been so hard when he left for Bar 717. I needed Jeffrey. He wanted me to come with him, but for all my conflict with my mother, I was incredibly close to her. I was her baby girl, and I always would be. If I left, it would destroy her. I was sad and angry to see him go again, but I couldn't betray her. Not yet. So Jeffrey ran away to live with Dad.

Over the next couple weeks I did everything I could think of to get my mom to kick me out. I talked back. I left my room a mess. I refused to do the dishes and was as annoying as possible. But she wouldn't throw me out. She adored me. I loved my mother too, but she was focused on pleasing the husband she loved and feared and needed, the same man I loathed.

Two weeks later push came to shove. I wasn't supposed to be on the phone after a certain hour. Lenny exploded into my room. He ripped the phone out of the wall and towered over me as I cowered in the corner of the room in terror. He was in my face, yelling at the top of his lungs, spittle flying, huge and vitriolic. The part of my brain that wasn't terrorized was thinking, *Really? All the shit I've done and you finally lose it about my phone curfew?*

Mom ran into the room screaming, "Get away from her!" She eventually talked him down and got him out of the room. Later she made the excuses that women who are abused make: *He was having a bad day; everything's okay; you're okay.* But I was scared for her and scared for myself. Lenny was a tyrant and he was only getting worse. I wasn't safe without Jeffrey there.

The next day my mother and I fought as I threw my clothes, albums, and toiletries into bags. I told her I was moving to Dad's. She cried, implored, commanded me to stay, but I was almost thirteen—about to become a teenager—and I was resolute. I loved her and didn't want to hurt her, but I had to get out of there. Finally she said, "Fine, just go!" and I said, "I will!"

and stormed out of the house. I'm sure she still expected me home by sundown.

Our building was right near Gelson's supermarket. As I walked past the parking lot I dumped my heavy bags into a stray shopping cart and pushed the cart a block down the street to my grandmother's house.

Whereas my grandmother on my mother's side could set a table for thirty-six with her two-hundred-year-old Haviland china and S. Kirk & Son Repousse silver, my dad's mother, Dini, was the social opposite: a full-blooded Cherokee Indian who was, as a child on the reservation, branded with a cross to prove she wasn't a heathen when she went into town looking for work. Dini was a stone-cold alcoholic whose poison was Scotch and milk and I loved her. I often stopped by her house on the way home from junior high. I'd walk in the front door and she'd say, "How was school? Want a Coors?"

So now, when I showed up at Dini's with all my worldly possessions in a shopping cart and told her I was moving to Dad's, she nodded and said, "Want me to call you a cab? Want a beer?"

The cab brought me to the door of the new mansion Dad and Genevieve had rented at 414 St. Pierre Road, near the east gate of Bel Air. I rang the doorbell. Dad answered the door in a tie-dyed caftan, smoking a joint. I said, "Pay the taxi. I'm moving in."

He said, "Sure kid, whatever turns you on."

Dad gave me my own wing of the mansion. It was that kind of place—a pink Italian palace that was designed by Paul Williams for Johnny Weissmuller, the Olympic swimmer and on-screen Tarzan. We also heard it had been rented or owned by William Randolph Hearst for his long-term paramour, Marion Davies. Whatever the case, the house was clearly built as a place for rich people to play. First Mick and Bianca Jagger had rented it at my dad's recommendation, and when they left, Dad and Genevieve moved in from the Chateau Marmont. Dad liked to live large, to show everyone what a big star he was. The ceilings were twenty feet tall. The moldings had hand-painted fleurs-de-lis. There was a mirrored hall and countless antiques. The vast ballroom was surrounded by Moroccan murals of guys on horses and temples with pointed tops. There was a stage, mirrors, a ballet bar, and a supply of wax to restore the floor to an optimal surface for dancing.

The house was furnished when Dad moved in, but he added a few personal touches. He brought a Zodiac Tiffany floor lamp that even at the time was worth thousands of dollars. Even more spectacularly, the living room was dominated by a twelve-foot-tall pop-art sculpture of a man standing on a massive platform that looked like a teacup from the Disneyland ride turned upside down. He was painted beautifully in rainbow stripes and he stood like Atlas with his legs apart, his arms spread tall above his head. But in his hands, instead of the world, he held a neon sign that said HOLLYWOOD. We called him the Hollywood Man. He watched over the mayhem with confidence and humor. I'm sure my father felt that way when he bought the Hollywood Man—like he had the whole industry in the palm of his hand.

My bedroom was painted powder blue with white wainscoting and trim. There were beautiful leaded casement windows that opened onto a spectacular stone courtyard on one side. On the other side French doors opened to a Juliet balcony overlooking the tropical backyard. The bathroom had a claw-foot tub and a shower with three showerheads that were original from when the house was built in 1931.

Dad had married Genevieve in a Chinese restaurant. The ceremony was presided over by a one-legged Buddhist priest. I sat between Jerry Brown and Mick Jagger. Dad and Gen's infant son, my baby brother, Tamerlane, was there, and I know his room was the only other one in my wing of the house, but I don't remember much of him from those years. He was mostly under the care of a nanny, and it's a good thing because the scene at Dad's was a constant party, child-inappropriate.

Much of the partying took place in my father's bedroom. In the center of the room was a huge brass bed made for tall people, beautiful people, with scarves draped everywhere. There were plastic molded chairs with built-in stereo speakers. Quadrophonic sound, I think they called it. In the sitting room of the bedroom suite was the baby-blue piano that Gram Parsons liked to play.

After I settled in, I wandered through the tropical gardens until I found my father lounging by the pool. I asked him, "So . . . what's expected of me? Is there anything I need to know about living here?"

Dad thought for a minute. "Here are the ground rules," he said. "You have to be home one night a week," he said, "and if you stay out all night, never come home in the clothes you left in. A lady never wears evening clothes during the day. It's cheap." That was it. The house rules. There was no phone curfew here. There was no curfew whatsoever. My brother and I were together again. Jeffrey wasn't afraid to ask for drugs. I wasn't afraid to ask for money. We got both. When it came down to it, the choice had been: live with my mom in a condo in Tarzana, do homework, heed my curfew, and follow Lenny's rules, or live with my dad in a mansion, hang out with the most famous movie stars and rock stars of the day, and have no rules whatsoever. Taking my love for my mother out of the equation, I thought I had picked heaven over hell.

Any time, day or night, there were at least six people in my dad's wing. A bunch of incredibly brilliant, well-spoken reprobates. They were like children. Rich, high children whose own children were just part of the ongoing party. I'd come in dressed in glitter, with shaved eyebrows and platforms. I'd start to sing with everyone and stay to get high.

Outside, there was a swimming pool that Johnny Weissmuller

must have had built so he could do his laps. To say the pool was long is an understatement. It was 301 feet long, but skinny, and winding like a snake through exotic landscaping and funhouse weirdness. An arched bridge crossed over the pool and led to a stone tunnel with Gothic windows. Near the tunnel was a wall of hand-painted stucco cabanas. All the structures, including the bottom of the bridge over the pool (the part you saw when you swam under it) were decorated with hand-painted murals. It looked like the hybrid child of an Italian church and a Hawaiian lagoon. At the end of the pool closest to the road was a massive waterfall.

What made the enormous, serpentine swimming pool most extraordinary was that it was kept empty. Who could maintain a pool that size? Dry and collecting dead leaves, it wound a deep, smooth path through the gardens with the mysterious aura of ancient ruins—the indestructible relic of other people's lives. It may have been empty and eerie, but we put that pool to good use. It would have made an excellent skateboard park, but we didn't have skateboards, so we rode Big Wheels down the length of it at four in the morning, racing back and forth in the deep darkness of the long, sunken pit. When that got boring we set off M-80s, the big-daddy fireworks that must have driven our Bel Air neighbors mad.

Like the pool, that ballroom on the bottom floor of the house also didn't go to waste, but was not exactly used for its intended purpose. My half sister Chynna was in a child-size wheelchair because she had a tumor wrapped around the muscle in her thigh. For some reason there were a couple of other wheelchairs rolling around the house. Jeffrey and I were friends with Marlon Brando's sons, Christian and Miko. We liked to take acid, sprinkle dance wax on the floor, and zoom around the ballroom in the household wheelchairs. We played chicken and figured out how to do wheelies. We called it "Wheelchair Follies."

Possibly the first time Christian did acid—he was really tripping hard—Jeffrey and I found some sparkly gold powder in

Genevieve's paint supplies. Jeffrey and I put the gold dust on our fingers and waved our hands in front of hapless Christian's face, saying, "We've been to Pluto." We told him that we had Pluto dust on our hands, and that if he followed us, then he too could visit Pluto. When we tired of taunting Christian, we all tried to ride the wheelchairs down St. Pierre Road.

St. Pierre Road goes down to Beverly Glen in a long, steep, blind curb. Riding down it in wheelchairs proved beyond even our daring, so we got the Big Wheels out of the empty pool and rode them instead. The steering was superior to the wheelchairs and we could skid the front wheels against the curb to slow down our descent. We flew down the road, tripping, in Big Wheels. If we'd learned anything from our parents, it was how to have a good time.

Years later, when Christian's life would take a terrible turn, when he was convicted for shooting his half sister Cheyenne's boyfriend and Cheyenne subsequently committed suicide, I felt heartbreak for the whole family. I was thinking, *That's my old friend.* Those boys were like us. We were kids of privilege who could have anything we desired except what we really wanted—a connection with our parents. Broken kids being broken together, trying to have fun in our broken Bel Air mansions.

I was supposed to go to school, but sometimes I had to hitchhike because nobody was awake or willing to drive me. I was allowed to go to school on acid if I wanted, and Dad signed a ream of blank sheets of paper on which I could write notes like "Please excuse Laura from class at noon today as she must see the doctor," or "Please excuse Laura from physical education today. She has a family obligation." I always wanted but never dared to write "Please excuse Laura from school as everyone is just too fucked up."

Stealing drugs from Dad became my not-so-secret habit. I'd sneak into his bedroom and help myself. One time I found a pretty purple pill in a small glass container. I didn't know what it was, but I figured it was acid, so I took it. Little did I know that the pill I had swallowed was in fact a legendary, legendarily scarce Purple Owsley. Owsley Stanley was a pioneer LSD cook, and the Purple Owsley pill from his now-defunct lab was Dad's prized possession, a rare, potent, druggie collector's item, the alleged inspiration for the Hendrix song "Purple Haze." It may have been one of the last hits of Purple Owsley on this planet. I'd really fucked up this time. When Dad discovered what I'd done, his face filled with a rage I'd never seen before. The father who had no rules was as angry as I'd ever seen him. It was as if I'd crashed some normal rich dad's Porsche. He said, "You took my last hit of Owsley. You're grounded." I think it was the only time Dad ever grounded me. And I don't even know if the acid had any special effect on me. I probably just went to school and tripped out in social studies.

What do you expect to happen if you teach your child to roll joints at the age of ten? How will she turn out if she is free to pilfer the lesser of your personal pharmacy? Who will she be if she is left to find her way among adults who are lost or hell-bent on losing themselves? My father didn't think about the consequences. He thought he was having fun, but to call it fun is to oversimplify the hunger and loss and anger that drove his relentless commitment to oblivion. And that muddle of emotions was passed from father to daughter. As I grew up there was something more powerful and formative at play than the irresponsible example my father set. I desperately wanted to be close to him. I needed him. I did what he did and said what he said. Of myself I wasn't enough. I couldn't just . . . be.

4

That summer my father and Genevieve decided to send me away to summer school. It all had to do with *American Graffiti,* a movie I'd shot the year before. How I got the part started with my seventh-grade band.

Dad did drugs, but he still made music. Like father, like daughter: being on acid for school didn't stop me from putting together a band in seventh grade. It was Chris, Laura (me), Adam, and Scott, and we called ourselves "Class." Mondays we played the open-mike nights for amateurs at the Troubadour in Hollywood. We'd written rock 'n' roll songs about being in prison, eating cold soup, and drinking beer. No one had yet told us, "Write what you know." I was the lead singer. For our first gig I wore a cool sweater with birds on it: navy blue, low-cut Landlubber jeans, a purple belt, and Wallaby shoes. I had long hair with bangs. My dad was in the audience. One of the other kids in the band had a father who was a big executive at Elektra Records. Another band member's father was an entertainment lawyer. There was rampant nepotism among us hipster kids of power-hippie parents, so nobody was surprised that Fred Roos, a film producer, was in the audience. He would later say that he saw me as a spunky kid with a good look and an instantly recognizable desire to act older than I was. Fred asked me if I'd like to be in a movie. I was a total Valley girl. I said, "That would be so cool!"

American Graffiti was the first audition I went to. I was up against 250 girls for the part of Carol, a bratty preteen—the youngest character in the movie—who gloms on to John Milner, a hot-rodding teen, on a summer night in the 1950s. It was a low-budget film that George Lucas, pre–*Star Wars*, wrote and directed.

I was still living at my mom's house when I found out I got the job. We were jumping up and down and screaming, but I didn't really know what the movie was exactly. Was it an educational movie? An after-school special? I'd played Santa Claus in the school play at Summerhill. Would it be like that? It just didn't occur to me that I would be filming a major motion picture.

Apparently, my parents didn't fully process that idea either. I remembered that when I worked on the movie I lived with the producer, Gary Kurtz, and his wife, who were very nice Quakers. But it wasn't until thirty years later, at an American Film Institute celebration of *American Graffiti,* that Gary said to me, "Remember when you arrived in San Francisco all alone?" I didn't know what he was talking about. He said, "Yeah, we met you at the plane and you were all by yourself. We asked where your guardian was, but you didn't have one." I assumed that I lived with Gary and his wife because that was the arrangement, but it turns out there was no arrangement. When I showed up alone they had to scramble around to get temporary guardianship.

I was the youngest in the cast by far. Most of the movie took place in the course of a single night, so we'd shoot from dusk to dawn. There were no dressing rooms and no trailers. We just hung out between takes at Mel's Diner, where a lot of the movie was shot. I was the little mascot. I was only twelve, but I knew my home life was good fodder. I'd tell stories about the Stones and other people who hung out at my father's. Sitting around late into the night, I learned to drink coffee.

Paul Le Mat played John Milner. For much of the movie he and I are driving around in his car, and the car was rigged with cameras facing in each window. We couldn't get out of the car between takes or during set changes because the cameras were in the way, so my memory of shooting the movie is mostly of being stuck in that car for hours and hours on end.

For a scene where John and Carol cover a car with shaving

cream, Lucas set up the cameras and said, "Just do whatever you want." That scene does a pretty good job of capturing what I was like then—I mean, I wasn't a screaming banshee, I was always respectful and well mannered, but I was wild and full of life. I never need a lot to be happy. I'm not a happy idiot, but I'm easily entertained. You can see it on the screen. I like it on this planet.

Apparently, there were comic and serious troubles on the set of *American Graffiti*. Rumor has it that people were arrested for pot, hospitalized for allergies, busted for arson. The usual drill. True or not, I was oblivious to the scandals. When our nighttime shoots ended, I went home to the Kurtzes' pleasant house and slept, as a teenager should. All I remember was that Paul Le Mat made a habit of climbing to the top of tall trees—I guess that was his way of getting high. I came to set one day and heard that Paul had climbed to the top of a Holiday Inn sign and refused to come down. He was a strange man. Years later, when I was eighteen (barely legal), shooting *More American Graffiti*, Paul and I would have a fling. He was married, instantly regretful, and distant for the rest of the filming.

After I shot the movie, I moved in with my dad and started running around L.A., hanging out in nightclubs, drinking, taking drugs. Then it was the summer of 1973, I was thirteen years old, and the movie *American Graffiti* was finally scheduled to be released on August 11. But at the beginning of the summer, before the film premiered, my stepmother, Genevieve, said, "Laura, I don't want to throw you to the lions." I think that was her way of saying she thought a young girl shouldn't be swept up in the notoriety whirlwind of a movie release, and maybe that was right, but it's just as likely that she was tired of having me around. I was a pain in the ass. Genevieve went on, "We're going to send you to a boarding school in Switzerland for the summer. Pretend you're an alien and your mission on this new planet is to learn French." Genevieve says stuff like that.

The boarding school, La Chatelainie, was a beautiful place. I was a crazy glitter kid, a David Bowie wannabe from Hollywood. And although I was in a foreign school where everyone spoke a foreign language, I didn't stop being a handful, to say the least. During lunch I'd jump on tables and do imitations of Donny Osmond. I sang loudly, called teachers names, and was generally obnoxious. At night my roommates and I would sneak out the windows, go into the little town nearby, and drink beer at the local pub.

My father's play *Space Cowboy* was now being developed as a Broadway musical called *Man on the Moon*. Andy Warhol was producing. Perhaps to facilitate his dealings with Andy, my father had a telex machine, the precursor to the fax, connected in the library of his Bel Air mansion. This was a time when ordinary people didn't have telex machines in their homes. But my dad was no ordinary mortal, as he proved regularly. One school day the headmaster came up to me and said, "I received this telex." He handed me a page. It was addressed to "Max," which was my father's nickname for me.

Dear Max,
My name is Can and I am the king
and I can do most anything
'cause it gives life a simple swing.
Some may say that being a king
Can be more fun and easier
than being a knape or a knave.
Who wants to be a slave?
If King Can shall, who shan't?
If King Can will, who won't?
If King Can do, who don't?
And if King Can can, who can't?
Love, Dad.

The headmaster looked pained. "What is this?" he asked. "It says it's from your father. What does it mean?"

I shrugged and said, "Oh, that's just Dad."

A few days later another telex came:

Dear Max,
Wee funky little bats have never played out in the sunshine. Hang by your heels in a cave and you will find truth to be blinding.
Love, Dad.

And Genevieve had told me to pretend to be an alien. Who needed to pretend?

When *American Graffiti* premiered in the States, Dad started telexing me reviews and telling me that I was a star and how proud he was of me. Nobody at school believed that I was in a movie, much less the biggest movie of the year. I had gone from anonymity to movie star overnight, but—as Genevieve had planned—for better or worse I missed the hoopla.

So I went to my classes, mocked the house mother, who had the unfortunate combination of long armpit hair and short-sleeved shirts, and was a regular, but not exceptional, nuisance, until the day the headmaster came up to me, this time with no incomprehensible telex in hand. He said, "Your father has not paid. We can't reach him. You have no ticket home. You can stay here, but you cannot participate in any more classes or activities." I was upset, but not unduly shocked. This was a new manifestation of the same old Dad—a barrage of endearing nonsense, some pride, then . . . silence. But abandoning me in a foreign country was a new extreme. In my own country I was now famous, but I was stuck in Switzerland. I couldn't do anything or go anywhere. If Dad was so proud of me, then why wouldn't he pay the bill—or get me the fuck out of there? One minute I was a spoiled, newly famous Hollywood brat. The next I was stranded in Switzerland while my new friends attended classes, went horseback riding, and left for daylong field trips. I wandered around the school all day embarrassed and depressed, abandoned. I waited for my MIA father as I had before and would many times again. Weeks went by.

Finally, Dad sent a plane ticket with a note promising to pick me up at the airport in L.A. The school put me on a bus from Neuchâtel to Zurich . . . or Geneva. What did I know from Swiss cities? I was fourteen and traveling alone. I just climbed aboard whichever bus they put me on, feeling like Paddington with his "Please look after this bear" tag. When I arrived at the Swiss airport, I tried to find my flight, but something had happened. The flight was delayed, or canceled, I couldn't tell exactly. I'd missed most of the classes, so my French wasn't great. I knew how to order oxtail soup at a small-town pub at midnight, but it was unclear to me how I'd ever get home. I sat on my suitcase in the airport and cried.

Eventually there was a plane. I made it back to the States, but I still had a layover at JFK before I flew the last leg home to L.A. As I disembarked the international flight at JFK, one of the heels on my huge, ugly, white plastic platform shoes broke. My many-hours-long layover had just begun. I had a full day of travel ahead of me, and all my shoes were in my suitcase, checked through to Los Angeles. I limped through the airport, one leg a good six inches longer than the other. People were glancing at me with recognition for the first time in my life. So it was true, I was a movie star. But I walked around JFK as alone as a girl can possibly be, in gimpy limbo—lost in an untethered nowhereland that was already familiar to me at fourteen.

At last I arrived at LAX. In a rare show of timeliness and reliability, my dad was actually there in the flesh to pick me up. He stood at the gate, always taller than I expected, with his long hair and beard, chamois suede pants and top, and a rhinestone belt. Alongside him were his best friend, Michael Sarne, and my cousin Patty. I was relieved and happy to see my father and overjoyed to see Patty. She was twenty, six years older than I was. We'd been little girls together in Virginia, living in the same apartment building and having family dinners at our grandmother Dini's every Sunday. While I was away, my aunt Rosie and her two daughters, Patty and Nancy, had moved to Los Angeles. When Patty met me at the airport she said, "Now I'm going to be your big sister." Then she gave me a Quaalude. Welcome home, kid.

5

Not long after I made it home from my ill-fated summer at boarding school in Switzerland, I went to see *American Graffiti* for the first time with my dad and Genevieve. It was a private screening for the cast, producers, and their invitees. I wore an amazing 1940s red-and-white polka-dot dress of Genevieve's, white patent leather six-inch platform heels, and short, spiky hair. I'd shaved off my eyebrows and painted on glitter lightning bolts. Dad wore hand-stitched suede pants, and Genevieve looked like a movie star, as always. Mom and Lenny were there too. It was my big night.

It seemed like ages since I'd first landed the part. Nearly two years had passed since I'd shot the movie, during which time I'd moved from the shadow of Lenny's scary dictatorship to the trippy glow of my father's hedonism. When I think of that night, it's as if I'm watching it on a TV screen. I can see myself stepping out of the Rolls in my teetery heels and walking into the theater, but I see it from a distance. I remember a lot of the major events in my life like this, as though I watched the moment instead of experiencing it. Maybe it's a side effect from years of drug use, maybe I disassociate because it's easier for me to digest my life from a distance, maybe I create memories from stories I've been told, or maybe I'm just insane.

Regardless, we walked down the red carpet and took our seats in the theater. My dad gave me a couple Quaaludes and I popped them all at once. All I remember of that first viewing is the opening credits, which started before the ludes kicked in. As they rolled, my name came up on the screen. The people in front of us said, "Mackenzie Phillips, who's that?" I practically had the same reaction—I'd been Laura Phillips my whole life.

When I got the part in *American Graffiti* my manager, Pat McQueeney, whom I'd met through Fred Roos, didn't like "Laura Phillips" and asked me what my middle name was. I told her it was Mackenzie. People have always thought I was named after Scott McKenzie, my dad's lifelong friend and one of my favorite people on this planet. Scott sang Dad's song "San Francisco (Be Sure To Wear Flowers In Your Hair)" to promote the Monterey Pop Festival, launching the Summer of Love. But the truth is that when I was born Scott McKenzie was still known as Philip Scott Blondheim. I was actually named after my great-grandmother on my mother's side, Sarah Mackenzie. When I told Pat my middle name was Mackenzie, she said, "Oh my God, that's it."

Now, as the people whose heads bobbled disruptively between my fourteen-year-old eyes and the screen wondered who Mackenzie Phillips was, Dad leaned forward and said, "You'll see." And after that the night is a blur. I was stoned off my ass. Maybe Dad felt guilty about the Quaaludes. He kept passing me little silver spoonfuls of coke to help me wake up.

No one expected *American Graffiti* to be a huge success, but it was an instant classic. The critics loved it and it was nominated for multiple Academy Awards that year. I was suddenly frighteningly famous. I already had some level of recognition as John Phillips's daughter, but after *American Graffiti* was released, I was a familiar face. And it wasn't just my face that was familiar. Suddenly everyone also knew me by the name Mackenzie Phillips. I thought of Mackenzie as my stage name, and for a while I continued to think of myself as Laura. People would say, "I know who you are, you're Mackenzie Phillips." I'd say, "Yeah, I'm Mackenzie, but everybody calls me Laura." But I'm so not a Laura. People were confused. It was too complicated. So I just decided, *Fuck it, I'm Mack.*

I was unabashedly thrilled at my new stardom. A few days

after I saw the movie with my parents, I went back for more. My cousins Patty and Nancy, a few of my friends from Highland Hall, and I hitchhiked to the Avco Cinema in Westwood to see it again. At the ticket booth I proudly announced, "I'm in it! I'm in the movie!" They let us all in for free. That was such a coup that we went back over and over again. We must have seen that movie thirty-five times. We'd be reciting all the lines of the movie and people would turn around to say "Would you kids shut up?" But then they'd see that it was me and smile. I guess if it was worth paying to see the rude, precocious kid in the movies, it was worth it to have the rude, precocious kid disrupting the show.

When I wasn't cutting school to watch myself on the big screen, I was back at Highland Hall. I'd left school to make *American Graffiti,* and then I'd spent the summer away. Now I was back and things were different. I was different. I'd been in Europe for a few months. The movie was out. I was famous. Highland Hall had a hippie vibe, but I was in the glitter scene, running around Hollywood, wearing dramatic makeup, and leading what seemed like a sophisticated life. At Highland Hall I had my first taste of how fame changes your regular life. I'd done something—it was just work, really, and had nothing to do with who I really was—but it changed how people saw me and dealt with me. There was an awkwardness, a hesitance. My friends—and family too—started treating me differently, like I had some new value or merit that I didn't have before. It felt odd and wrong. And it wasn't all them. I was still a kid, but I didn't feel like a kid.

Most of my nights were spent back at my favorite hangouts on the Sunset Strip. My friends and I were glitter kids, followers of British glam or rock acts such as Silverhead, Slade, the New York Dolls, Iggy Pop, David Bowie, Sweet, and the Stones. We were young hot girls who wore platform heels, fishnet stockings, and spiked Ziggy Stardust hair. We went to the Whisky, where my cousin Nancy worked as a waitress, the Roxy, Rodney Bingenheimer's, and the private upstairs club above the Rainbow Room, called Over the Rainbow. Rodney's was an underage club, but none of the others were. Mario Maglieri, who ran the Whisky and the Rainbow, had a signal. If the Alcoholic Beverage Control (ABC) came around looking to bust underage drinkers, he gave us the signal and we knew to throw our drinks on the floor.

I was hanging out with older people, wearing crazy clothes, listening to crazy music. Everyone knew I was Papa John's daughter, so the people who worked there and the musicians around all made it clear that they had my back. Mario would say, "Keep your hands off the Kid." There was an invisible barrier around me. Nobody messed with me. I was living it.

I often brought people back to the house at all hours. My room was gigantic, as was my closet. If I heard my dad coming down the hall, I'd hustle everyone into that closet. When Dad came in he'd just march straight to it, fling open the doors, and say, "Hello, ladies." I couldn't hide anything from Dad, but I also couldn't get in trouble. All the drugs I did, all of them were taken from Dad's vast supply, and he was not a man to set a double standard.

I was loved, but I wasn't protected. It was a carefree and careless youth, which was fantastic and liberating, but things happen. There are reasons for the standards society sets. Nobody was watching out for me, but someone was watching me. One night, leaving Rodney Bingenheimer's, my friends Billy and Jody and I hitchhiked with a guy we thought we recognized. I don't know how many times I made a mistake like that, but I was young and irresponsible, and there was no safety net. I climbed into the front seat of this man's car. Billy and Jody piled into the back. Just above Sunset Boulevard, the driver pulled off on a side street. I said, "This isn't the way to my house."

He said, "I think the gas cap's loose," and turned around to Billy and Jody. "Can you guys get out and check?" They hopped out. I started to get out too, but he said, "You stay here." I saw the glint of metal in his hand and knew in an instant that I was in trouble. I lunged for the door. Billy and Jody must have heard or seen something. Billy was at my door in an instant. He grabbed my arm to pull me out, but my attacker threw his arm around me, catching around my neck. Billy pulled at my arm, fighting to free me. Now I was half out of the car, between the open door and the seat, with the guy's arm around me and his knife at my throat. The threat of that knife felt like a band of fire, raging and unstoppable. The guy stepped on the gas. As the car pulled away Billy couldn't hold on any longer. He let go, and I was dragged between the car and the door for several long seconds. Once Billy and Jody were left in the dust, the driver pulled me back in, drove me up into the hills, ripped off my stockings, pushed me down on the front seat, a long bench seat, and raped me.

I was terrified, but desperate to save myself. I started talking, saying anything I could think of to get him to stop: "You don't have to do this. You're a really good-looking guy, a nice guy, you can get any girl you want." He said, "Shut up. I'm going to fucking kill you, you white bitch." *He was going to kill me.*

I said, "You can't kill me. You're going to get caught. I can't die. This is not going to happen to me. Oh Lord, please don't let me die." They were foxhole prayers. I knew as he was raping me that there was nothing to stop him from killing me. *I was going to die.* But when he finished, he shoved me out of the car and drove away.

The car pulled away and I stood on the side of the street, stunned. I'd been dragged between the car and its door. My fishnets were shredded, my legs scraped and bruised. I wobbled on my high platform heels. The straps were loose, maybe broken. I steadied myself, trying to figure out what had happened. He had said he was going to kill me, but then he'd let me go. Was I bleeding? Did he cut my neck? *Am I still here? Am I alive?* I was. I was alive, and at that moment, no matter what else had happened, that was all that mattered. I don't know how much time passed, but as soon as I realized I was still in one piece I started running down the street.

I was wearing a denim miniskirt, a tube top, my torn fishnet stockings, and the high platforms. I stumbled down the hill to Rodney's—it wasn't far. The police were already in front of the club, and Billy and Jody were crying. Dad showed up. They took me to the hospital to do a rape kit, then we went to my grandmother's house. This time, instead of giving me a Coors, she handed me a Valium. The more I saw how upset my friends and family were, the more upset I became.

My family gathered at Dini's. Everyone was wailing, and I was crying too. But when I look back on that experience it's not a lower low. It's an event in a box. This happened to me, I remember it, I do. But was it before *American Graffiti* or after? Did Aunt Rosie move into Dad's house because of the rape, or was she already there when I came home from Switzerland? Or did the rape happen before Switzerland? What is the chronology? What happened to that girl I was? Why does it feel like I watched it happen to her?

When she was young, my mother went to a finishing school in London called the Club of the Three Wise Monkeys. It was the place my grandmother hoped would purge my father from my mother's heart. The school emblem was the three wise monkeys—see no evil, hear no evil, and speak no evil. My grandmother worked at a jewelry store and she had a gold charm with three little gold monkeys made for my mother. As a child I always loved that necklace, and when I was in my twenties my mother gave it to me. I became fascinated with the concept and the expressive nature of monkeys, and I've been collecting depictions of monkeys ever since.

I own my memories, but I still sometimes see them from afar. I'm positive, I'm happy, I'm fun, and I can be these things because I refuse to take on the full weight of my experiences. I am the missing monkey, the fourth monkey, the feel no evil monkey. I learned to box up the evil and separate it from the joy of life at an early age, before the rape, before the kidnapping, before losing Patty, before what happened with my father.

There are many of these boxes. Unprocessed memories, sealed up and set aside. Sometimes they climb out unexpectedly. A night at Anthony Kiedis's father's house when I was thirteen or fourteen. I was with some older friends who instructed me to have sex with a forty-five-year-old actor. He told me what to do and how to do it. I was scared. He seemed like an old man. In the morning he insisted that I make the bed. He said, "Tuck the sheets in tight. I want to bounce a quarter off the bed." To this day I don't know why they told me to do it. It is a memory that bears no connection to who I am today, and so it feels like it happened to somebody else. I was there. I watched it happen to me. But I didn't let myself live the experience.

Feel no evil. There's an upside to it and a downside. But in the case of the rape, and similar but lesser ordeals, feeling no evil helped me stay alive. Over time I ran into discomfort with intimacy, wanting people close and keeping them far. But there was a cap on the fear and misery I was willing to experience.

The day after the rape I went home to my dad's house. That night Quincy Jones's daughter, Jolie Jones, was at Ben Frank's on Sunset, a diner where we'd hang out and ditch the check. Jolie heard two guys talking about how their friend had raped Papa John's daughter. Jolie told Quincy, and Quincy told my dad. Dad took a shotgun and disappeared for a day and a half. I have no idea what happened, and I never asked. I think, in a way, that I don't want to know anything more, because I don't want to learn anything that might change what I found out then: In a moment of crisis, Dad wanted to save me. In some primal way he wanted to protect me, to rescue me. I clung to that as evidence that for all the lax parenting, for all the hitchhiking to school and empty refrigerators, for all the joint-rolling and coke-supplying, I had a father who cared. I packed up and stored away the rape with dispassion, but I cradled that memory—Dad dashing out the door with his shotgun in a rage—as proof of his love.

PART TWO

MACKENZIE PHILLIPS

6

I was a recognizable face, out on the town, out of control, too close to danger. I was living an unprotected life, and now there was evidence, beyond a doubt, that I wasn't safe. But nothing could stand in the way of Dad's unabashed hedonism. He was driven to pursue pleasure—sex, drugs, cars, rock 'n' roll—and from the moment the Mamas & the Papas had made him a rich man he'd been hell-bent on living as high and fast as a man could live. He was a world-class partier.

The Mamas & the Papas had broken up after four short years, and Dad was ostensibly working on a play called *Space Cowboy.* Now I see it as a belabored project that was constantly delayed by Dad's chemical distractions and/or producers who lost interest when they saw how out there he was. But at the time I didn't concern myself with my father's productivity. I'd go hang out with the handsome young actors in the play, and when I say handsome, I mean Don Johnson. Literally. It was an older crowd, but those guys thought of me as my dad's little girl. The Kid. None of them touched me—until they did.

In 1974 Dad hosted a party to welcome home the returning veterans of the Vietnam War, although I'm not sure any of the "boys" were actually in attendance to be welcomed home. Like all of Dad's parties, this one took place in the courtyard of the pink palace and swept down the majestic stairway that led to the pool area. The weather had a magical quality that Dad seemed to order up for his parties—a temperature that matches your skin so exactly that you feel like you are floating. And most of the guests were, on the free-flowing booze or the trays of joints that were passed like hors d'oeuvres, or the audacious mountains of cocaine that were kept inside only to shelter them from the occasional, potentially disastrous breath of wind. There were musicians, artists, industry people, hippies in chamois and rhinestone belts, hippies in caftans with long hair, a Rolling Stone or two in tailored suits, scruffians—everyone from star-fuckers and hangers-on to rock 'n' roll royalty.

For this particular party, Dad strapped an ashtray to the head of a dwarf friend of his and called him the Human Ash-tray, which is only slightly less offensive when you know that the dwarf called himself Sugar Bear.

Even when Dad wasn't having a party, 414 St. Pierre Road was a crazy place to be, especially on acid. The dark, empty pool. The ballroom. The waterfall. The poolside arcade. The tropical gardens. The Hollywood Man looming large in the living room. I'd been tripping at home for years, but with my cousins Patty and Nancy, I rediscovered the house's secrets and surprises. We walked around saying "Oh my!" in amazement.

This decadent hipster nirvana was my world, and I assumed it would go on like that forever. Then one Thursday my dad, Genevieve, and their two-year-old son, Tam, took a trip to New York for the weekend, leaving me and Jeffrey in the care of their friends Marsia and Yipi. They were supposed to be back the following Tuesday. But Tuesday rolled around without any sign of them. A few more days passed. Then a week. Then another week. About a month later Dad bothered to call and let us know that he and Genevieve were in New York trying to make his play *Space Cowboy* happen. Marsia and Yipi didn't last long. Jeffrey and I were staying out till all hours of the morning, drinking bad wine and taking Tuinals, then calling Marsia to ask her to pick us up. Marsia would trudge out to the driveway only to discover that we'd taken her car. She'd called Dad to complain, and his path-of-least-resistance response was to send tickets to fly her and Yipi to New York.

And so it was that Aunt Rosie—Dad's sister—moved into the house in Bel Air. From the get-go Aunt Rosie was very strict compared to Dad. She made rules and expected us to stick to them, and at first we did. Kind of. I mean, when we took downers or acid and stumbled all around that amazing house, we weren't technically breaking our curfew. Though we hid our drug use from Aunt Rosie, we never really thought of drugs as illicit—we just thought Aunt Rosie wasn't cool or enlightened. My dad's friends were glamorous, they had money, they did drugs. Everything they did was worth imitating.

Aunt Rosie called Dad and Gen with increasingly aggravated reports: Jeffrey stole the car or broke something yet again. At some point Genevieve said, "Make him a milkshake and put ground glass in it." Aunt Rosie, who never got Genevieve's bizarre sense of humor, hung up the phone, stunned. "What is wrong with that woman?" she wailed.

The next time Dad checked in, Aunt Rosie informed him that the landlords were asking about the rent. The tug of obligation must not have appealed to Dad, because after that he stopped calling or even returning calls. As Dad would one day admit, he "sort of forgot about California and the two kids [he] had out there." Dad, Genevieve, and Tam never came home. *They never came back*. It's true that as the head of the household, my father didn't exactly run a tight ship. Bills went unpaid, kids went unfed. But he was still unquestionably the man of the house; he was the center of our family; *he was the center of my world*. He went away for the weekend and then never came back. He stopped communicating. He stopped paying bills. He stopped paying rent on the house. I don't know how to explain it. Dad had a remarkable lack of responsibility. Michelle would later say that when Dad wasn't using heavy drugs, he felt duty toward us and enjoyed being with us, but that when he got into heavy drugs everything else became secondary. I'm sure she's right and it is that simple. If Dad's behavior was because of the drugs, well, it's hard to say, since I never knew him free of that influence. Blame drugs or blame Dad—it makes no difference, since as far back as I can remember, drugs shared his body and soul.

When the rent checks stopped coming, the owners of the house were justifiably furious. After some months of nonpayment, they showed up at the house with a report documenting thousands of dollars' worth of damage to the house and its contents. Everything that could be torn, stained, cracked, broken, or hurled in a drug-addled fit across a room, had been. Hoping to recoup some of the back rent and damages, they confiscated most of our stuff, holding hostage in storage many precious and sentimental items, including my diaries and Aunt Rosie's slides of the family dating back to the mid-1950s. Aunt Rosie didn't want me to watch the scene when the owners came to go through the house making their claims, so she sent me to my grandma Dini's house. I came home from school to find the house half empty and in shambles. There followed a period of stress and tension at 414 St. Pierre. The great house had been filled with people and music and bustle and life. Now it was cavernous and scary. It felt like a ghost town.

My father was incommunicado, and without him we couldn't remotely afford the three-thousand-dollar monthly rent. Finally, after phone calls and demands on the part of the landlords, pleading and postponing on Rosie's part, and radio silence from my father, they kicked us out.

My father had lived in that house for almost two years. Before that he'd lived at 783 Bel Air Road for six years. He had always been a person who had a home. From that point on Dad was ephemeral. He developed a taste for transience, moving from rented penthouse to hotel to mansion without giving notice, without paying bills, without telling anyone his new number. He'd say, "Pay my bill, pack my shit, and meet me there."

Pay, pack, and follow was what he called it, and that is what he named his final album, recorded with Mick Jagger and Keith Richards in the seventies, but released after his death. My pay-pack-and-follow father left debt, belongings, family, lovers, and, eventually, thousands of used syringes in his wake.

For Dad the house may have felt like a burden, but Jeffrey and I lived there. For us 414 St. Pierre Road was home, and home was pulled out from under us.

Our whole lives we had known our father as a man who was always late coming and early going. It was in his nature, so his disappearance probably shouldn't have been the shock that it was. He hadn't really changed. But his absence also brought to light that in the time since I'd left her, my mother *had* changed. She was no longer the traditional mother who expected her children to be groomed and polite. Nor was she the warm, energetic person to whom I had been close all my life. Feeling trapped in a very difficult marriage, she had worn to a scared, vulnerable thread, doing all she could to hold the patches of her life together.

Maybe her own life was too overwhelming; maybe she felt dethroned by Rosie; maybe she was drinking too much; whatever the reasons, my mother, like my father, also abdicated—though it was against her nature. I had left her house, but now she had disappeared from my life. I missed her, and I resented her dismissal of me, but I boxed that up for later. She wasn't going to die tomorrow. The world wasn't going to end. My mother was still right there, a phone call away. I was fourteen. Not speaking to my mother didn't feel like a big deal. Besides, Rosie fed me, tried to discipline me, wanted to protect me. She attempted to do and be all that my mother had lost and given up.

Thank God for Rosie. Without hesitation my aunt stepped into a parental role that was otherwise empty at that point in my life. Our palace was gone, my parents were MIA, but my home was with my aunt and my cousins. After *American Graffiti* I had started making enough money through acting gigs that

I could now afford to rent a place for myself, Aunt Rosie, Nancy, and Patty. We went from a mansion in Bel Air to a funky, modest two-bedroom apartment in the Hollywood Hills that could have fit into my bathroom at 414 St. Pierre. Jeffrey moved back in with my mother and Lenny. The owners of 414 kept our belongings in storage, where they remain to this day, but we moved on. The new place was a relief after the trauma at 414. It felt like we were on an adventure.

Patty, Nancy, and I were the Three Musketeers, devoted to one another. We got our hair cut together—the same long shags for all of us. We dressed in the same clothes—our uniform was denim asymmetrical miniskirts with rhinestone stars or lightning bolts on them from Grills & Yang, halter tops, and platform heels. We all wore the same eye shadow, dramatic swipes of pink, then blue, then more pink. We helped one another apply it, declaring that it looked "like a cloud in the sky!"

I hate to unravel those moments, those amazing times with the cousins I loved dearly and still do. I'd like to leave them as they are in my head, young and blithe. To describe our early days together is to face that they were the beginning of something darker. The shadow of drugs was already over us, even seeping into us, forever changing who we were and what we could be, though we didn't see it or feel it. Drugs were a friend who would betray us, but hadn't yet. We loved life. Oh, Patty. She was beautiful, outgoing, and goofy. I loved her dearly.

At night we'd get all dressed up, practicing dance moves, trading clothes, and drinking wine. It took us hours to get ready. We'd wait for Rosie to go to bed, then around ten o'clock we'd creep down the stairs, right past Rosie's bedroom, and pile into the front seat of a tacky '57 white pickup truck that belonged to Nancy and Patty's older brother, my cousin Peter, and hit the clubs.

We'd spill out of the truck on Sunset Boulevard at the Roxy or the Rainbow. Sometimes by the time we arrived we were already fucked up and falling over and they wouldn't let us in, so we'd cheerfully pile back into the truck and head to another club.

Nancy, Patty, and I attracted a lot of attention. If we were sober enough, the clubs always found a table for the three of us (though the VIP sections weren't the velvet-rope enclaves they are today). I was still the Kid—men knew I was too young to hit on. But my older cousins were strikingly beautiful. We smoked and chatted and flirted. We choreographed elaborate pantomimes of Chicago songs like "Just You 'N' Me" and belted them out as we went through our routines. Patty was a brilliant singer, a karaoke star before her time. We were happy and fun, a sparkling trio.

After the clubs closed at two in the morning, everyone hung out in the parking lot to find a party. We became friends with a group of men who lived up on Mulholland Drive in great big houses. We'd leave Over the Rainbow and drive up Mulholland to Rico and Freddy's house. We called it "Freako and Reddies," and it was a real scene—pure seventies decadence.

Freddy and Rico were at least fifteen years older than I was—in their thirties. There was always a crowd of people at their pad, and vast quantities of drugs. Patty and I took tons of pills and did lots of coke. I smoked angel dust, the devil's drug, at that house and could not move for hours. We never had to pay for drugs; we weren't expected to have sex with the guys.

Our escapades made Aunt Rosie batty. She'd call up wherever I was and say, "Put her in a cab home this minute or I'm sending the police over to have you arrested for statutory rape." She'd scream on the phone, at her wits' end. But, for a while anyway, she had less to fear than she realized. Everywhere I went I was the Kid, the mascot, untouchable. It was the crumb of protection that Dad had tossed behind him before he disappeared: he put the word out that if anyone touched me he'd kill them, so nobody made a move on me.

We sometimes drove my other cousin Billy's orange Volkswagen station wagon, which we called OIG because those were the letters on the license plate. At six a.m. we'd drive home—but we'd say that OIG brought us home, because none of us ever remembered driving. Shoes in hand, we'd creep back into the house. Aunt Rosie was always there, in her dressing gown. She'd say, "Laura Mackenzie Phillips," "Patty Ann Throckmorton," "Nancy Elizabeth Throckmorton," pissed off and beside herself with frustration.

What could she do? There was Rosie, recently retired from a personnel job at the Pentagon. She'd recovered from a minor heart attack, moved to her rock-star brother's mansion, got kicked out, and took unofficial custody of a bunch of wild kids, one of whom was famous. How out of your element can you be? Aunt Rosie did a great job considering the circumstances, but she just couldn't make us behave. We'd apologize sweetly and swear up and down that we'd never stay out all night again, then we'd go out and do the same thing the next night.

In spite of my cautious aunt and somewhat protective cousins, there were some close calls. My old friend Danny Sugarman—who was the manager of the Doors and would become a pop culture icon in his own right—used to tell the story of the night we met. He was riding home from a Slade concert with Rodney Bingenheimer. Danny was in the front seat with Rodney and the driver, and one of the supporting bands was in the backseat. Apparently I too was in the backseat, making out with one of the band members, when they all decided to get in on it. Someone yelled "gang bang," and amid my protests the backseat became a tangle of arms and legs. Danny didn't like what he heard. He said, "All right, cut it the fuck out," and flicked on the overhead light. The band members sheepishly pulled back, the driver pulled over, and I hopped into the front seat to thank my savior.

Danny was nineteen—five years older than I—but we became partners in crime. He was handsome and fun, extremely bright and full of boundless energy. Between the two of us we had rock 'n' roll carte blanche. We had our table at the Whisky.

We could go backstage at any show. He knew he could count on me to behave myself, so he often brought me out for Chinese food with his father, to show that he was keeping company with a well-brought-up famous movie star. I gave him legitimacy in the eyes of his straitlaced father, who had no idea I was a wild kid.

My days were almost as busy as my nights. My turn in *American Graffiti* was a golden ticket. I was a well-known young actress. My ex-stepmother, Michelle, ended up being the one who took me on the auditions that constantly sprang up at inconvenient times. Michelle, who had a very busy and full life and career, stepped up when my mother couldn't or wouldn't. She invested herself in my career and my future. It was incredibly generous, but she did it with her typical matter-of-fact manner.

When she was married to my father, Michelle had been playful and warm, and I was a cute plaything for her. Over the years she'd developed into a cool Hollywood broad. She was also a mother now. She had a better perspective on my questionable upbringing and understood that children need protection and guidance. She did all she could to keep Chynna away from the insanity, and she tried to protect me too, in her own way. As we drove to one of my auditions she said, "Everyone in this town knows how talented you are, but they're calling you the next Judy Garland, and you're probably going to die just like her." Michelle was tough and frank. This was her way of showing love and trying to protect me. Michelle was worried about my safety, but I didn't take her seriously. The idea that "everyone in this town" even knew I existed was weird and incomprehensible to me. Besides, I didn't have a real sense that what I was doing was wrong or dangerous. I just thought she was being mean.

My mother wasn't completely absent. She must have called during this period, because I remember asking her to drive me to some of my auditions. She declined. And for me that was the last straw. It was more clear than ever that her life and her marriage were more important than I was. From then on, whenever she questioned me in a maternal way, asking what I was doing, where I was going, how late I'd be out, my response was—if not in so many words—"Where do you get off grilling me?" As far as I was concerned, she had given up her rights.

Thanks to Fred Roos, I auditioned for *Taxi Driver* and *The Exorcist,* both parts I didn't get—though in hindsight Jodie Foster's off-screen blowjob was a little too much for me, and Linda Blair's head spinning, well, I had better ways to make my head spin. But I landed plenty of parts. I worked constantly after I got the job in *American Graffiti.* While it was in production I did an episode of *Movin' On,* and a TV movie, *Go Ask Alice.* After the movie came out I did another TV movie—*Miles to Go Before I Sleep* with Martin Balsam—and single-episode parts in *Baretta* and *Mary Tyler Moore.* I also got a part in a film called *Rafferty and the Goldust Twins* with Sally Kellerman and Alan Arkin.

Alan Arkin was a great teacher and a gentle soul. How lucky I was to work with him at such a young age. Much of *Rafferty* was shot in Arizona. We all were there together. Rosie was my legal guardian on the set, Nancy was my stand-in, and Patty was my best friend. I became, at fourteen, involved with a stunt man in his thirties. Rosie, consistent in her distrust of older men, hated him and the trouble she was sure he'd cause. But we girls loved him.

When *Rafferty* came out in 1975 the attention was intoxicating. I flew to New York for the premiere, appearing in one of the first issues of *People* magazine. A profile of me in *Interview* said that I walked around like a young Bette Davis sucking on my cigarettes and flicking the ashes to the floor. I just loved my work. I loved what I did.

In New York I found Dad living in the Stanhope, a luxury hotel favored among celebrities that was on Fifth Avenue across from

Central Park. I walked into the room and he said, "Hey, Laura-bug, give your old dad a hug." This was the first time I'd seen my father since he left us to be evicted, but there was no drama, no accusations or recriminations. I was just grateful to have him back. This may sound strange, but it never occurred to me to be mad at him for disappearing. Anger didn't exist, not for me, and seemingly not for his other children, wives, friends, or Aunt Rosie. Dad was a remarkable man. He was so powerful and charming and brilliant that being around him, being in that orbit, was glory enough. We didn't expect him to adhere to the social standards of the common man. That wasn't how he lived. We knew that he never promised anything. It was hard to hold him accountable when he accepted no responsibility. He just was so clearly and consistently himself that for a long time we took him as he was and even loved him for it, in a warped way. Later, my family would have reason to be angry at him on my behalf, and even later than that I would excavate my own ingrown shards of anger. But in those days we all let it go.

Now, in my new incarnation as a press-worthy child star, my father relished the attention I was getting. It matched the high-flying life he and Gen were living, hanging out with luminaries like Colin Tennant, who owned the island of Mustique, and Princess Margaret. Besides, Dad was suffering a bit of withdrawal from the attention he'd received as the brains behind the Mamas & the Papas. He craved the limelight. Hitting the scene with his famous daughter more than doubled the buzz. We led a fancy life, going to Mr. Chow every night and to nightclubs.

When Colin Tennant rented the Kennedy compound on Montauk, Dad brought me out to stay. One of Andy Warhol's cronies was there with his niece. I got in big, big trouble for seducing the niece. I don't know exactly how it happened. She and I were friends, about the same age, and one night we started playing some rather innocent but naked games in my bedroom. In the morning her uncle pounded on the door, telling us to open up, while Dad appeared at the window. Her uncle was very upset, shouting, "How dare you? She's just a child!" I was kinda thinking, *Well, what am I?* After that I wasn't allowed near her anymore. For the rest of the vacation we'd wave at each other from across the room apologetically.

I didn't see how her uncle could judge me—he was flamingly gay—but I wasn't fazed. This wasn't my first same-sex dalliance and it wouldn't be my last. Like my father, I let momentary desire carry me like a current—I never drew lines at gender, age, circumstance. Later, when I was clean, I would discover that those lines existed, that they were coded in my DNA. At the time I thought my open sexuality was natural, but in reality it was the drugs. I'm straight.

Reviews for my performance in *Rafferty* were good and led to a pilot deal for a show called *One Day at a Time.* I didn't even audition. I just met with Norman Lear, whom I knew was the brilliant creator of *All in the Family, The Jeffersons,* and *Sanford and Son*, and the deal was done. At the time, landing the role of Julie Cooper seemed like just another exciting job to me—I had no idea that it would be on the air for the next nine years and would prove to be the defining role of my career. I came from a family with a father who left houses when he got bored or ran out of dough, a mother who was under the sway of a cruel husband, and a brother who was in and out of trouble. I had a recreational drug habit that was quickly becoming a way of life. For all the chaos in my life, *One Day at a Time* would prove a point of stability. It would be, in some ways, the closest thing I had to a home.

7

Originally *One Day at a Time* was built around me, the little starlet who was getting so much attention. I'd been on the scene for so long, in fact, that when Bonnie Franklin heard that she was going to play my mother on the show, her first reaction was that I was too old to be her daughter. Bonnie's character—Ann Romano—was supposed to be thirty-five. I was only fifteen—two years younger than my character!—so I definitely wasn't too old, but it had been three years since I'd shot *Graffiti*. I had a very public life. I was such a familiar face that she assumed I was much older.

Shooting the pilot wasn't momentous for me. It wasn't a new-enough experience to be nerve-racking or exceptionally exciting, and, as I've said, I had no idea how significant the role would be in my life. I don't remember rehearsing it, shooting it, watching it, or celebrating it.

Needless to say, my lack of awareness was immaterial. CBS loved the pilot, with one exception. In the pilot my character, Julie Cooper, was an only child. CBS's major note was that they wanted a sibling for me, so Valerie Bertinelli was cast as my younger sister, Barbara Cooper. Later they'd be patting themselves on the back for that wise and show-saving decision.

Valerie remembers the first time we met better than I do. She always tells it that we were in an elevator on our way to the rehearsal hall. I don't remember the setting, but I know that I was a lot taller than she was and different in every way. I remember seeing a cute little kid—we were only six months apart in age, but she seemed like a young child to me. Not only was she five inches shorter than I was, but I wore platforms that made me almost six feet tall. She wore sneakers. I wore tight jeans and leather jackets. She wore headbands; I wore shades. I was so young, but at the time I didn't feel like a kid, not with my work schedule during the day and the older crowd I ran with at night.

The encounter may not be burnt on my soul, but I can guarantee that Val greeted me as she always did, with a characteristically sweet and enthusiastic "Hi!" With my seasoned club-kid attitude I probably said something understated, like "Hey. So you're my sister." I wasn't trying to intimidate her, but apparently I did.

Julie and Barbara were basically the sanitized, Hollywoodized versions of me and Val. Julie was a rebel. In the pilot she wanted to go on a coed camping trip. She hitchhiked, she became a Jesus freak, she talked back to her mother, she ran away, and she . . . well, she may not have done anything terrible, but she sure talked back to her mother a lot. Julie also dated a man twice her age—in that case life was soon to imitate art. She may not have been rolling joints for her father at the age of ten, clubbing on Sunset Strip, or getting high with seasoned pros, but the part wasn't exactly a stretch for me.

The main difference between my character and me was Julie's attitude. Her parents had split up, and Ann, her mother, was trying to stay positive. But whenever she tried to bond with her daughters, Julie was like, "Can you get to the point? I got boys waiting for me outside." I was never rude or verbally defiant—actions got me in trouble, not words.

Also, I definitely thought of myself as way cooler than my character. I didn't have boundaries. Aunt Rosie had certain rules, but when I walked out the door of our house (which I rented) I could do whatever I wanted, and I did. I had freedom and I had money. I saw poor Julie as trapped in her dorky sitcom world of eye-rolling frustration and teenaged howls of "Mo-om!" Her life was specific and ordered by the powers that be. In that way—in her limited freedom and resources—the fictional Julie was more of a real kid than I was.

Barbara was Julie's clingy, perky, saccharine-sweet little sister. In Julie's mind poor Barbie needed to be torn up and spit out on a daily basis. Valerie was straight out of Granada Hills, just as bubbly, clean, and eager as Barbara. Val's innocence only made me feel more sophisticated, as I felt with most people my age. But I wasn't all confidence. After all, I was still a teenager and what teenager wouldn't feel ugly next to Val? My bad skin was a particular source of angst. Norman Lear, the producer, didn't want me to wear much makeup on the show because my skin was "teenage." Meanwhile Val had perfect, glowing skin that I couldn't help envying.

I don't remember re-rehearsing, reshooting, rewatching, or recelebrating the new pilot that included Val as Barbara any more than I remember the first go-round, but CBS was satisfied with the new ensemble and decided to put the show on the air.

That first season we shot fifteen episodes of the show, and we adopted a regular work schedule similar to that of most sitcoms. We shot one episode per week. On Monday we got the script for that week's show. We did a "table read," running our lines so the writers could see what was and wasn't working. Bonnie felt a responsibility to the character and always gave a million notes on the scripts. She'd say, "Ann would object to this behavior from the girls," or she'd point out that Ann wouldn't laugh off every single one of the slimy superintendent Schneider's advances, day after day. At some point Ann had to try to put a stop to it. Bonnie wanted to bring Ann's ex-husband, Ed Cooper, played by Joseph Campanella, into the show more in order to highlight the conflicts that arose there. Above all, she didn't want it to be sitcom fluff—she wanted it to deal honestly with the struggles and truths of raising two teenagers as a single mother. She never gave up. She drove the producers nuts. But she absolutely made the show better.

I had enormous respect for Bonnie's passion, but I was young and knew my place. Most of my notes were suggestions for how to make Julie's lines funnier or tweaks to her voice or reactions. I was from a broken family, so this was familiar territory for me. Sometimes, as I got the hang of things, I'd make suggestions about how scenes could be shot. Once, for a tough shot where they needed to look into our apartment but also needed a turnaround shot to see the wall, I suggested that they cut a hole in the wall. The director, Alan Rafkin, gave me the unofficial "Director of the Week" award for that idea.

After two days of rehearsal, on Thursday, we'd move to the soundstage, where the crew would start blocking the scenes for the cameras. This was tedious. We had to repeat scenes over and over so they could time the camera moves up in the director's booth. I was a teenager about it, letting my boredom show, but I never caused problems. My mother's instructions to be kind and polite to everyone came to the surface on the set. In an industry where some actors see themselves at the top of a hierarchy, I never saw it that way. I was always equally friendly with cast, crew, and guest actors. I welcomed strange faces and was happy to hang out with whoever was around. To this day, if I run into an actor who was an extra on the show, or a grip, or a gofer, he or she invariably tells me that I made him or her feel like a human being. Later there was much to regret about my behavior during my years on the show, but I was never, ever a diva.

Friday nights we taped the show before a live studio audience. In the afternoon, after a run-through, we'd get into wardrobe. I always made sure Julie looked cool. Often, I'd wear my own clothes—the opening credits had me in my own forest green leotard and tights doing yoga. I'd wear bell-bottom Landlubber jeans with Kork-Ease shoes—huge wedgie platforms with crisscross straps that I had in both pink and red. Under the strappy platforms I'd wear Hot Sox—bright socks with stripes, stars, or rainbow colors. I was the tallest woman in the cast by far, so you'd think those platforms would be verboten, but they liked to joke about my height and weight in the scripts. Pat

Harrington as Schneider would tease me that if I turned sideways in the shower I'd disappear, or he'd call me "a Q-tip with eyes."

We taped the show in front of the studio audience twice—actually in front of two different studio audiences—so that they'd have a couple different takes to choose from when they were editing the show. Performing in front of a live audience never bothered me—I finally had the attention I'd always wanted—and it taught me how to be a better actor. There is no faster way to learn what is working and what isn't. We could tweak a line through infinite rehearsals, but the true test was simple: did the audience laugh? Performing live taught me the importance of good timing.

Aunt Rosie was my on-set guardian. She was with me all day every day. My cousin Patty worked in wardrobe, and Nancy was my stand-in. All three of them were often in the studio audience to applaud me. On Sunday nights at eight we would watch the show at home together, often with friends, on CBS. (This was pre-VCR, pre-TiVo, in the hard-core days of appointment television.)

I read a lot on the set. My father had given me and my brother Jeffrey a list of must-read books for Phillips children. He wanted his children to be able to discuss literature and art. I dutifully read all of the books on the list, cover to cover, but come to think of it, I don't remember ever talking to Dad about any of them. The list included *Wuthering Heights, Jane Eyre, The Comedians* by Graham Greene, works by Byron and Shelley, and *Cosmic Consciousness: A Study of the Evolution of the Human Mind*, which was written by Richard Maurice Bucke in 1901. Also on the list were *The Picture of Dorian Gray* by Oscar Wilde and *Orlando* by Virginia Woolf, both of which deal with characters who are determined not to grow old. It was a notion that appealed to my father so much that he and Gen gave my brother Tam the middle name Orlando.

One time I was reading off-list—*Dune* by Frank Herbert—and Aunt Rosie picked it up while I was busy rehearsing and became engrossed. During my breaks I took it back, but Rosie took it back up while I was working. Every time I read a great book, I hate putting it down because it feels like the story will go on without me. As I rehearsed I kept thinking about my book in Rosie's hands, wondering what was happening on the planet Arrakis. Late in the afternoon, I glanced over at Rosie to see if I could tell by the look on her face whether ill had befallen the hero, Paul. For the first time all day she wasn't buried in the book. *Dune* was on her lap and she was chatting with Valerie's mother, Nancy. A surge of tenderness toward Aunt Rosie swelled up in me. She had given up having a life to sit on the set with me day in and day out. She was always there, a constant. I loved her for that and more.

Having family around bore quite a contrast to the days of *American Graffiti,* when I'd shown up in San Francisco all by myself. But Dad was still Dad. I was dying for him to see a taping of the show, and one Friday he and Genevieve said they'd come. I asked Pat Palmer, the producer, to reserve two seats for them and she taped off two chairs. When the warm-up comedian went out to get the audience riled up for the upcoming show, I peeked out from behind the curtain. The audience was full, except for two empty chairs. Dad and Gen were late. The comedian finished and we came out onstage to tape the first scene. I snuck a glance at the audience. The seats were still empty. All night, through both tapings, I kept waiting for my father, hoping he was going to show up, believing against all reason that he would. But he never showed. This happened many times.

Maybe Dad wasn't eager to see the show, but others were. We'd go to work on Monday mornings and they'd give us the overnights—the ratings for the night before. Back in those days there were only five networks, no cable, no computers competing for audience share. We regularly had an audience of around twelve million people—more than twenty percent of the total audience. It was huge. We were often the number one show of the week. The show was in the top ten, or close to it, for most of its run.

When I watch episodes of the show now, I cringe at my over-acting. Why didn't anybody say anything to me? But I guess the high ratings prove that broad, over-the-top comedy was the sit-com style at the time. I do remember Alan Rafkin saying things to Val like, "Valerie, can you hold up your hand so we know you're acting?" She took a lot of shit. It was not a critically ac-claimed show, but with numbers like ours nobody cared much. The powers that be just said, "Oh, yeah, right, but America loved it." Our show was another feather in Norman Lear's cap.

Val and I both went to school on set. We were supposed to do four hours of schoolwork per day, in twenty-minute increments or longer. I kept the same on-set teacher, Gladys Hirsh, from *American Graffiti* through all of *One Day at a Time*. I loved the Waldorf curriculum at Highland Hall and at first brought it with me, but Highland Hall didn't want a working student who only came to school during hiatus, our three-month break from shooting the show. So when we were on hiatus I started going to Hollywood Professional School while Val went back to pub-lic high school.

Hollywood Professional School was an odd place on Hol-lywood Boulevard a couple blocks east of Western. It was in a rank, dangerous part of Hollywood, a strange place for a school. The building was very old, with cement floors painted institu-tional gray and green. It was not fancy.

The students were all kids who thought they were going to be stars: ice skaters, jugglers, kids who did commercials, wan-nabes, and, randomly, Leif Garrett. One girl kept spray paint and a rolled-up sock in her locker. She'd spray the sock and huff the paint.

Classes took place from 8:45 a.m. to 12:45 p.m. so kids could go on auditions in the afternoon. The teachers were old and crazy. Mrs. Anderson, the creative writing teacher, regularly went off on tangents about her personal life in the middle of class. She'd say, "That reminds me of when I was in Mexico, there was a young man, he was beautiful . . ." and for the rest of the class we were hearing about rum drinks and coconuts. Meanwhile she criticized my stories for being too hard to believe. So much for "creative" writing.

Our civics teacher was even worse. She had white-blond hair and wore more makeup than a showgirl. Her face shone as if she had a coating of Vaseline on her face. Her idea of teaching us civics was to require us to copy the entire glossary of the textbook verbatim. While we wrote away, she played belly-dancing music and walked around with finger cymbals on. Eventually she was arrested for prostitution in front of the school. For all my absences, hitchhiking, acid-influenced attendance, and hippie schooling, I'd always managed to be a good student. But Hollywood Professional School was a joke. I was like, "Are you kidding me, this is *school*?"

Nobody, including me, was about to complain. Not that it would have mattered if we did. The school's principal, Mrs. Mann, had a beautiful house in Beachwood Canyon. She liked to have big parties for all the students where we'd play kissing games.

It was tricky to make friends at Hollywood Professional—we were all coming and going—but I did have a boyfriend. Two of my classmates were Andy and David Williams, identical twins who were nephews of the singer Andy Williams. They were lanky, with long, thick blond hair in matching shag cuts and strong noses. They were built like aristocrats. The twins wore turtlenecks with gabardine slacks, perfectly shined loafers, and matching Cartier watches with gold chains. They were musicians, trying to launch a twin-brother pop act that I don't think ever went anywhere. Andy was my boyfriend the whole first year that *One Day at a Time* was on the air, but it must have been one of those early, token relationships where we spent most of our time socializing in groups and hanging out together at parties. My only surviving memory of the relationship is how spectacularly elegant Andy was and what he would one day say to me when it came to an end.

Not long after I started working on *One Day at a Time,* I was invited to appear on the game show *Hollywood Squares.* I sat in the square next to the brilliant Paul Lynde. At *Hollywood Squares* they shot five episodes in a single day. The first time I did it everything went smoothly. Being a Square was fun—all the challenge of a game show but none of the pressure. When they invited me back again . . . and again, I was delighted. But before one of my subsequent appearances I ran into a little trouble.

I may have been a professional all day long, but I was still a kid when I hung out with my brother. Jeffrey and I liked to play a game we called Bicycle. We'd lie down on the floor, put our feet up against each other's feet, and bicycle as fast as we could. On this particular occasion—the night before I was due to tape *Hollywood Squares*—Jeffrey was over at our house and we had a Bicycle session that got a little rambunctious. Jeffrey's foot slipped and he kicked me in the eye. I had a shiner the size of California.

There was no way I could show up to *Hollywood Squares* with a black eye. Patty took one look at me and said, "Dr. Feelgood is your only hope." Our own Dr. Feelgood was the family resource for speed prescriptions. Family, friends, and associates went to him every week. The girls would hide rolls of quarters in their underwear to make sure they "made weight" for stronger drugs. Dr. Feelgood was the next best thing to a miracle worker, so Patty brought me to him. I don't know what he gave me, but the next day I was as good as new. Not exactly the life lesson I needed: it wouldn't be the first time Dr. Feelgood gave me something to get me through another day.

By day I was a prematurely employed young girl, throwing myself into the role of teen-dream Julie Cooper or going to school with my cute, clean boyfriend. On weekends I was living out Ann Romano's worst nightmare. I smoked pot, drank wine, and took Quaaludes (and maybe some barbiturates). But Aunt Rosie carefully supervised the part of my life that took place within her field of vision. I went to work every day. On hiatus, I went to school every day. I didn't party every night. Many a night Patty and I curled up next to each other in bed to read. For the most part I was doing what I thought most teenagers did—stretching the rules, experimenting, living through experience. It was fun, and I had no desire for the partying to escalate, no instinct that it was dangerous, no sense that it might lead to disaster.

8

After the first season of *One Day at a Time* aired, my father mentioned that I could spend the summer in London with him and Genevieve. Dad had a flat off Kings Road on Glebe Place. I leapt at the invitation—wherever Dad's party was, I would follow.

For the first couple days Dad and I sat around, mostly singing and doing coke. Then one afternoon Dad and Keith Richards (the Rolling Stone with a known heroin habit) came home and started crawling around on the floor looking for bits of heroin or cocaine. I helped. Still that same little girl who wanted to roll joints for Daddy's friends. Finally, disappointed, they said they were going to go score. As they hurried out the door, they told me they'd meet me at Redlands, Keith's house in the country, that night. A driver would soon arrive to pick me up. Then they left.

I packed a small bag and waited. And waited. Nobody came. Hours passed and night fell and nobody came. I was a confident sixteen-year-old, but it was my first time in London. I hadn't been there long and wasn't remotely oriented to being in another country, alone, without cash or friends or keys or food in the refrigerator. Late that night I went to sleep with all the lights on, expecting Dad and Keith to walk through the door any minute.

At three in the morning I woke up with a start. The power was out. The phone was dead. I was still alone in the flat. I found a single candle and lit it. I sat in front of my stepmother's vanity table, and when I looked in the mirror I saw the distorted, spooky shadow of my face, lit by the candle below. It reminded me of the slumber-party game where you turn out the lights, hold a candle up to your chin, and chant "Bloody Mary, Bloody Mary," waiting for the ghost of a woman who murdered her children to appear. But different specters appeared to me that night.

Here I was, waiting for Dad, again. He had abandoned me, I had found him, and now he had disappeared again. I knew full well that there was no guarantee that a driver would ever arrive or that Dad would walk back in that door. Why was he that way? What was it about me that made it so easy for him to leave? What was wrong with me? Was I invisible? Did I exist? I started writing in my diary, a thick blank book with a shiny silver cover. I wrote and wrote, in red ink by candlelight. Hours passed. So often my father had left me to fend for myself, but when I was younger it was an adventure. Now, in my melodramatic teenage mind, it was terrifying. I was more alone than I'd ever been in my life. Nobody was coming to get me. I had been abandoned. Was I even there in the first place? Was I real or someone else's dream? Was there anyone outside this flat? I was in a void, having lost everything but myself. It was like being dead.

That night I took measure of my life for the first time, and it seemed to be nothing but a series of random events that dropped me into a hole. Dad was gone again, in pursuit of personal nirvana, but the pure hedonism he envisioned doesn't exist. You always take others down with you. I try not to blame my father for being who he was, but he should have known or learned this. I think about my own son and I can't imagine how anyone could desert a sixteen-year-old like that. And in the same instant I think about what I did to my son, and the deep regrets I have, and I know how someone can.

I had been left, for the millionth time, told by my father's actions that I was worthless and inconsequential, that I couldn't count on anyone, that nobody cared what became of me, that I had to fend for myself and if I didn't, well, that was my tough shit. If ever there was a potential turning point, a moment in my youth when I might have been angry at my father, blamed him for forgetting me time and time again, dismantled his power over me, this was the moment. But I loved—or, more accurately, yearned—for him too intensely to be angry or to dismiss him. Instead, I turned my anger inward, self-destructing. *What was it about me that made it so easy for him to disappear?* I looked at myself in the mirror and cried and cried.

Days passed. I wrote in my journal, contemplating my own existence, page after page of distraught teenage fear and fury that would one day burn to ashes in a house fire. I ate some old bread and Marmite. I wept.

Waiting for Dad: It happened a lot. When I was growing up in Virginia he hardly ever visited. He became an untouchable, unattainable figure. I'd watch him on TV and say, "That's my Dad," but he wasn't a reality.

My sixth Thanksgiving: Dad was coming. Jeffrey and I were all dressed up, sitting on the couch, waiting for my father. My legs stuck straight out—they weren't long enough to dangle over the edge of the couch. I stared at my Mary Janes and ruffled socks, clicking my toes together. Click, click, click. We waited and waited. Then the phone call: "I can't come. I just took acid with Donovan."

My father was frequently four or five hours late, but this time stood out because when she heard he wouldn't make it to Thanksgiving, my mother lost it. She screamed, "That bastard," and started crying and yelling, storming around and slamming doors. Jeffrey and I sat there stunned. We weren't shocked that he wasn't coming. That was already a familiar disappointment. But my mom went off the wall. What followed was a quiet, terse Thanksgiving meal with the three of us, throughout which my mother drank buckets and buckets of whatever she drank.

An amusement park outing: Michelle and Dad promised they'd take me, six, and Jeffrey, eight, to an amusement park called Pacific Ocean Park. Like any kids would be, we were dying to go. Finally, the big day arrived. They drove us to the park, handed us a hundred-dollar bill, and told us to meet them in the parking lot at the end of the day. Then they left.

The trip to the Virgin Islands: Once Dad called in the middle of the night and asked Mom to bring me to the airport immediately. I was five years old. I flew by myself to Philadelphia, then boarded a Learjet with the Mamas & the Papas. They took me with them and a couple friends to the Virgin Islands for a trip that was to last until the money ran out. We camped out in tents on the beach for months. My dad and Michelle had a huge tent with an Oriental rug on the floor and candles everywhere. I had my own little pup tent nearby, where I got eaten alive by the bugs. I remember waking up one night with a spider crawling on my arm and realizing that if I didn't want the spider on me, I would have to be the one to get rid of it.

The whole group was on acid or speed all the time, from the moment they woke up. An unpredictable point in time that ranged from late morning to late afternoon. I remember walking through the forest with a bunch of them, including Duffy, the owner of the club in Saint Thomas where the Mamas & the Papas got their start. All the grown-ups were freaking out about the forest for some reason. I took Duffy's hand and said, "Don't worry, Duffy, I promise the sun will rise again tomorrow." There I was, a five-year-old, talking adults down from bad acid trips.

I couldn't afford to be shy—I was hungry. Literally. With all the partying and sleeping in and writing the songs that would make the Mamas & the Papas a world-famous vocal group, feeding the little kid wasn't top priority. I was a tough little survivor. I'd walk into town all by myself and go to church. I convinced some sailors to buy me breakfast and one man to buy me a new pair of shoes. (I could have used that boldness when my dad deserted me in London.) When I told my father and his friends what I'd done, they thought it was the funniest thing they'd ever heard and sent me to other camps to steal food for them—apparently we'd run out of money. I was happy to have a mission.

I don't want these stories to sound self-pitying. For the most part I was perfectly well cared for, and all the waiting added up to only a small part of my life. But those moments created a dynamic that forever dominated my relationship with my father. My dad was so tall. I was a tiny girl. I was always pulling on his pants leg, saying, "Hey, hey, hey," trying to get his attention like a little puppy, hoping someone would throw the ball for me. Dad would keep talking, oblivious to the tugging sensation around his knee. I so longed to be cherished.

I waited at his mansions for my guardian to show up. I waited in the mornings for someone to drive me to school. I waited on Friday nights for my father to watch me tape *One Day at a Time*. And now it was still happening: my trip to London.

Three days later Dad and Keith finally showed up in a Lamborghini. They announced, "We're here!" I didn't say, "Where the fuck have you been?" I was just relieved that I hadn't been completely forgotten. My gratitude for that eclipsed the rest.

Dad and Keith had my little brother, Tam, who was five, and Keith's son Marlon, seven, in tow. I deduced that they had already been to Redlands and now had used picking me up as an excuse to drive into the city and score more drugs.

On the way to Redlands Keith drove 125 miles per hour. Tam, Marlon, and I were in the backseat sliding back and forth and laughing hysterically. My dad, parent for the moment, said, "You can't drive that way—the children are in the car." He insisted that Keith pull over so he could take the wheel. In his head, he was a great parent.

Redlands was a gorgeous castle in Chichester, with big gates at the entry and rolling lawns. When we walked in, Keith's girlfriend, Anita Pallenberg, doyenne of rock 'n' roll wivery, turned to me and snarled, "Who invited you?"

I was thrown. I said, "Um, my dad?" The guy who drove me here? The guy I walked in with? First I'd been abandoned for several days, now I was apparently unwelcome. But I'd learned not to take what the grown-ups said at face value. The rudeness was random and meaningless. Indeed, eventually Anita and I would play dress-up together, with me trying on all of her seventies finery.

Not everything at Redlands was so innocent. The adults were partying. Tam and Marlon, little rug rats, ran around unsupervised. There were syringes in the cups in the bathrooms. Drugs were just another part of the posh rural retreat. Later, on another family trip to Redlands, my grandmother Dini came with us. Dini was a drunk, but when it came to drugs she was oblivious. Keith would come downstairs after doing a shot of heroin and nod out. Dini would say, "He's on drugs now, right?" And I'd say, "Yes, Dini, Keith is on heroin." She'd nod, and we'd go back to eating our lunch.

A couple days into the visit, Genevieve and I were sitting on the couch, enjoying the view out a vast picture window overlooking the countryside. There was a grassy hill that dropped off steeply enough that you couldn't see what was immediately behind it. Out of the blue, Genevieve said, "Oh, look at all the lovely white balloons." At first I didn't look twice. Genevieve was the queen of the non sequitur. In her high-pitched Betty Boop voice she'd say, "Laurie, I love it when you smile and your gums show." Or, "Laurie, you're like a bottomless lake, so deep." Then I noticed several white globes bobbing along the crest of the hill. As I watched, the white orbs rose up over the hill and I saw that they weren't balloons. They were helmets. Helmets atop the heads of several uniformed bobbies. I said, "Those aren't balloons. It's the cops," and ran to tell Keith.

Redlands had been raided before, and Keith had been tried for drug possession three times. We all panicked. As the bobbies approached, everyone scrambled around the house, flushing dope and hiding syringes.

Only a few crazed minutes passed before the doorbell rang. Keith sauntered to the door as I remembered the toothbrush holder full of syringes and hurried to hide it in a chest. The bobby-in-charge stood stick-straight in the doorway and politely said, "Mr. Richards, someone seems to have set off your burglar alarm." The little kids had unwittingly hit a hidden panic button that set off a silent alarm. We had called the cops on ourselves. They were very civil and everything was sorted out on the threshold. They never set foot in the house.

After we returned from Redlands, I found my footing in London. First I ventured out to shop in Soho to spend some of the great stack of traveler's checks I kept in my purse. I was walking down Kings Road in a paper minidress from Fiorucci when I got catcalls from guys. I'd gotten catcalls before, stateside, but these were different. *One Day at a Time* was a hit in the States. It was a huge show. I was completely recognizable—people called me Julie everywhere I went. Add to that my Dad's fame and *Graffiti*—when I got catcalls back home, I always assumed the attention came from my notoriety. And when I met people, part of me always wondered, *Do you really like me? Am I really cute or fun or sexy? Do you actually like who I am?* These Kings Road catcalls—from men who didn't know who I was—meant they actually thought I was just plain worth a whistle. It was a nice confidence boost for a self-doubting sixteen-year-old girl.

There was a heat wave in London that summer. It was humid and sticky and nasty. Restaurants notoriously skimped on ice cubes in drinks. The only way to escape the brutal heat was to find the surprisingly few bars and clubs on Kings Road that had air-conditioning. Now I was on familiar turf. At first I went with Dad and his friends. Then it happened that as I walked past a table at a club I was stopped by Lorna Luft, Judy Garland's daughter. Lorna said, "Don't I know you?" We'd met in L.A. I joined her table. That night Lorna introduced me to her boyfriend, Jake Hooker, and a guy named Alan Merrill. Jake and Alan were in a band called the Arrows. The Arrows were extremely hot—there was rampant Arrowmania in London that summer. Alan was the lead singer. I started hanging out with Lorna and her friends, and soon I started dating Alan. He was ten years older than I was and drop-dead gorgeous.

Alan and I had a hot, hot affair. There was a first kiss that I should remember, and I know I used to remember it because of the song I wrote for him about it after I came home:

Hey your pixie misses you
She wants it all to last
Hey your pixie kisses you
But our love grew too fast.
Our first kiss at the Bellgravia Fair
About that she reminisces
And runs her fingers through her hair

Alan Merrill and Jake Hooker were the center of teen-pop craziness. When I went out with them, Lorna Luft, Papa John, and Keith Richards, we had the run of the city. And we often had parties at the Glebe Place flat. At one of those parties Mick Jagger made fun of me for listening to the Don McLean song "Starry Starry Night." Another night, out at dinner with Dad and some other people, apropos of nothing, Jagger told me, "You have to exercise or by the time you're forty your ass will be at your ankles." He stood up from the table and demonstrated how to do squats. I didn't care what words were coming out of his mouth. I thought he was luminously attractive.

• • •

That summer was a coming-of-age for me Phillips style. My memory of that time has fogged over—I'm left with a blurry sense that it was bright and fun and a nonstop frolic. It's not that I was doing drugs that summer, at least not enough to account for the fogginess, but the drugs that came later obscured bits and chunks of my past. What I remember without doubt was that sex for me hadn't been anything too special until Alan. I loved having sex with him. I said as much in my journal, where I went into great detail about having sex all night in every imaginable position. And I remember Aunt Rosie finding my silver diary, ignoring the pages documenting the tortured days I spent alone, skipping to the naughty parts (who wouldn't?), and discovering that in spite of all the times she waited up late, screamed over the phone, and made threatening calls to various older male parties over the years, I wasn't a virgin. Poor Rosie.

It was a romantic, amazing, idyllic time. I was sixteen, I was in love, and I was totally free. I expected only more of the same ahead.

9

Home in L.A., when Rosie found my diary, she called me a slut. She told me that I had a personality disorder, that there was something terribly, terribly wrong with me. Now that she said it, I thought maybe it was so. When I was a little kid I'd sometimes wondered if I was different and nobody was telling me. Was something wrong with me? Was everybody hiding it from me? Were they suspiciously cautious around me? I'd been put on Ritalin for hyperactivity—Ritalin, which at least one study has linked to later smoking and cocaine use by children who take it. Now I was fully formed, successful, and newly confident in my sexuality, but still with underlying doubts that I could function like everyone else.

Meanwhile, during the first season of *One Day at a Time*, in the episode "Julie Goes All the Way," her boyfriend, Chuck, pressures her to have sex. He says, "Only freaks and weirdos don't make love when they feel the urge." Hmm. Wasn't that the exact opposite of what Rosie said?

Julie's life on *One Day at a Time* resonated with mine, not because the writers knew what went on between me and Rosie (or me and Alan for that matter), but because the struggles of a teenager chasing independence are so universal. Season two started with a four-parter called "The Runaways." In the course of those episodes, Julie runs off with Chuck, the sex-seeking boyfriend with a leopard-spotted van.

The guy who played Chuck, William Kirby Cullen, was myopic or something. He had terrible eyesight. When we rehearsed he wore glasses, but when we taped the show the producers would ask him to take them off. The guy couldn't see for shit. He'd be saying, "Julie, I love you," but instead of looking into my eyes he'd be staring deeply and soulfully at my armpit. It was all I could do not to grab his chin and say, "Hey, buddy, I'm over here!"

Julie runs away because her mother is trying to control her. She says, "Fuck you, I'm outta here"—or she would have if such things were acceptable on network TV. Then she and Chuck move into a seedy motel. Bonnie misses her prodigal daughter. She goes to find her and ask her to come home. Of course the comic relief is Schneider talking to Rest Stop Rosie on the CB radio as he and Ann hunt Julie down.

The showdown is a scene I loved doing with Bonnie. When Ann tells Julie she wants her to come home, Julie is living in squalor with Chuck. She's unhappy. She misses her family. But she is still proud and defiant.

She says, "My relationship with Chuck has to be what we want, not what you want. I see him when I like, go on trips with him, or do anything else we want to do. Mom, this is it. Either I run my life or I don't come back." Julie was describing the freedom I myself had been enjoying for years.

But Ann, hard as it was for her, said, "Okay, Julie. Don't come back." It was a powerful scene, and for me it was a brief window into a world where a parent says "No, you have to live in my house on my terms" and is heard and heeded. It was what Rosie tried so fruitlessly to do.

Rosie was increasingly sickly, and her three charges were increasingly wild. We lived in a big house that I'd rented in Beachwood Canyon. My cousins and I went to parties and entertained an endless stream of visitors she'd never met before. The inmates were ruling the prison and it took a toll on Rosie. She couldn't ground me—I had to go to work every day. The more Rosie tried to control me the more I rebelled. I never thought of it at the time, but it must have been hard for Rosie to feel powerful. Dad didn't contribute anything to our household. I paid the rent; I bought Rosie her car; I financed the household. I'd been paying for my own dentist appointments since I was twelve. I had dependents who were older than I was from the age of fifteen. How do you control someone who holds all the cards?

Still, it wasn't a constant battle. There were many times we all cooked together, went to movies, and acted like a family. We'd somehow accumulated sixteen canyon cats as household members: Sooty, Ginger, Andu, Midnight, Brains, and eleven others, whose names occasionally come to me in the middle of the night only to disappear by morning. Each evening at feeding time Rosie and I would stand at the kitchen counter opening can after can of cat food as feline bodies wove in and around our feet. We set down sixteen bowls of cat food and watched the nightly feast. Rosie taught me to take in, care for, and love strays, animal and human. But she never did get me to follow her rules.

Rosie's rules weren't the only ones I was breaking. After my dreamy summer in London with Alan Merrill, I came home to my boyfriend Andy. I hadn't intended to betray Andy, but Alan Merrill was unimaginably handsome. When I fell in love with him I felt so far away from Andy, from home, from Earth. Then I came back, and Andy could tell I'd been with someone else. He said, "Look, first of all you're high half the time. I can't even talk to you, and I don't find it attractive." That was shattering enough, but he wasn't done. "Second of all, you're off fucking other people. I love you, but I can't do this anymore." We were over. I was crushed. I cried; I told him my summer affair was just a fling; I insisted that I would change: "It's over. I'm done. I'm not going to do it anymore. I'm not going to get high." But I couldn't keep that promise. I took Quaaludes the way other kids might sneak a chocolate bar in the middle of class. One day I passed out on my desk during typing class. I thought it was kind of funny—would the "ASDF" that was imprinted on my forehead fade in time for rehearsal? But Andy had plans for his time and they didn't involve waiting around for me to wake up.

It never occurred to me that Andy might have a point about my drug use. I just thought he wasn't hip like me and my family. My whole life I'd had it drilled into me that I was different. I came from a subculture that ran parallel to mainstream life. My father always said, "First and foremost, you're a Phillips and the rules don't apply to you. You can get away with anything." Textbook megalomaniac. He was the king of a fiefdom where, for a while anyway, everything went his way. With Dad and his cohorts my drug use was completely acceptable, but I was finding out that with others, like Andy, it was not.

I started dating a lot—guys who'd guest-star on the show and guys who worked on the lot. I wasn't sleeping with those guys, but I'd had more than one serious relationship. Meanwhile, Val was probably still a virgin. No matter, Val and I formed a special bond in spite of our differences. We were the only kids working a full-time job together. Our days were stripped of the social life that most kids find at school. We had lunch hour off, when we'd relax at my house, each having a glass of wine poolside. On the weekends we had guys over and hung out with them by the pool.

One night we were at KC's apartment (of KC and the Sunshine Band). It wasn't long before Rick Springfield, already a teen phenom at the time, started hitting on young, beautiful Val. She was still fifteen, maybe sixteen years old. She came up to me and whispered, "Mack, we gotta get out of here." I said, "But he's so cute!" Still, we ran out the door and drove away very fast. She was freaked out, but to me the parties, the flirtations, the hookups, the mad-dash escapes—it was all a hilarious adventure. That would be our mismatched dynamic for years. I was impulsive, carefree, careless. Val definitely partied too, but compared to me she was restrained and responsible. Our differences—much like our characters—would grow more dramatic over the years and at times pull us apart. But, like the sisters we played on TV, we had a bond that would always exist, no matter what.

Valerie and I always laugh about the fact that when it came to guest stars on the show, I always got the guys. Until Scott Colomby came along. He was really cute, and he went for Val. They dated for several years. My on-set romances tended not to last so long. My boyfriends were all casual accessories. A handsome, soft-spoken guy named Robby Benson came on for an episode called "The College Man." In the episode he is my date, but he goes for my mother—and she seems to like the attention. After the taping, Robby asked me out and we started dating. It was all very chaste. We'd go to his apartment—it was by the beach somewhere—and he'd play me songs that he'd written. One of them, "Mr. Weinstein's Barbershop," got stuck in my head and never left.

Anyway, we'd been dating for about a month and hadn't had sex yet. I partied but I wasn't promiscuous, in part because I still thought of myself as the Kid. After a date, Robby was dropping me off back at my house when he said, "I have this itch, I really need to scratch it."

I said, "So scratch it."

He said, "No, you don't get it," and raised his eyebrows suggestively. After more eyebrow raises than any dignified man should have to exercise, I finally caught his drift. *That* kind of itch. I could feel Aunt Rosie's eyes boring through the closed door of the house.

I said, "Oh, I gotta go." Something in me shut down and I didn't go out with him again.

I was a good girl, but I had my moments. One of the most memorable came two years later when I was on hiatus in New York. Dad and Gen's latest digs in New York were a penthouse on the Upper East Side. I rented the penthouse next door. I was rarely there—I was clubbing at night, sleeping during the day, back and forth to L.A.—but I had more money than I knew what to do with. I never got around to furnishing that apartment, so I always ended up crashing at my dad's.

For New Year's Eve I went with Dad and Genevieve to a crazy party at their friend Wendy Stark's penthouse on Fifth Avenue. Mick Jagger and Keith Richards were there, the editor of *Rolling Stone* Jann Wenner, and other luminaries. Jeffrey stayed home at our dad's apartment. He wasn't as comfortable partying with Dad's friends as I was. At midnight, when the Central Park fireworks started going off, Dad got a call. It was Jeffrey, who said, "It's the start of World War III. There are bombs going off everywhere. There are gunshots. I'm hiding in the closet. I'm terrified." It must have been the cocaine talking. Dad just said, "Look, you're on your own, kid." That was one of his favorite expressions.

A few days later we went to a party at the gorgeous Central Park West home of our dear friends Lenny and Marsia Holzer. (The same Marsia who a few years earlier had, with her then-boyfriend Yipi, fled the chaos at 414 St. Pierre.) Lenny was Dad's big shooting-up buddy who has now been clean and sober for five million years and is a highly paid interventionist. Mick and Jerry Hall lived in the same building.

Jerry was on her way somewhere, maybe Central America. She stopped by the party wearing an elegant hat, said, "Now you all have a good time" in her soft Texan drawl, and left.

The party went on, but at some point in the evening Mick decided he wanted a tuna salad sandwich. Dad was a connoisseur of white-trash food, so he insisted on making the Phillips family tuna salad recipe for Mick. Dad, Mick, and I went down to Mick and Jerry's apartment. Mick opened a can of tuna, then looked for the mayo. There was no mayo. Thank you, Jesus, there was no mayo. Mick said, "John, go upstairs and see if Lenny and Marsia have any mayo." Dad left, and the minute the door shut behind him, Mick locked it and turned around to face me. He said, "I've been waiting for this since you were ten years old." I was eighteen. Eight years is a long time to wait. We went into his and Jerry Hall's bedroom and had sex in their bed.

In the middle of our tumble my dad came back and started knocking on the door, yelling, "You've got my daughter in there!" It wasn't "Look, you're on your own kid" this time, but I imagine he was more annoyed at losing the chance to show off his tuna salad recipe than genuinely concerned about the defiling of his daughter. We ignored him and he finally went away.

That night I slept in that lux, illicit bed. I'd known Mick since I was a kid, and maybe most people think that their parents' friends are old and gross. But this was Mick Jagger. Mick Jagger! He was hot. He had the most perfect ass in history. (I'm sure he still has a perfect ass given that he taught me how to do squats so many years ago.)

The next morning we put on big fluffy white robes. (You have to wonder if every girl who stayed at the Mick Hotel got one.) He went into the kitchen and came back with a tray carrying tea, toast, and fresh strawberries. The phone rang. Mick handed it to me. It was my father. He said, "I've been up all night worrying. Was he nice to you?"

I said, "Dad, I'm fine. We're having tea. I'll see you later."

I was proud of my conquest, or of having been conquested, but I never intended to make it public. And then, many years later, I was talking to a friend, Mary, from the TV Guide channel for an interview. I was so naive. I honestly thought we were off the record when I told her about my night with Mick, but apparently not. *TV Guide* ran that story as the headline. In quick order it turned into a tabloid free-for-all. It was in the *Enquirer.* Jay Leno joked about it in his opening monologue. I got it: inside dirt about a globally famous rock star is money. But it turned into something I never wished it to become.

I was a good girl, but I knew a golden opportunity when I saw it, even if it came disguised as a tuna salad sandwich.

10

The times when I was on vacation from *One Day at a Time* float to the top of my memories, the same way that for most people the details of summer jobs prevail over the day-to-day of high school math class. When *One Day at a Time* was on hiatus from its second season and I was seventeen, I spent a couple months in New York. Dad's apartment was a bold display of unrepentant drug use, a horror show. There were drug dealers coming and going day and night. The once-beautiful apartment had quickly turned into a slum. Papers, clothes, unfinished projects, food, trash—if something got put down on any surface, there it remained indefinitely. Dad and Gen had a double-sided adjustable bed. When it got stuck with one side down flat and the other side raised like a hospital bed, with the head up high and a bend for someone's knees, it remained that way, a disjointed symbol of their out-of-kilter life until they moved.

The apartment had a spiral staircase to the second floor, a cruel joke to play on heroin addicts. They fell down the stairs constantly. There was blood on the walls and needles on the floor. AIDS wasn't a fear yet, but junkies still liked to use new needles. Clean, new needles have sharp points, and sharp points are better for finding veins. And if you're using a new needle every time, and if you shoot up every twenty minutes, and if there are two or three of you, then you use up to 150 needles a day. You don't throw them away, because where are you going to throw away that many needles without attracting attention or feeling paranoid that you might? The needles accumulate quickly. You had to watch where you stepped in that apartment.

On one of the first days of my visit, I came into the apartment and found my six-year-old brother, Tam, alone. He was sitting on a windowsill using a syringe for a squirt gun.

My father made no secret of his heroin use. One time I knocked on his door to see if he was ready to go out and he said, "Not now, darling. Daddy's shooting up." He loved to tell that story. Dad was so fucked up. It was the junkie routine: sleeping for days, shooting up for days, spending time in closets, stumbling around—mundane on paper but painful to watch.

I was horrified at the scene I'd come upon. Richard, one of my friends in L.A., claimed to have invented freebasing—smoking cocaine in its base form—though it's likely that what he meant was that he introduced a whole bunch of people to the process. A dubious claim to fame. When I told him how worried I was about Dad, Richard suggested that we introduce him to freebase. I guess he thought that once someone did base they wouldn't need heroin. For some reason I bought that logic—I guess I was desperate for an answer, and cocaine, unlike heroin, was the devil I knew—so I flew Richard into New York to make freebase for Dad. Then Dad became a freebase head.

Dad wasn't alone: I had started using coke regularly too, though I never shot up—until I did. I carried around a vial of cocaine in my pocket as casually as if it were a pack of cigarettes. I often tried to mooch drugs off my father. Sometimes he complied, sometimes he said no. Did he think they were bad for me or was he concerned about his supply? My best guess is the latter. One night my friend Rae-Dawn Chong—Tommy Chong's daughter, who would later appear in *Quest for Fire, The Color Purple,* and many other movies—and I were going to Tavern on the Green, the famous restaurant in Central Park, for dinner. Before we left I found Dad asleep on the knees-up side of the broken bed. Excellent—when he was half asleep was always a good time to ask Dad for drugs. He mumbled, "Bindles on the bedside table." I grabbed one and we left.

Rae-Dawn and I were in a cab speeding through Central Park. We slid the partition between us and the driver closed, huddled on the floor of the cab, and snorted the coke. By the time we got to Tavern on the Green we knew something was terribly wrong. We were nodding out, running to the bathroom to throw up, knocking things over. We were both recognizable, both very young, and both accustomed to snorting shitloads of cocaine. But what we had snorted was definitely not cocaine. This was heroin. We were seriously fucked up. In fucking Tavern on the Green. It was a bad, bad scene. It wasn't long before we were asked to leave. And I don't remember anything after that.

I was concerned about Dad, but I wasn't worried about myself. I told myself that it was the needles that were the problem, though now I see that helping Dad, wanting to save Dad, was another way of avoiding my own issues.

In mid-July there was a blackout in New York. Rosie called Dad in a panic. "Where is she? Put her on the phone." My father couldn't find me anywhere. Hours passed with no word from me. Rosie kept calling, frantic with worry. Maybe I was stuck in an elevator somewhere. Maybe someone had abducted me! Dad called around, but nobody had seen me. The blackout ended after a day, but there was still no sign of me.

The next day I came out of the back bedroom, yawning. Dad and Gen ran to me, checking to see if I was okay and asking where I'd been for two days. I said, "I was asleep. Back there." I gestured toward the back bedroom of my father's apartment. I'd been right there in the apartment the whole time. I missed the whole blackout. Blacked out.

The drugs that had for so long set the scene for my family's festive, extravagant lifestyle were moving into a lead role. Drug use was no longer recreational. It was central. It was necessary. We were all in deep and it was starting to show. Genevieve, Jeffrey, and I were all entwined with the same lover—cocaine.

It was a complicated relationship, an endless cycle of give and take, the instant thrill and surge of ecstasy that cocaine promised, delivered, and revoked all in the course of half an hour—after which the race to recapture that unimaginably good feeling, which only cocaine could offer, and did, would begin, again and again, until the supply ran out and the thrill turned to a dark, hollow absence, a bleakness so opposite and dreadful that more cocaine wasn't just desirable, it was necessary.

That necessity became a driving force in the household. There were no boundaries whatsoever. My dad stole a bunch of money from me that summer. When I first came back to New York, Dad had taken me to get a thousand dollars' worth of American Express traveler's checks. You're supposed to sign them twice—once when you buy them and once when you sign them over to the person you want to pay. But my father had me sign all of them twice. He was the kind of person who made you feel like an idiot if you contradicted him—I never did. I just double-signed the checks. But I was no dummy. I knew what he was about, so I slept with my purse clutched under my arm. I woke up one morning and the checks were gone.

If I had any coke, Gen would swoop past, grab it, and disappear. Dad would chant, "Genevieve's a coke junkie, Genevieve's a coke junkie," but the playground taunting belied the escalating insanity. When you use coke intensely you go into cocaine psychosis, you start thinking there are things on you—bugs or threads or strings. Right after you shoot up you notice that something is on you, and you absolutely believe it's there. It's so real that no matter how many times you've come down off coke and realized it was a hallucination, no matter how many times you've talked to other cokeheads about it, read about it, written yourself notes to remind yourself not to believe the illusion, when it happens again you are convinced that no matter what went before, this time it is absolutely real. People tear themselves apart trying to free themselves from those imagined creepy-crawlies.

Dad and Gen both went deep into a coke-bug obsession. I came home after being on a several-day tear with crazy people. Dad said, "I've got to talk to you. It's very important." He led me to the library and sat down behind his desk. I was thinking, *Here comes the key to life*. But he leaned toward me conspiratorially and said, "I found out where they're coming from. My nose." He was talking about the coke bugs. Dad must have liked the expression of confusion and disappointment on my face because a few days later he sat me down in a similarly serious way and said, "I have something very important to tell you and I want you to remember this always. Fifth Avenue separates the East and West sides of Manhattan." Another time he sat me down for this weighty revelation: "The farther off from England, the closer is to France." Each time he did this I was really expecting something redemptive and life changing, the *I love you and I'm sorry* moment that should have been forthcoming. But eventually it dawned on me that he was just amusing himself.

So Dad made the historical discovery that coke bugs were coming from his nose, and he was a man of action. I went about my business, and the next time I came home, as God is my witness, I came into the apartment to find my father, naked but wrapped from head to toe in Saran Wrap. He had left slits for his mouth and nose. I was sixteen, and for all the unorthodox parenting I'd experienced, I wasn't in the habit of seeing my father naked, and I expected to keep it that way. I said, "What are you doing?"

Dad said, "I'm killing the bugs. They can't breathe."

Okay . . .

I was happy to be back in L.A., back at *One Day at a Time,* back with Rosie, Patty, and Nancy. One night soon after I came home, my cousins, Rosie, and I were sitting around cooking dinner. We had an ongoing fixation with artichokes. We'd already made our favorite dip: Miracle Whip mixed with Spike (a spice mixture), and there were four artichokes steaming in the pressure cooker. The den of that house in Beachwood Canyon was classic seventies. There was a built-in bench bordering the TV area. *Bench* doesn't quite do it justice—it was so deep that if you sat with your back against the wall, your feet didn't reach the edge of the seat. There were cushions that made it loungy, and the whole thing was covered in brown shag carpet that spilled over its edge, down to and across the floor.

We relaxed on that comfortable built-in, drinking wine while the artichokes cooked. Then, all of a sudden, the top of the pressure cooker blew off. It narrowly missed decapitating Rosie. Artichoke went everywhere—the crew on *One Day at a Time* couldn't have planned an exploding artichoke scene better. The four of us rolled on the floor, clutching our bellies, we were laughing so hard. When we finally pulled ourselves together, we spent the next two hours picking artichoke out of every inch of that brown shag carpet. It was a mess, but it felt like good, clean fun.

I loved living with my aunt and cousins, but I was almost eighteen and ready to live on my own. My manager, Pat McQueeney, found a beautiful house in Laurel Canyon for me to buy. It was a small house with a galley kitchen, but it had great big windows, a terraced backyard, and an amazing view of L.A. Pat and I went shopping for fabrics and carpeting, and our purchases reflected a compromise between Pat's elegant sensibility and my thrift-store chic vibe. I chose carpeting in hunter green, a color I've always loved, and Pat selected custom drapes to match the custom bedspread and shams.

My cousin Patty and I ventured to an auction to buy chairs for my living room. I'd never been to an auction before, but I'd seen a photo of these dwarf wing chairs covered in a Missoni-inspired knit fabric that had subdued green tones matching my carpet. At the auction, I was so nervous to bid that I kept shoving the cards with the numbers on them to Patty so that she could bid for me. Finally, she summoned the courage to win me my chairs. We put them on either side of the living room fireplace.

Just before my birthday, Rosie moved out of Beachwood to a place in Venice where she would live for the rest of her life. Patty went to live with her boyfriend Brad, and Nancy got her own place. Before we all dispersed, we had a crazy Say Good-bye to Beachwood party that did my father proud. There were people running through the hills on acid, chasing coyotes. And then I turned eighteen.

I celebrated my eighteenth birthday in a private room upstairs at a posh Beverly Hills restaurant called Bistro Gardens. The pictures of me from that party show me wearing a backless black jersey dress and blowing out my candles. I danced with John Travolta, who was wearing a white suit. I was young and happy, beautiful and carefree. But I was about to get my first wake-up call.

A week after my eighteenth birthday I was out with my dad's old friend Yipi. He would later date and live with my mother, but now I was hanging out with him. I had taken some ludes and now we were going clubbing.

We were driving up Robertson Boulevard when Yipi pulled over to pick something up at a club. I stayed in the car. But then, for reasons that clouded over before they were ever clear, I got out of the car. I was incoherently wasted, which wasn't a daily state for me. I mean, I could usually go clubbing on ludes, but this time it wasn't to be. I seem to remember flagging down the police because someone was bugging me. But then—as you sometimes do on ludes—I kind of crumpled. I just slid to the ground like a marionette whose strings had been severed. By the time Yipi came back to the car, the police were standing over me, a sorry heap of youth on the sidewalk.

The cops said to Yipi, "Do you know this woman?"

Yipi said, "Yes, this is Mackenzie Phillips, the TV star. I'll take care of her." According to Yipi, when he said my name a light went on in the cops' eyes. They promptly arrested me and took me away.

When Dad found out I was arrested he said, "It's about time. Now you've proven that you're a real Phillips."

I was raised as an alien. Aunt Rosie made a real effort to teach me how to be a human being on Planet Earth, but on my home planet, with Dad, there were no rules. I was wild. I said whatever I felt like saying. I did whatever I felt like doing. I knew this way of life made me something of a space traveler, but I never thought the humans would find me out and arrest me for it. The police report said that I kept asking for coke, which is just plain nuts. No matter how fucked up I was, I would never ask a policeman for coke! I must have wanted a smoke. They also said I was found in a gutter, which is really just a disparaging way to say I was right outside my car.

Somebody bailed me out. I was so high I don't even remember being released, but when I got home I was really freaked. The next day my arrest was on the front page of the *LA Times*. On the ABC evening news Rona Barrett reported that I'd been arrested with enough Quaaludes in me to kill a horse. I was horrified and embarrassed.

The ongoing press was so relentless that Michelle, whom people always assumed was my mother, had a T-shirt made for herself that said, "No, I'm not Mackenzie's mother." Being hounded was bad enough, but Michelle was only fifteen years older than I was. To presume she was my mother was to age her. Any self-respecting actress would have taken offense.

It was nearly Christmas and Pat McQueeney wanted me out of town, out of the media spotlight for the round of Christmas parties. Sending me to rehab didn't occur to anyone. Instead, they put a Band-Aid over the problem. Two days later Pat's daughter Barbara and I took off in Barbara's International Harvester—the precursor to the Range Rover—with her three dogs. We drove straight to Mexico.

Barbara and I camped out in tents and stayed in youth hostels. I had all the money in the world and no affinity for camping, but Pat didn't want me to be seen at resorts. Still, Barbara and I managed to party in Mexico. We sat on the beach, smoking joints, drinking sangria, and collecting new friends, as I did wherever I went. For Christmas Barbara went out and caught a baby pig for me to have as a pet. I named it Rapido. Rapido became our faithful companion. He came to dinner. He came to midnight mass. I thought we had something special until the night Rapido ran away with a bunch of big pigs and was never seen again.

When we got back to L.A., work resumed. The rehearsal hall had a mockup of the set, with tape on the floor outlining the walls. Tables and folding chairs stood in for the furniture, the bar, and the sink area. It was only a twenty-two-minute show, so there was plenty of time between scenes and between run-throughs for breaks. The days spent rehearsing were my favorite part of the job. I snacked on dill pickle spears, cheddar cheese, and V8 juice and chatted with my costars, but Pat Harrington, who played Schneider, took his breaks much more seriously—if he took anything seriously.

Harrington laid claim to one corner of the vast room. With our prop guy Tony Jacobucci he hung curtains from a rail on the ceiling, cordoning off his area. He hooked up a phone and declared it his office. You could always hear him through the curtain, on the phone making deals, and you had to knock on the closest wall if you wanted to enter his space.

When Pat wasn't wheeling and dealing, everything that came out of his mouth was funny. He did an impression of a creepy guy who always held one of his hands shaking near his crotch. He'd say, "Wanna see a dead bird in a shoe box, little girl?"

Nanette Fabray played our grandmother on the show. Her special talent was that she could iron a man's button-down shirt in under a minute. She was minorly famous for this obscure skill and regularly demonstrated it on talk shows. One day she had the prop department bring out an iron and asked Wardobe for a shirt. After much hype and anticipation, she ironed that shirt in thirty seconds flat while singing a song. Indeed, it was amazing.

One Day at a Time was everything an actor could wish for in a job. There were endless moments like that—small, funny bonding moments that added up for me the way school days might add up for someone else, days that strung themselves together into a time that I remember as happy and fun, free and inspiring.

It was the best time of my life, and I could have made that my whole life, but I hadn't changed. I started going out on the Strip all over again. When does a recreational habit turn into a problem? If there is a line, it is different for everyone and impossible to recognize for yourself. Drugs give a false sense of reality and well-being. Then, without warning, they turn on you and take control of your reality instead of enhancing it. You're on the fast track to endless demoralization. But you're the last to know you're completely out of control.

My buddy Danny Sugarman got a frantic call from my brother Jeffrey, who told him that a limo driver was waiting outside to take me to the studio, but I was wigging out on coke and refused to come out of the bathroom. Jeffrey told Danny, "She needs some heroin or she won't come out." I wasn't into heroin, but any cokehead knows that if you're too wired to function it can bring you down.

Danny drove to my house. My brother let him in, and after convincing me to open the bathroom door, Danny fixed me a shot. I was shaking too much to inject myself, so he shot me up, then tied himself off. But before he could do his shot, he noticed that I was leaning up against the tank of the toilet, staring at the ceiling. "What are you looking at?" he asked. No answer. He asked again, but I just slid silently to the floor. I had OD'd. Danny cursed, shot himself up (because we all have our priorities), then shouted for my brother.

I wish I could have watched them attempt to rouse me, because—near-death circumstances aside—it was like a bad comedy. Danny needed something cold from the refrigerator. Jeffrey claimed it was empty. Danny looked for himself and came back with cold milk, but when he threw it in my face all that came out was cottage cheese—the milk had curdled.

Frantic, Danny ignored the sour milk curds and tried to administer mouth-to-mouth. I started turning blue.

Danny was a planner, a leader, a can-do guy. And we loved each other. He was not about to let me die on his watch. He threw me into his convertible and started to drive to the emergency room. At every red light he pounded on my chest, then listened to my heart to see if it was beating. The pounding worked, but a block later he'd check, find my heart had stopped again, and pound until the light turned green. All the while Danny was trying to decide whether, when he finally arrived at the emergency room, he was actually going to carry me in. The way he saw it was that if I died in the car, he would lose me and everyone would blame him. And if I went to the hospital and lived, I'd lose my job and blame him. He was damned if he did and damned if he didn't.

So he drove around with a mostly dead TV star in his car, pounding my chest like a maniac until I finally woke up and told him to stop hitting me. Danny was always there for me. He was a true friend. But as Danny told it, after I came home from the studio that night, I called to bawl him out. I'd gotten to work two hours late and it was all his fault, the bastard. Some thank-you.

I still didn't think I had a problem, but I was all too aware that my arrest had changed things at work. Not only was I on unofficial probation, but when it became clear that I was bad press, not to mention a bad influence, Valerie started backing off. I can't blame her. She was doing the right thing for herself emotionally and for her career. It makes sense to detach from someone who's having so many crazy problems. But it hurt me. I always loved her. Still do.

One Day at a Time should have been my salvation. It was exactly what I needed. Coming from a fragmented family, to have a place to go every day where everyone's talking, laughing, telling stories, bonding, and creating was heaven. It was the same sense of community that I'd felt so briefly after the earthquake of 1971. I was one of a group, not a weird kid who was whisked away in a stretch limo, but someone who fit in. I finally had a family.

But as time went on and my demons started taking over, holding on to that feeling of belonging was like trying to grab smoke. Close as we were, I was still alienated from the other cast members. They were all conservative, normal people. In the beginning I often curled up with a book to escape feeling odd and alone on set. But soon I started to use during the day. Part of me thought it was a perfectly normal thing to do—outside of work everyone I knew did plenty of drugs. But I had the instinct to hide it from my colleagues. I knew it would separate me further. There was an internal conflict I didn't see at the time: I saw this new, warm family and wanted to be a part of it, wanted it to come to life. But at the same time my family, my background, my history pulled me away. It was a tug-of-war between two factions, and a third party was about to join the fray.

PART THREE

GIRLFRIEND, WIFE, DAUGHTER

11

I met Peter Asher at the American Music Awards in 1978, shortly before I turned nineteen. A few dates after Peter and I met, we were at my house in Laurel Canyon and I put on some music. I knew he was a record producer, and I didn't know what he'd produced, but I had plenty of opinions about music and production. So we were listening to a Linda Ronstadt album and I told him what I thought of it. He said, "You know, I produced that." I said, "Oh. Well. That doesn't change the fact that the vocal is too far behind the mix."

Whatever was missing in Robby Benson and the boys before him was there in Peter. I fell for him hard. He was intelligent and well educated. We'd lie in bed and he'd explain the Doppler effect or parabolic reflectors. He wasn't classically handsome, but I thought he was really cute with his English accent. He was serious and stern, but also playful and irreverent. He was endlessly patient with me. In many ways Peter would be one of the great loves of my life.

Peter and I led a pretty sensational life. We went in limos everywhere, to parties and events, from hip hotel villa to Malibu mansion. We drove his Rolls-Royce Silver Cloud to a drive-through for burgers. I went to the Oscars, the Grammys, the Emmys. At heart I was still the eighteen-year-old in skintight jeans with a Newcastle T-shirt and a baseball cap, but when I went to events I had to present myself in a certain way. I made sure to wear the right clothes and to carry the right bag. I wasn't the Kid anymore.

Peter was recently separated. He had left his wife, his house, and the life they had built together and was living in a villa behind the Chateau Marmont on Marmont Lane. It was a serious rock 'n' roll scene. The musicians Peter produced and managed—James Taylor, Linda Ronstadt, J. D. Souther, Andrew Gold, Bonnie Raitt, you name it—hung around that villa, as did some of the powerful music executives my dad had known when I was a child. They may have been a little uncomfortable partying with me since they knew my Dad, but I was trying as hard as I could to live up to my dad's bad reputation. If being a Phillips meant getting high and running fast and being a star, I did my best.

When Linda Ronstadt went on tour, Peter went as her producer and manager and I tagged along as her pal. I'd perch sidestage on a road case, sauntering backstage to refresh my drink. I got spoiled—who wanted to go to a concert if you had to sit in the audience? *Rolling Stone* did a story on Linda. Jimmy Carter was president, and the magazine referred to me as the Amy Carter of rock 'n' roll.

After the concerts, back at the hotel, there was always plenty of coke around. Linda's guitar player, Waddy Wachtel, slept a lot, and the only way to rouse him was to tick a razor blade against a mirror. The tinny sound of the possibility of cocaine woke him every time.

We had vast financial resources, Peter's more endless than mine, and my partying was at an all-time high. Boy, did we have the life.

But there was a flip side. In the midst of our wildness, I found myself pregnant. It was the first time I'd ever been pregnant, and I was scared and upset.

Peter was angry at the news, and not at all nice. He said, "How dare you? How could you do this to me?" Our relationship was steamy and salacious. It involved lots of Quaaludes, cocaine, and kinky sex. I didn't always want the wild sex—I was kind of like, *Can't we just make love? Why all the bells and whistles?*—but I followed his lead. Attaching those acts to the idea of conception was hard for me, but apparently it was more upsetting to him.

I couldn't conceive of having a child at that age and time, but I felt the weight of having an abortion. I hadn't spoken to my mother for a year, but I went to her. I lay down on her couch with my head in the pillows, sobbing. Mom rubbed my back, telling me everything was going to be okay, that she was going to help me. She arranged an abortion.

The day after the procedure, Peter and I flew to Tahiti.

Tahiti was idyllic. It was the first time I'd gone on a vacation with a boyfriend, staying in a hotel, eating meals together. It felt so grown up. The Kia Ora Village had little bungalows right on the beach. We spent whole days sitting on the porch of our bungalow, getting up to swim, snorkel, or take long walks down the beach. I walked around topless and we swam in the ocean. There was a little fly in our bungalow that I adopted and named Wings, and I called the feral cat that howled for food Legs. I couldn't have sex right away because of the abortion, but Peter had novel solutions to that dilemma. I thought, *Do we really have to do this?* But I loved him.

Evenings, we'd walk a long stretch of beach, up to a restaurant at the top of a hill. I fell in love with pomelos, a fruit that tastes like a grapefruit-orange hybrid. I ate as many pomelos as I wanted and let the sweet taste cleanse the memory of the abortion and what it implied about my relationship and how I was living my life.

After that, Peter and I went to Tahiti every few months for a week. We liked it, so we did more of it. That was pretty much how things went. I could go anywhere, do anything.

At the same time, I had an adult job that came with adult responsibilities, and it was getting more and more difficult for me to make it to work on time every day. Along with the villa at the Chateau, Peter also had a beautiful house in Malibu Colony, right next to one of the houses that my father had rented when I was a child. In fact, the master bedroom overlooked the Pacific . . . and the courtyard of my father's place.

Staying in Malibu meant a longer drive to work, which meant I was later than ever. It wasn't a convenient commute, but who wouldn't want to live in Malibu? Before I knew it I was going to my house only to pick up clothes. We walked on the beach, listened to music, and drank champagne or Stoli. It was the early days of remote controls and I thought it was very fancy that there was a garage door opener to draw the curtains in the morning. The TV was on a hydraulic lift at the foot of the bed.

For my nineteenth birthday, Peter gave me roller skates and I skated exuberantly around the living room. Then, later, we were sitting on the bed and he tossed a brown paper bag at me. I opened it up and found beautiful diamond studs. I squealed and started jumping on the bed. Peter played it cool. He said, "You like 'em?" with no smile on his face, but I knew he was putting on his professor airs. He got me—both sides of me—the sophisticated young woman who could behave appropriately at events, and the silly kid who bounced on the bed for joy. It was the perfect pair of presents, recognizing and honoring the child and woman in me.

One Day at a Time was now, amazingly, in its fourth season. The episode that aired on Christmas Day of that year, 1978, was one of my favorites. In "Girl Talk," Julie, Barbara, and Ann go to a cabin for the holidays and get snowed in. Of course. And then the heat fails. Naturally. It's cold, and the three of us are sleeping on a foldout sofa, cuddled up and talking about boys, and mom's divorce, and Barbara and Julie's relationship as sisters. I loved the way it played. It was one of the purest, sweetest moments that we had on-screen. Watching it, you can tell that we are family, that the feelings between us are real. My family has always made a big deal out of Christmas, and now I was sharing that spirit with my onstage family.

But that warmth belied the increasing stress that my life was putting on my work. Peter was the third party who had entered the tug-of-war between my grown-up job and my freestyle high living, and he had added his figurative weight to the high-living side of the rope. I was always crashing around, trying to get out the door to work after being up half the night. Every day I drove from Malibu to Hollywood, and every day I was late.

One morning I was running as late as ever and my eyes were burning from a night of partying. I said to Peter, "Babe, where are the eyedrops?"

He said, "In the bathroom cabinet." In a rush, I grabbed the eyedrops, put some in my eyes, and got in my car to drive to work. Ten minutes later my vision went blurry. I could not see. Each time I came to a stop sign or a traffic light, I rear-ended the car in front of me—gentle vision-impaired taps that incited honks and obscene hand gestures but no exchange of insurance information. It took me an hour to get to work. When I finally arrived, the producers saw me feeling my way down the hall and assumed I was completely fucked up. They were used to me being late, but they weren't used to me being blind. I called Peter and said, "What the fuck?"

He said, "Oh, no. You didn't use the eyedrops in the brown bottle, did you?"

Oh yes I did. It turned out that those particular eyedrops were from when one of our houseguests had gonorrhea of the eye, a disease I sincerely hoped wasn't caused by some sexual act that I couldn't even conceptualize. My vision was blurry for the rest of the day. I couldn't see to read the script. I couldn't work. My rock 'n' roll lifestyle already made me look like a big enough fuckup at work—the last thing I needed was gonorrhea eyedrops compounding my already compromised reputation at *One Day at a Time*.

The tide of trouble on the set was slowly creeping toward the flood line, but the dam that held my mother's life together had already broken. Now that my mom and I were speaking again, I had to face the reality of her situation. She was drinking a lot, taking

Quaaludes, and doing coke. I was scoring for her, which wasn't exactly helpful, but that was the least of my concerns. Lenny, never a lamb, had turned brutal. He called me up one night at Peter's and said, "Listen to this." I heard a stomping sound.

He said, "This is the sound of my foot on your mother's chest and I'm not going to stop until you get here." Why did he call me? Why did he want to bring me into their domestic strife? Maybe in some way he was trying to stop himself, but all I knew was that he was crazy, my mother needed help, and I'd just taken two Quaaludes and was too fucked up to rescue her.

I called Melanie Griffith, who was a close friend at the time, and asked her to go to my mother's house. Then I called the police and had them meet Melanie there. But when they all arrived, my mother sent them away.

There were more midnight phone calls, more injuries, more threats, but finally I persuaded her to divorce him. I hired a lawyer for her, she came to live at my house in the canyon, and I moved what belongings I still had in my house to Peter's place in the Colony.

It was the right thing to do, but my mother went really crazy in that Laurel Canyon house, all alone. The house had large picture windows looking out on the woods of the canyon. Lenny would hide in those woods, watching her through the windows, stalking her. That was enough to freak anyone out, but my mom was more fragile than most. She had been beaten within an inch of her life. The abuse and drugs did a number on her. She tells a story of how she got out of bed in the middle of the night, put on Genevieve's five-hundred-year-old wedding jacket and cowboy boots, and walked around the house otherwise naked. She came across a giant rat, which she chased around the living room, attacking it with hairspray until it died. Sometimes I'd come home late at night and find her surrounded by candles. She'd call me Mom. She was on the edge of insanity until the divorce was finalized, Lenny moved out and backed off, and she was able to move back into her condo.

I was parenting my mother, I had an adult job, and I had an adult social life. But I still hadn't finished high school. Most kids remember graduating from high school as a major milestone, one that the whole family notices and celebrates, but my father was off on a drug rampage and my mother had sunk into a boozy depression. Both my parents had spun far away, vague constellations of worry and fear. Then again, when it came to my high school graduation, they didn't miss much. Actually, they didn't miss anything.

I'd done well at Hollywood Professional. I worked with a tutor on the set when the show was shooting, so I didn't spend much time on the campus, but my senior year I was the Bank of America Scholar of the Year and was on the honor roll or something like that. So I expected to graduate with some kind of honors and recognition. But then I did an interview for *People* magazine. There was a glamorous picture of me sitting on my couch in a strapless black evening gown and beautiful high heels. In the article I said that the Hollywood Professional School was ugly, boring, and a firetrap. I was immediately expelled. Can you be expelled for being an entitled teenage TV star? What did I care? I was like, *Well, fine, I don't need a high school diploma.*

The school later offered to give me my diploma for $750, but I declined. Fuck that.

Sacrificing my diploma for an obnoxious quote didn't faze me, but the *People* interview wasn't the only time I got myself in trouble doing press. My appearance later that year on *The Tonight Show* was an embarrassment that lingered for a long time. David Letterman was guest hosting. I don't remember why I was invited to be on the show, probably for being Julie, but I was very excited. So excited that I celebrated my appearance in advance by doing a ton of coke. By the time I got on the show I wasn't in ideal form. My nose was running. I was wearing a low-cut dress that kept flapping open. I got nervous and panicky. David Letterman had been told that I was a good speller, so the first thing he did was give me a little spelling test. I'm not sure what words he gave me, but I got every one wrong. You can misspell words with charm and grace, or you can do it as I did, with overblown enthusiasm and awkward jokes. I was completely off my game.

After the spelling debacle, Letterman and I sat down to chat. I nervously babbled on about being in a relationship with a married man. I was obviously fucked up, I had no media training, I said all the wrong things, and I was a perfect target for Letterman's teasing. I can spell "abysmal." And afterward there was no comfort from Peter. His primary concern was how his wife would react to what I'd said about my relationship with him. He gave me shit about my performance, more like a father lecturing his daughter than a lover comforting his mate. Our age difference wasn't so spicy that night.

I wasn't oblivious or self-centered. I completely dug how hard it was for Peter's wife, Betsy. When the well-known, fast-living, eighteen-year-old star of a hit sitcom starts dating a thirty-four-year-old separated-but-still-married mega music producer, it's big news. Betsy, a thirty-seven-year-old, had to watch her not-yet-ex-husband conduct a very public relationship with a teenager. I'd seen my mother go through the same thing with Michelle. Plus Peter and Betsy had been together for a very long time, and now I was hanging out with all their musician buddies—people who must have felt to Betsy like part of the marital property they were still dividing. Betsy wanted to attend Linda Ronstadt's shows, as she always had, and under no circumstances did she want to run into me. But the way Peter handled it showed no care or respect for me. We'd be backstage at a show or at the studio and Peter would get a call from Betsy saying she wanted to come by. He'd dismiss me and I'd leave to wait for him at home alone. Or a distraught Betsy would call and he'd leave me to go to her house. It happened over and over again. I felt confident that he wasn't having sex with her, but it still made me feel like a piece of furniture, moved out of the way when necessary. I understood it, from all sides, but I didn't like waiting for my boyfriend in empty houses the way I'd waited for my father for all my childhood.

For all my frustration, I never complained. I had no idea how to stand up for myself. I didn't like to make a fuss. I was developing a less confrontational method for dealing with my emotions. It worked for my parents, and it would work for me: drugs and disappearance.

12

Our conflicts ran like quiet poisonous subterranean rivers, but Peter and I continued to live the high life. James Taylor was doing a free concert at Sheep Meadow in the middle of Central Park in Manhattan. Peter and I arrived at the gig by helicopter, which itself was more memorable to me than the show—not because I didn't love James Taylor, but because attending rock concerts had quickly become as common to me as going to the movies.

What happened after the concert doesn't make sense, except in that cocaine was involved, and the only thing that out-of-control cocaine use consistently guarantees is an irrational, impulse-driven life. Peter and I were staying at the Pierre, a landmark hotel facing Central Park. Back at the hotel, the phone rang. It was Anita Pallenberg, Keith Richards's girlfriend who had once greeted me with disdain at their country estate. Anita was staying in a suite a couple floors above us. She invited us upstairs. Peter didn't want to go—it was late and he was flying to England the next morning to visit his mother—but I said, "Come on, let's go. I haven't seen Anita in years."

Anita wasn't clean yet. A guy named Jeff Sessler was working for Anita and taking care of her son Marlon. I don't remember the scene Peter and I walked into—I can't tell whether my memory lapses are the fault of years of drug use or whether they mark memories so painful that I've hidden them from myself—

all I remember is that Peter whispered, "These people are so bizarre, let's get out of here."

I was fucked up on coke, in general and on that night in particular. I was pissed off about all that had been going down with Peter, how he snubbed me for Betsy, how he made me feel incidental. Peter was bright, worldly, well educated. He treated me like a disciple, and I was over it. I was angry, and the antidote was obliteration. I said, "I'm just going to hang out for a little while longer." So Peter went to bed, and I stayed. And stayed.

Then I noticed an odd light coming through the curtains. It was morning. *Oh, fuck.* I called down to our suite, but Peter didn't pick up. I went down in the elevator, the shame shadow starting to cross over me. When I let myself into the suite there was utter silence. It was too quiet. Peter was gone. His suitcase was gone. There was a note on the desk that said, "I'm going to the airport. Where the fuck are you?" Shit. I called the Ambassador's Club at American Airlines and had Peter paged. When he came on the line he said, "You didn't come home last night."

I said, "I know I didn't and I'm sorry." I *was* sorry. I loved Peter and couldn't bear disappointing him.

But then I missed my plane home. And I stayed in New York with Jeff Sessler for five days without bathing or leaving the hotel. Whereas Peter was professorial and distant (albeit in a loving way), Jeff was silly and irreverent. He was a kindred spirit. We had the same urge to chase fun, consequences be damned.

For all our excesses, Peter and I led a life with a certain domestic rhythm. We both went to work every day. We ate together. We made commitments and kept them. When I cast Peter aside, I also lost the last vestiges of a stable life. Compared to what was about to happen, the life that Peter and I led was about to look downright Puritan.

Jeff and I decided to fly to Florida to see his father. I knew Jeff's father, Freddy—everyone knew Freddy. He was the drug man for the Rolling Stones. The bag man. Freddy ran a weight-loss clinic in Florida that was actually a speed dispensary. Jeff and I told people we were flying to Florida so I could meet his mother, but we both knew our real reason was to get prescriptions for speed from his father.

In Florida Jeff and I decided to get married. Through his father he had access to pharmaceutical cocaine, which for me was the equivalent of marrying into royalty. Sure, I knew that our five-day-long affair was an unreasonable basis for marriage. In fact, I'd always thought marriage was a bogus institution. Why would you need to be married in order to be with someone? It seemed limiting and formal. But I was almost twenty and took pride in being impetuous. If Jeff and I wanted to get married, what or who could stop us? Nothing and nobody. Jeff's mother had us over to her house for dinner. After we ate, his mom, Liz, pulled me into the kitchen. She said, "Mack, don't marry my son. He's an asshole." It wasn't the only time someone had said that I was making a mistake with Jeff. His younger brother also tried to stop me. Jeff was the black sheep of the family. I knew he could be a cocky jerk, but I liked his bad-boy vibe. Besides, he only ever treated me like a princess. At some other point even Betsy Asher—Peter's ex—called me on the phone. Betsy, the last person with any reason to care what happened to me, said, "Please, don't do this. Don't go with Jeff. Go back to my husband."

I didn't listen to these people, who had every reason to be telling me the truth. But there was another messenger en route, with a new, nefarious means of voicing his opinion. My father.

Lately my father had been particularly fly-by-night. I referred to him as an area code, because his was different every time I tried to find him. I knew Dad was still shooting up coke. He had come to stay with me in Laurel Canyon. He and Genevieve were to perform a campy, Burns-Allen comedy/musical act at the Roxy. Dad flew in before Genevieve and was staying in my room while

I slept in the guest room. I went back into my room for something and found a bag of syringes under the bed. There were needles and spoons. But when I confronted him he cut me off, as he did so well, saying, "Aw, kid, everything's fine. It's nothing to worry about, just a little chipping." What could I do?

Then, months before Jeff and I met, when Peter and I were staying in the penthouse at the Chateau—the same suite where I'd first tried cocaine with my brother—I realized that I hadn't spoken to my father in months and months, and I suddenly became convinced that Dad was going to die. It was one of those sudden, certain, gut-wrenching convictions—if I didn't find him, help him, I would lose him forever. I couldn't get him on the phone; nobody could get him on the phone. He was avoiding everyone. There in the penthouse I started making calls, the calls I always made when I had to track him down—friends, family, known accomplices, dwarves—but this time nobody knew where he was. He had disappeared into the ether.

Finally I called Mick Jagger. Something about him—his wisdom, his status, his power, his money—made it seem like he could find anybody anywhere on earth. Unlike the other friends who just told me they didn't know where Dad was, Mick said, "Look, I can't help you because I can't help John. He's going to do what he wants to do. You're not going to pin him down. He's running away from everyone. I can't find him for you."

I said, "But Mick, he's going to die."

He said, "You're going to have to let him die. He's a grown man. Stop doing this to yourself. Stop it."

I fell back on the couch and thought, *What do I do now?* My father was lost.

Now, in Florida, on the eve of my wedding to Jeff Sessler, my elusive father showed up. Dad, who chased my rapist with a shotgun. Dad, the unreliable ghost, seemed to appear whenever I stumbled. Or was he the only person I wanted to catch me? Did he rush to rescue me or did I ignore all other options in favor of his scarred arms of salvation? I never thought about it then. All I knew was that when the dad I longed for emerged from the clouds, I ran to him. I always ran to him.

Dad came to Florida with Bob, an old friend of his, determined to stop the union. They checked into our hotel, staying in a room a few doors down from Jeff and me. The night they arrived, Jeff was sleeping and I went to visit Dad and Bob. Bob was asleep too. I had tons of pills and Dad had tons of everything too. Dad and I got high on downs, and eventually I passed out on Dad's bed.

Then this: The biggest, worst moments of our lives never announce themselves. A car wreck suddenly changes everything terribly and forever. Words that destroy a relationship spill out unexpectedly but can't be unsaid. Actions, emotions, missteps, mistakes—no matter who is to blame, there are tiny hints and billowing flags of warning, but we are powerless to wholly predict and self-protect. I loved my father and I still do. But he was not a man with boundaries. He was full of love, and he was sick with drugs. He drew me to him and pushed me away. He wanted to rescue me, to protect me, but he also wanted me to reflect his greatness.

It's complicated and it's simple, and neither makes it right, and neither gives it reason, so simple will have to do. I woke up that night from a blackout to find myself having sex with my own father. I don't remember how it started or, thankfully, how it ended. There is only a vague memory of the middle, of waking up to a confusion and horror that I was unable to stop, change, process. Bob was watching from his nearby bed with a face I couldn't read. Was it the first time? Had this happened before? I didn't know and I still don't. All I can say is that it was the first time I was aware of it. For a moment I was in my body, in that horrible truth, and then I slid back into a blackout.

Your father is supposed to protect you.

Your father is supposed to protect you, not fuck you.

• • •

I was the feel-no-evil monkey, the child whose rape settled quickly into a dispassionate truth. The year before, in my relationship with Peter, I'd miscarried a fetus I didn't know I was carrying into a toilet. I scooped it out into a cup. It was the size of my fist. A moment passed, the moment in which I realized, *I was pregnant; I've miscarried; something that I didn't know was happening is already over.* And when I saw that it was over, I boxed it away, poured the contents of the cup back into the toilet, came out of the bathroom, and told Peter, "I need to go to the hospital." But before I left I stole two grams of cocaine from James Taylor, because even the feel-no-evil monkey needs a little help from her friends.

So my father had sex with me, and when I came to next to Jeff the next morning, I saw nothing, I said nothing, I heard nothing, I felt nothing. I put it aside for the moment and went on. My marriage to Jeff didn't happen. Dad didn't stop it. I didn't take a stand either way. The notion seemed to pass as impulsively as it had appeared. Bob and Dad and Jeff and I flew back to LA. Jeff and I had sex in the lavatory of the first-class section before we even took off, because that was how we rolled.

13

Back in L.A., Peter had moved all of my stuff out of our house and back into my house. It was fucked up, and I was fucked up, and now, at home, the reality of what had happened with my father started to hit me. It was so wrong. I had to do something. I told my mother. But she said, "Are you sure?" My mother had always been in love with my father. She loved me too. She couldn't process this. I went to Aunt Rosie, who believed me and was furious. We talked about what to do—me, Rosie, Mom, friends—and I wondered if I should press charges. Wasn't that what you did when somebody wronged you? Shouldn't he be punished? But Rosie helped me realize that if I took action against him, it would not only ruin my father's prospects of ever finding success again, it would also taint me. And my family. I would be dragging the family name through the mud. It would destroy us. The general consensus was that yes, it was terrible; no, it shouldn't have happened, but there was nothing for me to do but let it go.

Months later, in New York: The room was dimly lit. My father sat in a rocking chair. I said, "Dad, we have to talk about how you raped me."

He said, "Raped you? You mean when we made love?" And that statement, more than anything, captures my father. He wasn't a liar. He wasn't in denial. He didn't try to blame me. None of the tricks or excuses you'd expect an abuser to make. He simply lived without rules. If sex happened, and nobody protested, it was consensual. If sex happened between a father and a daughter, and nobody protested, there was no problem. If it felt good, it could be done, and if nobody put a stop to it, it could happen again, and again, as often and whenever it was convenient for him.

So I made Florida into the only kind of memory that was bearable—a bad dream. And in some ways that was all it was. Are the mistakes that you make real when they take place under extreme influences? If you fix them, undo them, ignore them, can you make them disappear?

I went back to work, and Peter and I met at the Chateau during a lunch break. We decided to get back together. I returned to the studio relieved. I belonged with Peter. I called Jeff to tell him it was over.

That night I went to another James Taylor concert with Peter. We were backstage at the Forum when the familiar call came. Betsy wanted to come backstage, so I had to leave. I went back to the Chateau, really pissed off. If I'd hoped my dalliance with Jeff would fix this part of our relationship, I was wrong. I was hanging out with my dear friend Rick Marotta when Peter called to say that he had to go to Betsy's place after the show because she was upset. It was already late; I'd been waiting for Peter for hours. Rick saw what a state I was in. He pursed his lips thoughtfully and said, "You gotta do what you gotta do. I don't see this changing."

I waited up late for Peter to come home that night. We went to bed angry and the next day I left for work before he woke up. After work, I headed to Malibu because Peter and I were taking a helicopter to a gig in Irvine. On the way I stopped in Venice Beach, where Jeff was staying with a friend. I wanted to give him the last of his stuff—a pair of shoes that he'd left at my house in the canyon. When I came into the Venice bungalow, Jeff said, "Marry me."

We were cokeheads, craving the rush of drama and control. A spontaneous wedding—what could be a brasher display of our renegade spirit? It didn't really matter who Jeff was or whether I imagined us together forever. Jeff was intense and passionate and made it absolutely clear that he wanted to be with me. I was still angry at Peter for the previous night, and here, standing before me, was revenge. Or the antidote. I didn't know which I wanted or which was driving me. It didn't matter. I said, "If you want to marry me you have to marry me right now."

"Come in," he said.

We looked in the phone book and found a place that would marry us that night. Jeff was staying in his friend Michael's apartment. We asked Michael to stand as our witness; the three of us got in my car and we drove away. The chapel, if you can call it that, was a little backyard garden next to the airport in Inglewood. I was wearing skinny jeans, a gray cashmere sweater of Peter's with a T-shirt underneath, and red satin tennis shoes. There were deafening jetliners zooming overhead. The minister broke up his words to let the planes pass: "Do you take . . . this man, Jeff Sessler, to be your . . . lawfully wedded husband?" It was slow going, but we finally got through the ceremony. The minister said, "I now pronounce you man and wife. Ms. Phillips, may I have your autograph?"

It wasn't exactly a dream wedding, but Jeff and I thought getting married was hilarious. Our families, my managers, everyone wanted us to do one thing and we were doing the opposite. We loved bucking expectations.

I was married, but nobody knew I was married except Jeff, our witness Michael, and my fan the minister. Then Peter called. He wanted to see me. After work I went over to the Chateau, to the penthouse where I'd lived with him. I came into the apartment and as we said hello I slid my hand behind my bag, hiding the diamond band, a ring I'd already owned, that was now on my ring finger. Peter said, "I see your hand, you know."

I said, "Yeah, I married Jeff."

Peter paused; he took both my hands in his and looked into my eyes. He said, "I wish you would understand that the night I got home from being with Betsy I finally asked her for a divorce. You left while I was sleeping. I was going to ask you to marry me." *Bullshit.* My heart flip-flopped, because I was nineteen and I loved him and I wanted to believe him. But he wasn't saying "Leave Jeff, because I want to marry you." He was saying "Now that you're married to someone else, I can torture us both with the pretense of devotion."

In my father's already dramatic life this was a notably insane period. He and Genevieve were now living in Newport Beach, California. His friends were trying to keep Dad and Gen off smack, but whenever my brother and I visited they were all high. So much for reliable sponsors. Dad had somehow gotten his hands on my limo account and charged thousands of dollars on it. Dad and Gen fought constantly—she hit Dad over the head, on separate occasions, with a guitar and a baseball bat. Michelle and Aunt Rosie were so worried about my brother, Tam, who was only nine years old, that they went to court and Michelle got custody. My father and Gen were soon to kidnap Tam back and flee across the country, but before they did so Dad somehow got it together to throw Jeff and me a reception.

Dad rented John Wayne's yacht, the *Wild Goose,* for a twenty-four-hour wedding bash. We sent out invitations that Genevieve helped design. They were black and white with pressed wildflowers and fancy, cursive script. They weren't exactly my style—I always liked thin, deco-y thirties fonts—but it didn't matter.

Tons of people came to the party. I wore a gauzy mauve dress. Dad held court in a white captain's hat and a double-breasted blue blazer with brass buttons and insignia on it. My mom was there, my cousins Patty and Nancy, Aunt Rosie, and a bunch of Jeff's friends from Florida. Michelle even let Tam and Chynna come.

It was a wild party, a blast, with drugs, sex, music, and booze. There was champagne and excellent food. We were out on the water, on a beautiful yacht. Racer, a band that Jeff was friends with, set up on the deck and started playing seventies rock. I sang with the band, and as my dad somehow recalled for his book, apparently Jeff and I made love in John Wayne's stateroom. We probably did. What I remember more vividly was that John Wayne had only died a couple months earlier and all of his personal effects were still in the stateroom. His clothes were in the drawers. His toothbrush was in the bathroom. His prescription pill bottles were in the medicine cabinet. He wouldn't be needing those anymore. I wanted to steal one as a souvenir, but it didn't seem right.

At some point my father said, "Excuse me, dear. I'm going to go downstairs and abuse the Zulu." That would be Genevieve, who was very into Zulu culture.

After the party, there were piles of wedding gifts that we somehow managed to cart up to my house in Laurel Canyon. My mother-in-law, Liz, stayed at my house to cat-sit Brains, the one cat I'd brought with me from Beachwood Canyon, while Jeff and I went on a honeymoon to Hawaii.

In Hawaii Jeff and I ordered room service and picked the most exotic food on the menu. We rented a cabana every day, sipped tropical drinks, and had races in the pool. Jeff put all the umbrellas from the tropical drinks in his hair and I adored him. I loved that goofiness. We made love all the time. We were perfectly matched sexually and had great fun in bed. It wasn't kinky as it had been with Peter, just pure passion. Jeff and I had a real connection. There was something about him that made me willing to throw away everything I had with Peter.

No matter how impromptu and misguided our union, we were really happy . . . for those first few days. Then we were in our hotel room watching the Pineapple Bowl on TV when the station broke in with a special report. There was a fire in Laurel Canyon. They announced that my house was on the damaged list. The honeymoon was over.

Jeff and I caught the next plane home. The band REO Speedwagon was in first class with us and the lead singer, Kevin Cronin, tried to help Jeff comfort me. I drank cognac from Hawaii to LAX. We took a limo back to Laurel Canyon. It was nighttime, and as we drove up the winding road of the canyon we saw bright flames shooting into the sky. We drove until the police stopped us. There were fire engines everywhere. They wouldn't allow cars up the small winding canyon road, so we climbed out of the limo and ran up toward the house. I prayed that it would still be standing. As we approached my driveway I breathed a sigh of relief. The house next door was still there!

We ran on—but mere yards away, the lot where my house had stood was completely empty, a pile of charred wreckage. My house was gone. My mother-in-law had escaped just in time, but my cat, Brains, was lost and all my possessions were ashes. There was nothing left standing except the dishwasher and the fireplace.

Jeff and I checked into a penthouse suite at the Chateau Marmont—the same suite where I had tried coke for the first time and where I had lived with Peter Asher. All I had left were the few clothes I'd taken with me on my honeymoon—shorts, flip-flops, some T-shirts, a light dress—and a husband whose true (dark) colors would soon emerge. Everything was gone. I took stock of all that I'd lost. My beloved cat, Brains, was never seen again. The new wedding gifts were the least sentimental items—they were still in their boxes. But I'd been the family archivist. I had my sister Chynna's bronzed baby shoes, a classic record collection, the Madame Alexander dolls that my mother gave me every year. Genevieve's five-hundred-year-old wedding jacket, countless photos and negatives. All my diaries, including the big silver one that I turned to in my father's flat on Glebe Place when he and Keith Richards forgot about me. It never occurred to me that as a newlywed I might have found enough joy and happiness in another person to overcome the material loss. Jeff was fun to frolic with, but he wasn't that man. I was truly destroyed. Jeff and I went to score coke that same night, and in the weeks that followed I snorted mountains of cocaine. Oblivion was how I dealt with shit. With the help of coke I disappeared into myself for a long time after the fire.

We eventually rented a lonely house above the strip on Franklin Canyon Drive. Since we had no dishes or furniture, we rented it fully furnished. Some time after the fire I went back to the ruins of my house. I found slips of charred paper, a melted bowling ball, and one of the roller skates Peter had given me for my nineteenth birthday, with its wheels grotesquely melted. I took the dishes out of the dishwasher. No matter how many times I reminded myself that most of the loss was only material, the fire felt bigger than that. The sum was greater than the parts. It was a devastating blow, and a bad omen for the marriage.

14

When I came back to *One Day at a Time* after my honeymoon, I didn't show my castmates photos of Hawaii, and they didn't congratulate me. The fire, which had been all over the news, overwhelmed the rest—and none of them were exactly enthusiastic about Jeff anyway. I'd married him so quickly, and those who met him saw only his obnoxious side. They expressed their sympathy about the fire, and I thanked them, but I was distant. I was traumatized; the impermanence of everything weighed heavily on me. I'd put a statue of St. Francis of Assisi in the front courtyard of the house to protect my cat, and if even St. Francis couldn't protect poor Brains, then I couldn't count on anyone to protect me. I should have felt safe in the arms of people who knew and loved me. Instead, my drug use escalated, as if the fire were still burning, destroying whatever lay in its path.

The house in the hills became a major drug hangout. The scene was reminiscent of my father's mansions growing up. The digs weren't so luxurious, but I had a great deal of money, and Jeff and I spent it on shitloads of drugs. Perhaps not surprisingly, it turns out that free-flowing drugs attract a pretty nasty crowd. There were always ten or more people partying in our house, but whereas my dad's friends had been stoned and mellow, our friends were freebasing like crazy. Half-strangers crawled around on the floor, smoking bits of the carpet, picking stray rice kernels out of corners, hoping they might be crumbs of base.

I was still friendly with Linda Ronstadt, who was now dating Governor Jerry Brown. They dropped by once. I was in the upstairs living room with a bunch of the usual suspects. There was an open stairway, and as people came up the stairs their heads would appear in the room over a ledge. As I sat there in the living room I saw Jerry's head pop up above the short wall like a little gopher. He looked around, saw the scene, and his head retreated right back down the stairs.

We often flew to my dear father-in-law's drug clinic in Florida to stock up on pills. On one of these occasions Jeff and I were photographed outside our hotel. The photo was published in the *Enquirer,* and it was less than flattering. I looked like Keith Richards on a bad day. So burnt out—gaunt and weird—I didn't even look like a girl. Size zero was loose on me. I didn't like the photo or the bad press that followed it, but what was I supposed to do—change? That wasn't an option.

I still thought I was having fun. In the beginning, in spite of the drugs, Jeff and I behaved like a couple of kids in love. But the money and the drugs started to affect Jeff. He had been struggling financially. When we got married, he suddenly had access to an unending supply of cash. Jeff just spent and spent and spent. There was often a three-foot line of cocaine running down the mirrored wet bar. We hemorrhaged money on drugs, travel, hotels, cars, and musical equipment. I paid for everything. Pat McQueeney and her daughter Kathleen, who were managing my affairs, told me that the outflow was too high and I was going to go broke. They kept telling us to stop spending, but I didn't pay attention.

Jeff also started to be more possessive. At first he'd just ask, "Where are you going?" and I'd say, "I'm going to buy bras—why? Do you want to come with me?" The questions grew more intense, but the change was gradual and I didn't notice right away.

Jeff dreamed of being a rock 'n' roll producer, so we started a band. I was the lead singer. But I still had my job at *One Day at a Time,* which was just starting its fifth season. So I worked on the show from ten to five every day, then went into the recording studio with Jeff and the band from evening till dawn. The schedule fueled my habit. I was so tired during the day that I had to do coke to stay up, then so tired at night that I'd do even more. I felt like a wind-up doll.

Patricia Fass Palmer, a producer on the show, saw me weaving and bouncing down the hall. Alan Rafkin, the director, said I was "wonderfully easy, but when [I] was under the influence and talking to a wall . . . it wasn't registering."

I couldn't go on like this. Jack Elinson and Dick Bensfield, the executive producers of *One Day at a Time,* called me into their office for a meeting. It sounded like I was being called into the principal's office—though I never had been, not even in the days when I showed up at junior high on acid. I sat down in the office across from Dick's desk and they cut to the chase. They said, "You're looking tired. We're going to give you a sabbatical. Take some time for yourself. Put on a little weight. Get well. Come back in three weeks." Things were different then. They didn't say "We know you're taking drugs" and send me to rehab as they might now. Rehab wasn't in the news every day. I was a pioneer celebrity kid drug addict, and nobody knew what to do with me. They didn't know, and I didn't know.

I felt bad, just as I'd always felt bad when I disappointed Aunt Rosie by staying out late. So during the time off I cleaned up my act—stayed away from coke, got my teeth cleaned and my hair cut and colored, and bought some new clothes. Three weeks later I came back: "Ta-da!" They said, "Oh, you look great," and the show went on.

In October 1979 I came back to *One Day at a Time* and found out that while Julie and I were gone from the show, we'd fallen in love. I was introduced to Michael Lembeck, who would play Julie's husband. Michael was so handsome, so funny, so sexy. A perfect husband for Julie. I loved him immediately, and loved his wife too. I didn't socialize regularly with anybody from the show, but Michael and Barbara had me over for dinner a couple of times. My character and I were married months apart, but Julie the rebel cleaned up for her big day. She wore a white lacy wedding dress with a high neck, a brooch, and a hat. I had worn red satin tennis shoes. And that was just the most obvious difference. By now my life was so far removed from Julie's that any parallels in our lives were lost on me.

I came back to the show with renewed energy. I didn't want to disappoint anybody. But weeks later, without thinking of it as a lapse or a failure, I was back to using again. Val says she saw me on the monitor, standing on the set, nodding off, unable to keep my eyes open. She stood there thinking, *Please, somebody help her.* Even my cousin Nancy, who had partied with me plenty, said, "Everyone wanted the best for her. But she was so sure that what she was doing was right. She was an independent, grown-up person." I didn't think I had a problem. I certainly didn't think of myself as an addict. I just continued to live the way I wanted to live, regardless of what anyone else wanted me to do. Same as I had done with Aunt Rosie.

It was the beginning of 1980. I was twenty and about to face one fucker of a year. It began with my grandmother. Dini was very sick. She'd had a stroke and was in the hospital, dying. My father and Gen were off the map—soon after my wedding party on the *Wild Goose* they'd fled to the East Coast with Tam. Nobody knew exactly where they were and Michelle and Rosie, who had temporary legal custody, had reported them to the LAPD, who turned the case over to the FBI. It was a messy, painful situation and it is Tam's story, not mine. But when I went to see Dini, I asked Aunt Rosie, "Have you called Dad?" She said, "To hell with him. He doesn't care. He won't show up." Rosie, Michelle, my mother—they were all mad at Dad and Gen for leaving with Tam and for what had happened between Dad and me in Florida. These women—strong, loving women who made a practice of forgiving my father—were angry at last. They had been wronged many times in many ways, but now they saw his children being wronged and they couldn't accept it. It was unforgivable. I said, "She's his mother! You think he's fucked up now—just wait until his mother dies without us telling him."

Aunt Rosie said, "We don't want him here. Don't you dare tell him." It amazed and infuriated me that people could let this personal stuff get in the way of a mother and a son. I wasn't a parent yet, but I knew what my father meant to Dini. She was born on a reservation in Oklahoma. She saw the world in plain terms. It didn't matter how fucked up her son was, he was her life. I understood that my family had lost respect for my father. He deserved that. But nothing could justify depriving him and his mother of their last good-bye.

The decision to contact Dad was thorny enough, but finding him was nearly impossible. Once again I went into overdrive, dialing every number I knew and saying, "His mother's dying. You have to help me find him." Finally, before I had to call Mick Jagger again, I found Dad in New York. I said, "Look, Dad, Dini's in the hospital and I think you should come." Dad and I were both drug fiends, but at this point he was broke and I had money to burn. I bought him and Genevieve first-class plane tickets and met them at the airport in a stretch limo.

I don't know how long it had been since my father and his mother had seen each other, but when I picked him up at the airport, Dad was a mess. My father grew up with a father who was a mean drunk. My grandfather spent days, nights, years drinking bottle after bottle of Four Roses bourbon in the locked cellar while his wife, my grandmother Dini, carried the weight of the family on her shoulders. As damaged as my father was, his mother had been his salvation. My family was against me bringing him to the hospital, but a man as tortured and complicated and fucked up as my dad was—this moment was deeply important to him. I couldn't let it go by. We went straight from the airport to Dini's bedside.

When we arrived, Dini wasn't conscious. Dad, kneeling at her side, was still almost as tall as I was. He said, "Mom, Mom."

When my father spoke, my grandmother came to. She opened her eyes and said, "My boy, Johnny, my boy," then let her lids fall again. It was clear to me that this woman had been waiting to see her son. Gen was being a drama queen, as always. She said, "Oh, Dini, Dini!"

Dad looked at her and said, "Shut the fuck up, Gen. Get out of here." Gen left the room and Dad put his head down next to his mother and stroked her hand. He stayed with her that way for a good long while. It was a tender scene. How could anyone be angry enough to deprive these two of that moment? I could never be that angry.

Dini died shortly after we left the room. It was January 20, 1980.

About a month later Alan Horn, the head of the production company, called me and Pat McQueeney into his office. I didn't know what the meeting was about—maybe to renegotiate my contract or to say "Good job, kid." I knew that ratings had skyrocketed since my return from suspension.

Alan fired me.

I was shocked. This may be equally shocking to those I worked with, but I didn't know I was creating a problem. I knew I was doing drugs. I knew I was late every single day. But I was under the impression that my performance wasn't suffering.

If I'd been older and wiser, maybe I'd have gotten the message when Alan Rafkin had custom coffee cups made for everyone. Mine showed me running and had excuses written all over it: *The traffic was bad; My alarm didn't go off; I got lost.* (He tactfully excluded *I used gonorrhea eyedrops* and *I had a miscarriage.*) I should have seen the writing on the cup—I had run out of excuses.

I always found energy for the show. I always got it up for my performance before the studio audience, but that wasn't enough. My exhaustion showed at rehearsals and between takes. I wasn't a positive presence. And my drug use had taken a toll on my appearance. I was painfully thin and my skin was terrible—acne exacerbated by malnutrition. It was increasingly difficult for them to shoot me. Skinny wasn't joke material for Schneider anymore. For as long as I can remember, little old ladies have come up to me on the street and said, "I'm praying for you, dear. I've been praying for you since you were a little girl." People who used to watch the show tell me they tuned in to see how fucked up I was, how skinny I could get. They saw that I was disappearing, body and soul.

On *True Hollywood Story*, Alan Rafkin recalled what happened from his perspective: "I had been told that the next time she came in unable to perform I was to call and they would send her to a doctor for a drug test and proceed from there. On March 3, 1980, she came in clinging to a wall. She sat in the makeup chair making no sense. She failed the drug test. Within hours she was fired."

I was the last to know how fucked up I was. Clearly there was a time when things got out of control and it was obvious to everyone but me. I don't remember being mean or rude, but I do remember being defensive, saying, "I'm fine. What are you guys talking about? Everything's okay." I'm sure I was out of it, apologetic, defensive, making excuses, justifying. The show, all its employees, the ratings, the money it earned—it all relied on me, and I was the thin and thinner embodiment of unreliability. There was a lot at stake, and I was a loose cannon. But I don't think stabilizing the show was the only reason they fired me. Everyone knew I was in trouble. Firing me was their attempt to help me.

I felt like my family was kicking me out of the house for dropping a fork. Obviously what I was doing was much more destructive and unprofessional than dropping a fork, but that's as close as I can come to how it felt—the people I loved were giving up on me way before I'd given up on myself. Nonetheless, I treated the firing as if it was something as trivial as losing my phone book. I loved the idea of being on the show, but it had fallen into my lap. So much had been handed to me that for all I knew, life would go on like that. Everything would be okay. I had no idea how many bridges I had burned and no idea what I had lost. The show had been the most stable, constant part of my life for six years that began when I was still an eager teenager full of energy and promise. Now I was a different person, and though I didn't know it yet, I had squandered my best opportunity.

I think they wrote Julie out of the show by having her run away. I can't be sure—it's not like I celebrated being fired by having viewing parties to watch the show go on without me—but I believe that Julie ran out on her husband, and it was about time for me to do the same.

Jeff was waiting for me in the parking structure when I came out of the meeting. I climbed into the car and said, "That's it. I'm fired." We went straight to the dealer's house.

When I was fired from *One Day at a Time,* I didn't realize what I had. I thought, *Fuck them. I'll get another job.* But I'd already dug my grave. Drugs were expensive and my paycheck was gone, but I had no luck getting work. I'd hear about jobs that sounded right for me, but nobody could get me an appointment for an audition. Word was out in the industry that I was unreliable, and nobody wanted to hire me. I was blacklisted. And they were right. I was completely out of control. And we were running out of cash. Work had been a stabilizing force, and once it was gone, my life began to crumble. Now that I wasn't leaving for work every day, I was home. Home in the marriage that had begun with a flameout of destruction and ruin. Home with Jeff, the man whose own mother had warned me against him.

In the beginning Jeff was cocky and confident, which was attractive until it veered into excess. We had an amazing sex life, but now that wasn't enough for him. We'd have threesomes and I'd have to watch him fuck other women. To watch the man I loved have sex with other people was painful, and to see him take glee in my sadness was heartbreaking.

When I still had a job, Jeff had started to become controlling and possessive. When I went to work I had to take my pager so he could reach me at all times. Even so, I'd come home to an interrogation: *Where have you been? Who did you talk to? Who was that guy?* He was afraid of losing me.

Now that I was home, he grew more threatening. I had known women who were abused by men, and now I saw how it happened. My attentive, doting husband was becoming one of those men. I don't know if his abusiveness was triggered by marriage, money, drugs, or all three, but suddenly he was no longer the silly, loving man I'd married and I was a prisoner. If I stood up, Jeff wanted to know where I was going. If he didn't want me to leave, he'd say, "You're not going. Sit down." He told me, "If you leave me, you leave with half a face." He slept with his hand under my thigh. He didn't let me see anyone he didn't want me to see. My family was worried about me—so they fell into the category of people he didn't want me to see.

By the time I realized what was happening, my relationship had blown up in my face. Our home grew increasingly violent. Jeff threw me down the stairs. I kicked him in the balls. We got into a huge fight on a night when Jeff's father and his girlfriend were staying at our house. I called to his dad to help me but the man wouldn't help. I never liked that man.

Jeff was out of control, doing crazy drug stuff, spending all my money, fucking other girls in front of me. One night I woke to find him shaking my shoulder. As I opened my eyes, he asked me to sign a blank check. I rolled over and socked him in the nose. It wasn't the money, though he was bleeding me dry, it was the inhumanity. I'm not a violent person, but I had never had anyone try to put me under his thumb like that. It came really close to breaking my spirit. I put up a front, pretending that everything was fine, but I was falling apart. I lost all sense of myself. I was a walking skeleton. A zombie. I felt soul-sick.

It all came to a head one weekend. Jeffrey and I had bought a huge amount of cocaine that he was planning to sell at a profit. Soon he was hoovering it up, while insisting that I not use the "merchandise," which I did anyway. Maybe all druggies have this battle, trying to turn their passion for drugs into a business, wheeling and dealing, stealing and cheating themselves, resenting one another for diminishing the supply. Whatever the case, between our two out-of-control selves, we ended up doing all of the cocaine that we had planned to sell.

Jeff said, "Go to McQueeney's and get a check." He wanted me to get money from my manager, Pat McQueeney, so we could pay our dealers for the coke. It's one of those moments I see from above, as if someone described it to me, but nobody else was there. I was wearing red overalls, a short-sleeved Hawaiian shirt, and sneakers. I gave Jeff a kiss and got into my car. This was my chance, the first time he'd let me leave the house alone in weeks and weeks. I was about to save my own life. I beeped the horn twice on the way down the hill, like I always did. I glanced over my shoulder at the house. Many times I had stayed up all night and become delusional at that house. I never went back.

I drove straight to Pat McQueeney's office, burst through the door, and told her, "I'm half dead, so unless you want to finish me off, file for divorce right now."

I was broken, distraught, lost. From the outside the marriage may have seemed doomed from the start, but I had been too wrapped up in it to see that. Since I had sacrificed Peter, I had to believe that Jeff was the love of my life.

Running away took all my strength, but once I made the

break, I did everything I could to make sure it was permanent. In seven months of marriage I had lost seven hundred thousand dollars, much of it to drugs and Jeff's spending. My bank account was drained, my house was gone, and I knew that if nothing changed I'd be destitute, drug-addicted, and married to an asshole. I told Pat to cut Jeff off, and to repossess his car and everything he had that I had bought.

Jeff was going to be mighty pissed. I had to get out of L.A. I called the person who, in my twisted mind, represented safety: my father. I knew my father wouldn't say I told you so. I knew he wouldn't judge me. I had pushed the rape aside. It didn't matter in this moment. I knew that this was one of those times when Dad would come to my rescue, and he did. He said, "You're coming to New York. Go to the airport, there's a prepaid ticket waiting for you."

I arrived at the airport, and there was no ticket. And the flight he'd told me to take was full. I should have put it together that Dad couldn't afford a plane ticket, didn't even have the wherewithal to arrange one. Countless times throughout my life, he'd promised me plane tickets. I always arrived at the airport expecting them to be there, and they never were. I had only myself and my stubborn willingness to believe in him to blame. I whipped out my trusty credit card and got on the next flight.

When I arrived in New York there was no one there to pick me up. I waited a long time, hours, trying in vain to reach Dad. This, if anything, was the message my father sent me over and over again in the hours I spent waiting for him, wanting his attention, craving his love: *I love you. I will rescue you. Don't count on me.*

15

I'd been with Jeff for half a year, and during that time I'd lost Peter, my house, my grandmother, my job, and, it seemed, my soul. A fire had swept across my life and left only ashes. But the worst was far from over.

After I'd been waiting for hours at the airport in New York, a driver finally showed up and took me to Connecticut, where Dad and Gen were now living. Let's see, what was new with them: Gen was hugely pregnant with her second child, and Dad was hooked on heroin. He was working some scam where he brought blank prescription pads to a pharmacy on the Upper East Side of Manhattan, and in return they gave him boxes and boxes of narcotics and syringes, which he'd turn around and sell or trade to street dealers for heroin or cocaine. My father was no longer a stoner musician, or even just a flat-out addict. No, Dad was too smart for that mundanity. He was trafficking drugs, big-time. All hell was about to break loose in that house, but regardless of the drugs, my dad, the loss of Dini—the next cloud to shadow me was brought on by nothing but my own fucked-up, warped self.

In my dad's Connecticut house there were loaded syringes hidden everywhere. When you're a needle freak, there's comfort in knowing that next time you need a shot, there will be one ready and waiting for you. Besides, I think Dad had to hide them from Genevieve. My dad was at least half a foot taller than anyone else who might come into the house. And so in that beautiful old house he kept them stored on top of bookshelves, balanced on top of window ledges and door frames, stashed out of sight above the refrigerator. Syringes were stowed anywhere normal-size people couldn't see them.

Never one to shy away from dispensing fatherly advice, Dad kept telling me that shooting coke was a better high. He said it was like being smacked in the face with a cocaine truck. I'd never shot up before, but the line of fear that I'd drawn at using needles was fading. A better high . . . that sounded good. Yes! A better high was what I wanted, and I wanted it more than anything. I wanted it so much, in fact, that I couldn't quite remember what was so bad about needles. There's a natural progression in anything you do. As you become comfortable at a certain level, the next level becomes more accessible. This is a good thing, say, if you're skiing. As your skill increases, the expert hills don't look so steep. But after two years of smoking freebase, I found myself at the unfortunate juncture where shooting up was just skiing down a slightly steeper hill, and I was ready.

As a child my father's boundless world had been fun and carefree, like the song "Down the Beach," which he wrote about Michelle: *Things are cooler in my castle . . . everything is stoned and groovy . . .* I went from being attracted to the liberal ease of it all to being attracted to the dark danger of it. As my dad went down an alternative path, he didn't lose his appeal. I just switched to what he was doing. Nobody grows up thinking, *I want to be a junkie,* but in a weird way I did. I wanted to be whatever it took to fit in with my dad, his friends, and his life.

Where does a girl turn for help when she doesn't know how to shoot up coke? Daddy. To be fair, once I finally wanted to try it, my father was a little reluctant. After all, it wasn't exactly teaching your kid to drive a car. But eventually there we were, in the master bathroom. With a look of anticipation, Dad put some coke in a spoon, poured some distilled water into a syringe, and squirt it into the spoon. Then he flipped the syringe over and used the plunger to mix the powder and water. He tore the cotton tip off a Q-tip and dropped it into the solution to filter out impurities. He pulled the liquid through the cotton into the syringe, flicked it, and we were ready. He had on half glasses, the reading glasses he wore to see close up. I put my right arm out. He tied me off. He was squinting, trying to see the vein, but when he pushed the needle through my skin he missed. It's common to miss; maybe I was holding my arm at an odd angle, maybe my vein rolled, maybe, just maybe, he was nervous to be shooting up his own child—but whatever the case, he missed. I was pissed off. I knew that missed veins caused scarring. I'd seen my father's arms, covered with dark track marks and thick with white scar tissue. Dad, maybe a little bit relieved, said, "I'm not doing it again. Forget it."

I went back to my room with one of his loaded syringes. I wanted to shoot up in my ankle because I didn't want to ruin my arms. I timidly poked myself a couple times, but I had no idea what I was doing. Then my father walked in. He took in the scene: I was on the floor in an awkward crouch. The needle was tentatively aimed at my ankle. I'd forgotten to make a tourniquet. He said, "Aw, honey. You're not doing it right. But I'm not going to do it."

I said, "Talk me through it," so he did. And I was off to the fucking races. Daddy's little girl, all grown up.

I was happy to be where I was. With my Dad. Doing drugs all day and night. I tried to shoot myself up a few more times, with varying success. Dad wouldn't prepare syringes for me, and I was scared that the loaded ones I found around the house would be too much for me and cause me to overdose. So I'd try to do part of one, or I'd chicken out midshot and miss my vein. But there were plenty of new, colorful pills to lab-test on myself. Every so often I'd join Dad for the drive in to New York to pick up drugs and supplies at the pharmacy. Otherwise, I just stayed home and partied with Dad and Gen. I had escaped Jeff, and now I lived a much more palatable version of terrible with people I knew and loved.

Dad and Gen had won custody of Tam. Dad, true to form, had convinced the courts that the situation with Tam was all a big misunderstanding—he and Gen *weren't* junkies. They loved their son and wanted nothing more than to provide a good home for him in the fancy Connecticut home that they would soon litter with umpteen needles.

In Connecticut, they had forged an odd friendship with their next-door neighbors. The Thurlows were a young, friendly, well-rounded, churchgoing family. When I showed up they invited us all to dinner so their young daughter Katie, who had acted in school plays, could meet the TV star next door. It was the night of their son Michael's first Communion. I showed up several hours late, on downers. I sat next to Katie, laboring over weighty decisions like how to get a fork up to my mouth, but before I could eat much of dinner, I passed out, face-planting in a plate of mashed potatoes. Katie must have been shocked to see this whole new side of Julie Cooper. My dad, for once at a loss, tried to blame my behavior on antibiotics. He needn't have bothered trying to sustain the charade. That night he left a trench coat at the Thurlows with a bloody tourniquet and prescription pad in the pocket. All I can hope is that the Thurlows dined out for years on their tale of the degenerate neighbors who spoiled their son's Communion dinner. We owed them that.

Though Dad's supply seemed endless, he controlled what Gen and I used. She was his pregnant wife, I was his daughter—could be that he wanted to protect us, but more likely he just relished being the drug master. On April Fools' Day, Gen and I found a Dilaudid, an opiate stronger than morphine, on the floor, hiding in the carpet behind the door like a little chocolate Easter egg that somehow stayed hidden through all previous hunts. I suspect Dad had dropped it there. He liked to plant little surprises for us to find.

I snapped the pill in two, and in true Genevieve fashion she snatched half and ran. Who knows what she did with hers, but I immediately shot up the other half. Dilaudid is synthetic heroin that's given to terminal cancer patients for pain. I felt the instant surge of euphoria and went upstairs to lie down. A few hours later I woke up to hear a commotion downstairs. I came to the top of the stairs, but Dad yelled up for me to stay where I was. Gen had just given birth to my little sister on the couch.

Bijou was born tiny. It was spring, but snow was falling, and the volunteer ambulance guys who finally showed up had no oxygen and no heat and they were hell drunk. They rushed Bijou to a nearby hospital and she was soon transferred to the Yale–New Haven Newborn Special Care Unit.

The first time I saw Bijou was in the hospital. She was so small, all wiry arms and legs, hooked up to a million monitors in a special crib. She may have been born into irresponsible, reckless hands, but Bijou was a beautiful, perfect, heavenly light sparkling through the clouds. We loved her—we all loved her immediately, deeply, and relentlessly.

Dad, Gen, Tam, and I moved to a hotel right near Yale–New Haven to keep vigil on our little jewel. My father was self-righteous about his drug use, but he didn't want to lose Bijou, and he knew that he had something to hide from the powers that be. When we went to the hospital, Dad hid the track marks on his arms with long-sleeved shirts. But that didn't cover the track marks on his hands. An old junkie trick is to cover up track marks with a layer of toothpaste, then spread makeup on top. Effective *and* thrifty. Every day before we went into the special care unit I covered my dad's tracks for him. They kept the nursery warm for the newborns, and when Dad put on gloves to hold Bijou, he'd start to sweat and the makeup would get gooey under the gloves—it looked like his hands were melting off inside them. I think of those sweaty, goopy, destroyed hands, the hands that held Bijou so gently, the hands that made music, the hands that reflected a life of contradictions and despair.

There's a song from the fifties by a band called Lambert, Hendricks & Ross called "Bijou." I'd sing it to her—*ma petite bijou*—while I rubbed her tiny feet and tiny legs. Little Bijou—she has triumphed over incredible odds. Her story is her own, but my culpability is part of it. I witnessed the dangers of Genevieve's pregnancy. I shot up with her. I was there, complicit, the night of Bijou's birth. My brother Tamerlane was about ten years old. He and I shared a room at the hotel near the hospital, and while I prayed for our sister's survival from a drug-wrecked birth, I did coke in front of him many times.

I had no sense of the hypocrisy in how much I loved my two younger siblings and how damaging my actions may have been to them. I watched them endure horrific parenting; I behaved irresponsibly in front of them; and later I would make essentially the same mistakes with my own son. There are people in the world who do these things, and I was one of them. We all survived, but barely.

Then, out of the blue, Dad decided that I needed to go to rehab. I was taken aback. *Excuse me? I need to go to rehab? What about you?* But Dad had a point. While he was preoccupied with Bijou, his control of my drugs slackened and my use escalated dramatically. I think Pat McQueeney must have chimed in to persuade Dad to get me help, and he in turn convinced me to go to a psychiatric facility called Silver Hill. It was a country club–like rehab in tony New Canaan that Dad thought was cool because Truman Capote used to go there to dry out. I agreed to go—I'd reached a point where the drugs weren't fun. I was just stuck in a cycle of needing more and more and I wanted out. Silver Hill didn't have much experience with drug addiction—I believe I was one of the first cocaine patients they ever had—but they took me in.

My father came to visit me. It pissed me off that I was in rehab when his habit was worse than mine, though any sensible person could've seen that it wasn't a competition. I said, "You know what? This isn't fair. You're as bad off as I am." I made him check in and join me as a patient. It's safe to say that neither of us was wholly committed to recovery, but I, at least, was clean. Dad, on the other hand, asked me to pee in a cup for him and hide it in the woods so he could hand them my pee when they drug-tested him. Eventually he just checked himself out. Maybe they caught him swapping pee cups. I don't know how it went down.

I met a guy at rehab named Dolfi Aberbach. Like me, he was in for cocaine. He was tall, elegant, and charming. I thought he was the cutest thing I'd ever seen. Dolfi and I spent a lot of time talking and becoming close friends. After a couple of weeks, Dolfi signed himself out, which meant he was leaving without completing his rehab, against medical advice. The next day I signed myself out. So much for staying clean. As I left, the staff said, "Say hello to Dolfi."

Genevieve came to pick me up in a limo and the first stop was to buy cocktails for two. Because cocktails are an excellent way to celebrate ditching rehab. When we arrived home we did shots of tincture of morphine. Morphine: more celebration. Later that day we took a car into Manhattan to see Dolfi, and I stayed.

Dolfi and I didn't even pretend to want to be clean. In Connecticut, at Dad's, I'd never gotten the hang of needles. Now, in a matter of days, Dolfi taught me to shoot up for real, and we proceeded to shoot outrageous amounts of cocaine together. We were young. We were rich. Money from reruns and/or syndication was accumulating now that Jeff had stopped draining the coffers. We could go anywhere and do anything we wanted. We chose to sit around and shoot coke. Sometimes we drove to Connecticut to see Bijou and Tam and to partake in Dad's wares. We'd crouch down in the back of the limo, shooting up all the way. We visited Betsy Asher, my ex-boyfriend's ex-wife, at her hotel and snuck into the bathroom to do a shot. Coke was all we did day and night.

Back in L.A., my cousin Patty was getting married, but I

didn't go. Patty had been in a relationship with a cinematographer named Bradford L. May for years. Bradford used to come with Patty to tapings of *One Day at a Time,* and he had a distinctive, honking laugh. When I watch tapes of the shows, I can still recognize Brad's funny laugh. Patty and Bradford were domestic, nesting. I went over to their house a lot before I lived with Jeff—before I stopped seeing most of my family—but now there was no way I'd make it to her wedding. I should have been there. I should have been a bridesmaid, but I was too out of it to go through the motions of civilized life.

Dolfi wasn't a devil in disguise. Of all people to instruct me in the bad habits that I was already chasing, Dolfi was as sweet and warm a companion as one might find. That was part of the problem. We think of users and dealers as scuzzy people who scam and manipulate, but so many of my drug companions were dear, dear friends, people I enjoyed and loved. It wasn't a matter of good and evil, black and white. So I kept at it.

16

The drugs kept running out and I kept calling Pat McQueeney from New York to ask for more money. Finally, she refused to send me anything but a ticket back to L.A. I moved in with my mother in Tarzana, where my brother Jeff had also landed with his own rampant drug habit. Neither of us was in good enough shape to live on our own. I'd been shooting coke day and night for months. I was painfully thin, and my arms ached. I'd been a human pincushion and the result was clogged veins, dying and collapsed veins. Every morning my mother massaged my arms and legs to restore my circulation.

One morning when my mom was rubbing my arms she looked up at me and said, "Your eyes look yellow." By the next morning my skin was yellow too. I had hepatitis B. At St. John's Medical Center in Santa Monica, I was put in isolation. All attendants and visitors had to wear face masks. Most of the time I was alone, and I lay in the bath amazed at how bright yellow I looked against the white ceramic tub.

It had only been two months since Bijou was born. In that time I'd been in and out of rehab. I'd had a sweet but drug-infested love affair and come back home. But 1980 wasn't over yet, and there was more trouble ahead. On June 9, I was at the recording studio where I'd worked with Jeff Sessler, hanging out with my friend Lisette. I received a call from my cousin Nancy. She was sobbing, but she managed to tell me that my cousin Patty had died. I sat there in shock. The memory of that moment breaks my heart every time.

Patty was six years older than I was, twenty-five, a beautiful girl who always wore a pendant that was the hand of Fatima. Two weeks earlier she had married Bradford, her youth and beauty and their happiness masking her drug problems. I remembered how when we were teens we'd sometimes drive into Hollywood to explore, just peeking into stores or walking down Hollywood Boulevard, staring at the sparkly bits of quartz in the sidewalk. Patty said, "I do believe we're in the City of Glitter." The whole world felt like our Oz, our playland, and we spent days with each other just wandering around tripping.

Patty, who was my companion for years, my happy sidekick in the City of Glitter. She could sing like nobody's business. She was funny, quirky, my beloved sister, and now she was gone.

What happened to her could have happened to me on any number of occasions, except that it didn't. She was at a party and apparently some guys gave her a hotshot, a lethal injection of drugs, so they could take advantage of her. Patty passed out and a friend—a sketchy girl whom we never found after she told her story to the cops—brought Patty back to her apartment, put her on the couch, and went to sleep. When her friend woke up in the morning, Patty was still out cold. The friend left for work, and by the time she came home Patty was dead.

The last time I had seen Patty was at my house in Laurel Canyon before it burned to the ground. Jeff and I had just gotten together, and things hadn't soured yet. Patty came over and in the course of the evening she got progressively more fucked up. We were playing a board game, of all things, on a glass coffee table, and Patty was out of it in a sloppy, barbiturate way, bumping into things and slurring her words. It's best to be in that state when you're with others in exactly the same boat. When you're not wasted like that and someone else is, it's kind of gross. I told Patty to go to bed. I said, "Come on, you're going to hurt yourself. You're going to break something. Just go lie down." But Patty wanted to play and kept knocking things over. It was unattractive. I've been that way myself, and I'm sure that people told me to go to bed just as I'd told Patty. But on this particular night I was sharp to her, saying, "Go, I love you, but just go to bed." Now, after all those years of being so close, I was stuck with that as my last encounter with Patty.

That night I did anything and everything to remove myself from reality. I stayed at Lisette's and slept with her and some guy. The next morning I scored a bunch of street Quaaludes (meaning they were fake, not pharmaceutical) and took them. By the time I arrived at Patty's funeral I was really high. Everyone looked at me as if to say "How could you? How could you show up here like this?" And I thought, *How couldn't I?* I'll never forget the moment I saw Aunt Rosie, from behind, walking into the funeral parlor. She was bent in half, crying. She lost one girl to drugs, and another of her girls was to all appearances on her way to the same grave. I know I added to her pain that day.

Michelle and Pat McQueeney shuffled me into the back of a limousine and insisted that I wait in the car during Patty's memorial service.

After the service, Michelle started telling me I was overdosing and had to go to the hospital. Michelle was always a presence at family events, a voice of reason, a stabilizing force. She was afraid for me, again, always. This time she had black hair for a part in a film and was wearing a Spanish mantilla made of black lace. I was too creeped out by her Addams Family look to defend myself. They took me to have my stomach pumped. I have no memory of that part at all.

The following weeks were a blur of sex, drugs, whatever I imagined would mask my pain. I was grieving for Patty. I am still to this day.

Two years after Patty died, Aunt Rosie gave me a framed picture of her, heartbreakingly young, smiling, caught forever in the time when we were so happy and blithe and sure that we could have as much fun as we dared without risking anything. I move that picture around my house, onto my porch, as if to bring Patty with me, a sister-guardian. On the back, in Aunt Rosie's handwriting, it says:

Tell me then must I perish—
Like the flowers that I cherish?
Nothing remaining of my name?
Nothing remembered?—oh no!
I know to all who loved me—
I'll always be young!
The songs I sang will still be sung!
And there will be flowers;
And poems;
And pictures with pretty smiles.
RAT 2/82

After Patty died, my brother Jeffrey and I moved in together. It was a cute two-bedroom apartment in Hollywood where our friends came to hang out. Danny Sugarman, Jeffrey, and I shared needles and drugs. Ah, friends and family.

When I wasn't using, I was busy with my divorce. I had had Jeff Sessler evicted from the house, all accounts canceled, and all cars repossessed. But Jeff, who had spent as much of my money as he possibly could, countersued. Pat McQueeney had wanted to arrange a prenuptial agreement but I forbade it, saying that Jeff wouldn't ever hurt me that way. What a trusting, blind fool I was. I'd been under Jeff's spell when we were married, but now I saw our relationship for what it had been. Jeff was a wannabe. A wannabe producer, a wannabe rock star, a wannabe drug dealer. He saw me, or at least my money, as a ticket to these things. I do think he loved me, but it was a sick, controlling passion that sucked me dry emotionally, physically, and financially.

Ours must have been one of the first high-profile divorces in which a man was asking for alimony from a woman, because it caused quite a stir. We were in the courthouse in Beverly Hills every day and the evening news reported on it every night. Connie Chung was standing outside the courthouse talking about my divorce. It was surreal.

Weirdly, in spite of our court battle, Jeff and I never behaved like real enemies. We always said hi in court. Yes, he'd been bleeding me dry, but I was bleedable. Yes, he was trying to take me to the cleaners, but he was entitled to alimony under the letter of the law. I didn't feel hatred for that. I had been in love with Jeff. I was married to the guy. The love didn't just disappear because it all fell apart. No matter what hidden sides had emerged, he was still the person I had fallen in love with. I don't believe in cutting people out of my life or erasing experiences. I am who I am by way of where I've been. Jeff was a terrible mistake on the road to many terrible mistakes, but he was part of an experience that I refused to regret. I didn't blame him for who he turned out to be. I just needed to get out, and that's what I was doing. But the old love made it hard, and the press made it harder. The whole thing took a toll on me. I was already so wrecked physically and emotionally.

The night before a particularly big day in court, my brother and I stopped by his pill doctor and picked up some Tuinal. We went shopping to buy me a new dress for the occasion, then home to get high. I took a few pills, and then I took more. I wondered how many I'd had. Was this my second round, or had I already had seconds? How many had I taken the first time? It didn't matter. All I knew was that I wanted to be more high. As what I thought was probably my second round started to kick in, I went into my bedroom to lie down for a moment.

Apparently, my new boyfriend Mark, a beautiful Spanish boy, arrived some time later and asked where I was. He came into my room and found me unconscious on my bed. My cigarette was burning a hole in the blanket. I wasn't breathing. When they tried to rouse me, my head flopped like a rag doll. Mark and Jeffrey called the paramedics. I know it sounds like a movie cliché, but I remember floating above the scene of the paramedics working to save me. I saw my brother and friends gathered around in tears. For a moment I felt like I had a choice to either go back or die. Next thing I knew I woke up in the ICU. I was released later the next day, and I was high again within hours.

I had overdosed, and I had nearly died, but so much other shit was going down that nobody made a big deal about my near-death experience, including me. We all attributed it to the stress of the divorce. We didn't connect it to Patty's death. We didn't see that I had been right behind her. I don't remember feeling scared for myself, scared of death, or scared that it would happen again. The truth is, I was doing everything I could to make sure I never felt anything at all.

It had been a year of marriage and divorce; rehabilitation and self-destruction; birth and death; love, drama, and pain. Something had to happen to pull us out of the tornado that had sucked me, Jeffrey, Patty, Bijou, Tam, Genevieve, and Dad into its vortex. And it did. In July, nearly a year after I married Jeff and everything went downhill, Dad was arrested for trafficking narcotics. His mother was dead. His niece was dead. His three-month-old daughter's health was still compromised. Dad had been injecting himself with cocaine every twenty minutes for a year. And now he was facing forty-five years in prison. We were all scared and upset—even Dad, who had treated my arrest at eighteen as a rite of passage. Now he changed his tune.

It wasn't exactly a wakeup call—nobody said, "Wow, what we've been doing is really, really unhealthy and wrong. We need to clean up our acts." But nobody wanted Dad to go to jail for forty-five years. Dad and his lawyers started jockeying to change the charges and reduce the sentence. He immediately went into rehab, which would show the court that he was repentant and reformed. Then he called me and asked me to come into treatment. He thought it would look good on his record if he was not only trying to clean up his own act but also helping his own daughter with her vices.

I was using and living like a pig with my brother. When I wasn't getting high with someone or trying to get cash or pulling myself together for a court date, I was sleeping or watching *General Hospital*. It was the summer of Luke and Laura on the run. I stayed in bed for days on end. Empty tequila bottles and pizza boxes littered the floor. When Dad called to ask me to come into treatment, I laughed at the suggestion and went on my merry way.

Days later Dad called again and I heard something different in his voice. He needed me. This time it was Dad who was calling me for help, and I would do anything to keep him out of jail. Anything. I arrived in New Jersey and for once Dad was actually there to meet me at the airport. The storm of that year—the drugs and helter-skelter and tragedy—was over. We were going to get better, and we were going to do it together. That, at least, was the image we wanted to present.

PART FOUR

PAPA'S NEW MAMA

17

My father was on trial for conspiracy to distribute narcotics. The potential for that forty-five-year sentence motivated him to get clean as nothing before ever had. Together with his doctor, Mark Gold, Dad hatched a plan designed to land him the most lenient sentence possible. He would first have a very public and zealous rehabilitation and then take a very public and convincing stance against drugs. He would be reformed, and the world would know it. As part of the plan, Dad and Dr. Gold thought that if I stood by his side, equally reformed, it would look like he had spearheaded the recovery of his whole family.

Dad was the center of the family, of our lives. If orbiting around him meant going to rehab, then there was no question I would do it. I became a day patient at Fair Oaks Hospital in New Jersey. For six weeks I went there every morning for group counseling. At that time Fair Oaks kept drug addicts and alcoholics apart. We went through treatment separately; we even ate separately. I'd look over at the alcoholics in the dining room and think, *You wimps.* I know it's warped, but I had junkie pride. The alcoholics were lightweights, soft-core. They didn't know what a good high or a bad addiction was. We had the best and worst of it. We'd been on the world's scariest roller coaster, while they'd only ridden the kiddie rides. That roller coaster, in a junkie's fucked worldview, was the whole point.

Here's my favorite part: for some reason the well-intentioned doctors at Fair Oaks Hospital decided that it was perfectly fine for us drug addicts to continue to drink alcohol. Because alcohol wasn't our drug of choice. Well, that was handy.

I became friends with a girl named Sue Blue who was working for my dad. Sue Blue was and is a wonderful photographer. She and my father had met in the Hamptons when he was walking down the street with Mick Jagger. Sue Blue asked to photograph them, and she and Dad became friendly. She was talkative and opinionated, but sweet. Before I met her, Dad told me I would be friends with her forever. Sue Blue walked into the kitchen, a New York girl with fuzzy hair and big glasses, and the minute she opened her mouth I got it. Dad was right. We would be friends forever.

After a long day in drug treatment, Sue Blue and I would drive around in her car and drink wine. In the evenings I'd come home to the "Big House," a huge house that my father had rented in New Providence, New Jersey. Living there were my dad, Genevieve, Jeffrey, Tamerlane, Bijou, and I, and three counselors from Fair Oaks to keep an eye on us.

Soon enough Dad, Genevieve, and I discovered that booze helped fill the hole that cocaine (for me and Gen) and heroin (for Dad) had left. But the hole was deep, so it took a lot of booze to fill it. Most of the time we were all drunk off our asses. Even our in-house counselors drank. Because they were *drug* treatment counselors, so they didn't have a problem either.

Still, even with the infusion of alcohol, I was cleaner than I'd been in a very long time. I'd been taking pills so consistently that when I took my birth control pill, I found myself waiting for it to kick in. Nonetheless, I was proud of having stopped. Backstage at a Stones show, I was in the dressing room and Keith Richards came up to me carrying a mirror with a pile of cocaine on it. He said, "Can you say no to this?"

I took a deep breath and blew that mountain of cocaine into his face. It was one of my shining moments.

The three years we spent in New Jersey was the first time I really felt like I was part of a big, warm family that wasn't going anywhere. There were dogs and cats and a boisterous group of people who gathered on stools around the big island in the kitchen. Dad made breakfast every morning: scrambled eggs and fried bologna or pancakes and sausage. Chynna and her little friend Dilyn came to visit. They went to ballet classes and put on shows for all of us. We played basketball in the driveway. There were all kinds of noise and play that made it feel like a big family home. It was closer to normal than my living situation had ever been since we left Virginia.

Though Genevieve's mother had come from South Africa to care for Gen's kids, I often spent time with Bijou, who was a little angel. I'd feed her, change her diaper, take her places, play with her for hours. Tam was going to Catholic school and was supposed to wear a tie every day, so he'd come down for breakfast with crazy rumpled hair and his tie on crooked. He was brilliant—he subscribed to the *Wall Street Journal* at age nine—but he was no Alex P. Keaton. He was a wild and beautiful spirit, a firecracker crashing around dangerously, hurtling across the room and plowing into you at high speed, running, jumping, building forts, and wrestling with the dogs. But the minute Bijou entered his radius, he'd calm down, stroke her cheek gently, and kiss her sweet head.

There were still some indications that this wasn't exactly *The Brady Bunch*. There were clear gaps in the parenting. One day Sue Blue and I came home to find Bijou in the den on her blanket, cheerfully chewing on a pack of Marlboros. She must have had sixteen cigarettes in her mouth. I gently worked them out of her mouth and scavenged out the remaining bits. I can still see that pack on the floor, torn and surrounded by bits of saliva-covered tobacco. No wonder Bijou turned out to be a smoker.

Genevieve was a wild card. She was drinking like the rest of us, but she was not what one would call a happy drunk. I can't pretend to know what was going through Genevieve's head when it came to her children. The only time I saw her express something resembling concern or regret for introducing them to a world of instability and drugs was once when I was sitting by the fireplace in the library at the Big House. Genevieve came into the room, said, "It's your fault that Bijou's retarded," and kicked me as hard as she could in the small of my back with her cowboy boot. I flew across the room and lay sprawled on the floor. Genevieve walked out of the room.

As anyone who has met, seen, or heard Bijou knows, she grew up to be as smart, beautiful, and talented as she promised to be from day one. I imagine Genevieve was referring to the fact that she and I had shot up together while she was pregnant with Bijou. If violence and aggression were her way of confronting those painful memories or expressing guilt and regret, it didn't surprise me. Genevieve was an unstable woman who did heartless, abusive things while on drugs, but thankfully in later years she got clean and developed a great relationship with both her kids.

After I finished my six-week outpatient treatment at Fair Oaks, I became a counselor on the adolescent ward of the hospital, helping to evaluate the kids who came in with psychological, drug, or alcohol problems. Dad was also "recovered," and the two of us manned a cocaine hotline. When people called I tried to talk them into treatment, explaining that they didn't have to live that way—there was a way out and this was it.

Dad and I started doing a lot of antidrug publicity. We shared the cover of *People* magazine for an article about kicking our drug habit. We appeared on *The Dick Cavett Show, The Tonight Show* with John Davidson as the guest host, and *The Phil Donahue Show*. We traveled all over the country to appear on local TV shows and to speak at schools. The media ate it up. We were photographed together going here, going there, flaunting our new, cleaned-up selves. What a heartwarming story of shared recovery.

Jeffrey and me as happy kids.

I cut my own bangs—
bad idea.

Me and my
beautiful
Mommy,
April 1969.

Jeff Noone and me—
scary hairdo.

An old headshot of mine.

Me, Dad, and Jeffrey,
1967.

Me at 12 years old. So young—where did the time go?

Me, Aunt Rosie, and Patty when Kork Ease Wedgies were all the rage.

CBS/LANDOV

One Day at a Time cast photo: Pat Harrington Jr, Valerie Bertinelli, Bonnie Franklin, and me. We're all in our places with bright shiny faces. *(Photo by CBS/ Landov)*

This was taken after my mom got a terrible beating from Lenny. I knew nothing at the time. Poor Mom.

Tam, me and Chynna in the Fair Oaks Hospital days, 1981. *(Photo by Suzanne L. Sinenberg)*

Dad, me and little Bijou.

New Mamas and Papas: Spanky, me, Scott, and Dad in four part harmony.

Mick Barakan and me. We were so much in love. *(Photo by Suzanne L. Sinenberg)*

A very 80s version of us. *(Photo by Suzanne L. Sinenberg)*

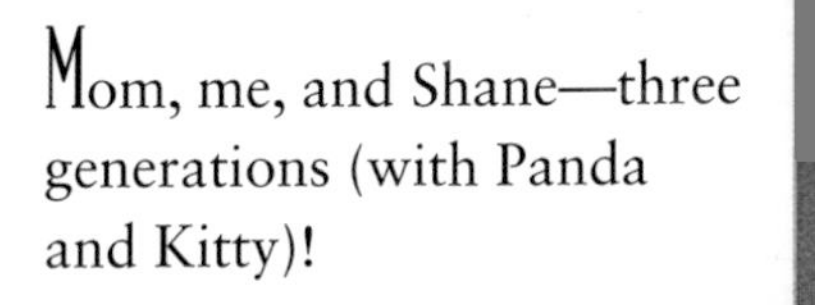

Mom, me, and Shane—three generations (with Panda and Kitty)!

Our wedding day, me and Mick with Shane.

Post liver transplant Dad and sober me. *(Photo by Neal Preston)*

Papa John and four of five kids—Dad, Chynna, Bijou, me, and Tam. This photo makes me sad. *(Photo by Suzanne L. Sinenberg)*

This is the last photo taken of Dad and me, 2000. I knew he was very ill, but tried to smile anyway.

Chynna, Bijou, me. The Sisters

Me, Shane, Mom, and Jeffrey, May 2008. Three months before my arrest. Shane is so handsome!

At times the public exposure became discomforting. It was so personal. Phil Donahue got my father to show his arms to the camera. Dad's arms were a crime scene of black lines and cavernous scars—every one seemed a twisted testament of debauchery and self-torture. It was telling too much, showing too much. I pulled Dad's sleeves back down, saying, "Leave him alone. Don't do that to him." We were already discussing our problems with the world. Wasn't that enough? But for the most part I did whatever Dad and Dr. Gold asked me to do. This was the first time my father had asked me to help him. He needed me—and that was all I needed.

My father's trial was still ahead, but he was already planning for life after his sentencing, and, tellingly, he didn't plan on being a volunteer antidrug counselor and publicist forever. There were a lot of us in that house, and someone needed to finance the happy commune. Dad saw the press surrounding us and wanted to strike while the iron was hot. His idea wasn't exactly inspired, but it was promising. He would put the Mamas & the Papas back together.

There was a big market for reunion tours at the time. The Turtles, the Association, Gary Puckett—all pop bands—were capitalizing on it. There was state-fair work across the country, international markets, Vegas. If you could swallow your pride enough to accept the label "revival act" and realize that the second time around was never going to match the first, then the money could be pretty good. But putting the group back together wasn't exactly easy. He couldn't raise Mama Cass (Cass Elliot) from the dead, and Michelle had moved on. She was in Los Angeles, an elegant Beverly Hills lady with a flourishing career as an actor. There was no way she'd come back. As soon as Dad started talking about how he'd reconstitute the group, I said, "Not without me, you're not." I'd always dreamed of being a musician. Here was a way to be with my father, to make music, and to earn a much-needed paycheck.

Pat McQueeney was against my joining Dad in his new

group. She said, "You need to be in L.A. You need to be auditioning." McQueeney was a force to be reckoned with. A tall, beautiful woman from a cultured, horsey Connecticut family, Pat knew the industry inside and out. She could get anyone in Hollywood on the phone. She was the one who promoted me, protected me, and did damage control . . . a lot of damage control. But it wasn't all business. After all these years, Pat was like a mother to me. And she hated my father. In part she felt that his spectacularly bad influence undid all her hard work, but she also saw him as simply a bad parent. She believed—not unreasonably—that if he hadn't been around, my life would never have spiraled out of control. Dad, on the other hand, felt threatened by Pat, and the quiet power struggle between them finally culminated in Dad telling me to fire her. He said, "She's so uptight and straitlaced—how could she possibly understand you? She's holding you back."

Pat was my advocate. She'd invested years in me and my career. But my father told me to fire her, so I fired her. If he'd asked me to walk into a burning building, I would have done it. The look on her face when I told her our professional relationship was over haunted me for years, and even in that moment a part of me knew that what I was doing was a mistake. I would spend years missing her and all she did for me, and all she was to me. But with Pat gone, there was nothing and nobody to stop me from joining the New Mamas & the Papas.

When I was seven or eight, I snuck into the recording studio that was hidden behind a wall panel in Dad and Michelle's house at 783 Bel Air Road. The Mamas & the Papas were recording the vocals for the title song on their album *People Like Us*. When they sang four-part harmony perfectly in tune, there was an overtone that was its own voice. They called that magical fifth voice Harvey. Now I hid behind a huge, freestanding sound baffle and sang along with the four of them, "People like us, so much in love." When they listened to the playback the mike had picked up my little voice, and it wasn't exactly Harvey. One of the sound guys said, "Hey, what's that?"

Dad listened for a moment, then started tossing aside the huge paisley pillows in the vocal booth, saying, "Where are you?" I peeked over the sound baffle and was promptly banished.

Now I was going to be part of the scene I had eavesdropped on throughout my childhood. I would be singing Michelle's parts, the parts of my ex-stepmother. With me on board, Dad next called his fellow former Papa, Denny Doherty. Denny was freezing his nuts off in Canada. He had nothing better to do, so he flew down to New Jersey with his very pregnant wife, Jeanette, to join us in the Big House. That made three of us.

Then Dad tapped Spanky McFarlane, the lead singer of Spanky and Our Gang, to sing most of Cass's parts. Spanky is a bigger girl with a powerhouse of a voice. When I went with Dad to pick her up at the airport, she walked off the plane wearing a red beret with multicolored feathers sprouting out of it, a rainbow of eye shadow, and a voluminous red cape. I thought, *Wow, who the heck is this?* Spanky and her kids moved into the Big House too. The New Mamas & the Papas was assembled.

With a full house, we set about re-creating the sound of the Mamas & the Papas. We rented a rehearsal space above a bar called the Bunch o' Grapes and started having long, boozy rehearsals. For all the hard-core partying and incompetent parenting, when it came to his music, my father was a taskmaster. He demanded perfection. We rehearsed our parts over and over, singing for hours every day. We tried to be faithful to the original arrangements of the songs, but nobody was as young as they used to be. With age comes decreased vocal range, so for some songs we had to lower the key. We wrote new songs, worked out arrangements, and, with our longtime friend Marsia, designed a wardrobe for the group. Days passed in which we never left our rehearsal space—Bunch o' Grapes sent food and beers up at regular intervals. We had everything we needed.

When the time came for my father's sentencing, our whole crazy family came to court: me, Genevieve, Tam, Bijou, Gen's mother Audrey, Jeffrey, Spanky, Denny, Dr. Gold, and all the counselors. It was a dramatic show of support. Dad stood up before the assembled and said, "I'm the head of this family, and they all look to me to show them the next thing to do. For all these years I've been showing them the wrong next thing to do. I need to stay out of prison so, for the first time, I can show them the right next thing to do." The publicity blitz Dad had orchestrated between his arrest and his sentencing paid off. Out of a possible forty-five years, Dad was sentenced to thirty days in a federal work farm. When they handed down the sentence, Genevieve screamed "John! John! Oh, John! Yay!" a little too loudly. But she couldn't have been drunk in court . . . Well, who knows? We were all so happy that we had a party that night at the Big House, the likes of which the court might have been disconcerted to see. But we didn't use drugs.

It soon came time for Dad to serve his time. *Entertainment Tonight* was at the house to film the good-bye as we took him to jail. They set up their gear in our courtyard very early in the morning. Dad and I got into the car, and the cameras watched us as we drove away.

On the way to jail, Dad asked to stop at a bar for one last drink. We pulled over, had a vodka and orange juice, then got back on the road. But the next time we saw a bar he wanted to pull over again. We stopped at three different bars. Dad got shitfaced on his way to prison. Thirty days later, I came to pick him up and we got equally shitfaced on the way home.

With the new band members and their families, the Big House started to feel small. Spanky, her kids, and I moved out and got a pretty house together on a street called Sherwood Forest Lane.

From then on her son Matt was Friar Tuck. Dad was the sheriff of Nottingham, and so on. We had all of our furniture shipped across the country from L.A. In the living room we put the imitation deco rattan furniture that had been in the apartment where I lived with my brother during the divorce. In my bedroom I had a deco dark wood bed with matching nightstands and a vanity table with a round mirror. The cheerful communal spirit that we'd discovered in the Big House continued in my house with Spanky. After rehearsing all day, we'd come home to cook dinner and eat with the kids. Every night Dad, Denny, and new neighborhood friends would hang out, singing and tooling with guitars—the mellow happy hippie vibe I remembered and idealized from my Dad's pre-heroin Los Angeles days.

I loved having roommates and could have gone on like that for a long time, but the New Mamas & the Papas were raring to go. Dad was on a roll, rearranging old hits, writing new songs, and directing our harmonies. We were starting to sound good, so we went into a studio in New York to start laying down tracks. We recorded demos for an album just as the original Mamas & Papas had—before ever performing. I'd been acting for years, but this was my musical education. I sang four-part harmony, which is no easy trick, for the first time. To be with these talented musicians—in rehearsal, onstage, in the studio—was an incredible learning experience.

After four months of rehearsing and a warm-up gig at the Bitter End in the West Village, the New Mamas & the Papas had our first big gig in Princeton. Lots of industry people, friends, and media had been invited. I wore an amazing dress that Marsia made, a light green chamois suede halter dress with a Peter Pan zigzag hemline. Over it was a huge jacket covered in dark green rhinestone-studded leaves. I really did the eighties justice with that jacket. I looked like the Jolly Green Giant. I knew I looked fabulous, but before we went on I was so nervous that my knees were shaking. I'd acted in front of a live studio audience for years, but I was too young for stage fright when I started. Now I was starting something new at an age where I was old enough to be self-conscious.

That first night in Princeton we opened with "Straight Shooter," the same as the original Mamas & the Papas had, and the same as we would for every show from then on. "Straight Shooter" has a great vamp that the band repeated as we came out onto the stage. The crowd cheered. We played "12:30 (Young Girls Are Coming to the Canyon)," one of the most vocally beautiful songs my dad ever wrote. I started forgetting my anxiety and enjoying the music. Then we played a rockabilly version of the theme song from *One Day at a Time,* bringing my worlds together. The crowd went wild, and I felt a surge of giddy joy. This was the thrill of live performance.

We closed with "Monday, Monday" and "California Dreamin' " as encores. I'd first heard these songs in the Virgin Islands as a child, when the Mamas & the Papas were trying out their material at Duffy's. Often, when Dad put me to bed in the apartment above the club, I'd lie awake for hours, listening to the new songs until I fell asleep. Now here I was, singing my childhood lullabies in front of the first of thousands of people. It felt like a new beginning.

The New Mamas & the Papas took off. Our booking agents set up gig after gig, first in New York, then across the country, then around the world.

One reviewer of the band thought that John and Denny looked like artichoke pickers from Salinas, and another one said Dad looked like a woozy Errol Flynn. One said that I was obviously trying way too hard to be a rock star. Whatever. We weren't perfect. To sing a four-part harmony was such an exact science. If one person was off, we were fucked. Some nights the harmony would be pristine, and some nights it was, *Oh my God, I had to live through that?* Good or bad, nothing stopped us. There were countless fans dying to hear the Mamas & the Papas, even if in reconstituted form, and we were determined to fulfill that demand.

We were warriors. Tam and Bijou, Denny's kids, Spanky's kids, they all stayed back in New Jersey like army brats while we toured all over the world for the next decade. We went to England, Germany, Denmark, Norway, Hong Kong, Japan, Brazil, and all over Canada and the United States. We played cruise ships. We played state fairs. We played in Vegas for months at a time. Sometimes Michelle came to visit us on the road, stepping onstage to sing "Dedicated to the One I Love," which was her most famous solo with the original group. We'd play three weeks on—a different city every night—then one week off. We toured for 280 days one year. We were always on the road. Touring constantly was my job now. It was how I made a living and I loved it. We drank, we went onstage completely fucked up, and the audience loved us. Those were fun days, some of the best times of my life. I wouldn't trade them for anything.

The New Mamas & the Papas was in many ways a dream come true for me. I was performing, which I'd always done. I was in a world of music, which I'd always wanted. And, above all, it was the first time in my life that my father was fully available to me, for hours and days on end. I was no longer chasing a phantom. Now I was part of his trip.

18

As far as the world knew, my father and I were clean. They'd read it in *People* magazine—that touching cover story about our joint rehabilitation. The producers of *One Day at a Time* wasted no time in calling to invite me back as a recurring character. The show's ratings had declined in my absence, and the producer Patricia Palmer later said that Julie added a rebellious conflict that the show needed. She put it simply: if I could come back and be okay, they wanted me. The irony was not lost on me. Being a rebel was great for ratings, but not for real life. Still, I was overjoyed and gladly accepted the offer. Close to the beginning of season seven, Julie came home because she was having troubles with her husband, Max, and just like that I had my job back.

The first day I came back to work, I found that some things had changed at the show in the year-plus that I was gone. I walked reflexively to my dressing room, but stopped short when I saw the name panel on the door. It said "Valerie Bertinelli." Valerie had my dressing room, a slightly bigger corner dressing room. Then, the first time I watched the credits roll at the beginning of the show, I saw that her name had replaced mine for top billing in the credits. These things weren't important to me in and of themselves. I'd never felt competitive with Val about our status at the show. But they were an ungentle reminder that Val deserved these things and—obviously—I didn't. I'd been fired, my character had been written out of the show, and the space I'd filled had closed up behind me. My colleagues had gone on without me, living their lucid lives.

I don't think that when I left, people washed their hands of me, *good riddance*. They liked me, they worried about me, they wanted the best for me. But over the years I had become a topic of whispered worry: *How is she? What's she on? Has she lost more weight? Is she going to show up? Is she going to make it?* Nobody wanted to see me go, but I'm sure everyone was relieved when I did, because all that concern and instability went with me. When I was gone you could breathe again.

When I came back, Valerie and everyone was nice to me, but they had known me for years during which I'd only ever been a person who often came to the set tired and out of it and just as often left at the end of the day to get high again. I'd go away, come back promising I'd reformed, then tear the house down. I was the black sheep, the prodigal daughter, on-screen and off. They were understandably wary of my ability to stay clean. In addition, my behavior threatened their jobs. It threatened the show and everyone who worked for it. Now that they had seen that the show could survive without me, why in the world would they want to bring that threat back into their lives? The dynamic in which I was not a peer but a source of speculation revived at my return. I could feel it. People were careful about what they said and did in my presence. I didn't blame them, but I missed the comfortable familiarity I had squandered.

In addition to the justifiable distrust, I felt judged, by Bonnie and others. Times were different, and I don't think anybody who hadn't experienced addiction in his or her family or life understood my behavior as a sickness. Drugs were for Bowery bums, people with a bottle in a paper bag. It was hard not to think that the addict had a choice, that the addict was a fuckup, that the addict should *just stop*. I felt a little defensive. Yes, I was most definitely fucked up. And yes, there was also accountability. But hadn't I gone away and done exactly what they'd asked me to do? I had worked hard to fix myself. I was still young, and it was hard for me to accept that all wasn't instantly forgiven and erased. Little did I realize that all their doubts and concerns would soon be justified.

I never saw a shadow of doubt or aggravation cross Pat Harrington's face. He just saw me as a young famous girl with lots of money who was living the life. For all those years, he loved me and treated me as someone who was just doing her thing, though later he would say that my return caused tensions and misgivings. And Norman Lear—the show's creator—was amazing. He was so kind, so supportive. He never talked down to me. He saw me, heard me, and recognized me. But I would break his heart. Again.

The close working relationships I might have formed at *One Day at a Time* were at one time my best shot at a real, functioning family and support system. I saw that Valerie and Bonnie had become extremely close over the years. They often had dinner together and even traveled together. I envied what I saw between them. I looked up to Bonnie, and maybe if things had been different, she could have been the parental figure that I so needed. But night after night I had chosen drugs over human contact. My conversations with Bonnie were formal and restrained, mostly limited to talking about the show and the characters. Now, after seven years, Bonnie and Val had a long-term friendship and all I had was a relationship with evil, addictive drugs.

I came back to a changed show, and I myself was changed in more ways than being clean. When I left the show I was rail thin. The coke, which kills your appetite, had brought me below one hundred pounds. But during the time I'd been in New Jersey, substituting wine swilling for cocaine snorting, I'd gained an enormous amount of weight. As we were blocking one of the first episodes after my return, I sat down on the arm of the couch. From the control booth the director Alan Rafkin said over the PA, for all the cast and crew to hear, "It used to be cute when you sat like that, when you were thin. Now it doesn't look good, so sit up straight, okay?" I felt like a big fat pig. Now, when I look back at the "fat" episodes, I see how warped my perception was. I was still Hollywood-slim. But I can't fault Alan Rafkin for his harsh words. He had been through hell with me. I'd gone so far over the line so many times that he had earned whatever frustration or resentment he was venting.

As soon as my return was announced, the show's ratings went up again. I knew people wouldn't be watching just to see what happened in the plot of the show. All eyes would be on me: Was I thin? Could you see the psychic or physical scars of my past? I wanted to succeed, for myself and for the show.

Success meant doing what I'd always done without trouble—acting. Julie was in my bones. Stepping back into her character should have been like getting back on a bicycle, but I felt a huge responsibility to perform as well or better than I ever had. Without drugs I found that I was able to calm down and focus on making my character feel more real to fit into the evolving style of the show. It was no longer the hypertheatrical overacting that had been popular on sitcoms when it launched. I had a thrilling sense of rediscovering acting, but at the same time I was newly self-conscious. I'd never performed without having my substances waiting backstage to congratulate me. The first time I went out before the studio audience without drugs as my security blanket, it was almost as if I was truly aware for the first time that I was saying lines, and that they could be said in a million different ways, that I had infinite choices as an actor, and that those choices could hit or miss. These thoughts were distracting and dangerous onstage. I forced myself past the feeling, but it wasn't easy.

These days rehab programs look at the pressures of post-rehab life and ask you to think about how you will handle them. But back then, once you were clean, you were on your own and good luck. My appearances on *One Day at a Time* were squeezed into the New Mamas & the Papas' already busy schedule. At one point we had a long run in Vegas; I would perform in Vegas at night, zoom back to L.A., and arrive on the set of *One*

Day at a Time the next morning. My schedule was tight and I was tired a lot. The schedule, the exhaustion, the pressure to be thin—after a year I had all the classic pressures that lead people to start using again lined up like an army of pro-drug rebels. And then I went to New York.

Around my twenty-third birthday, just before Christmas of 1982, I visited my friend Susan in New York. It was the eighties. Everyone was doing coke, and it was all about the club scene. Susan and I were hanging out at Limelight, Area, Danceteria, and Studio 54. The club scene was my coke scene. Without drama or fanfare, coke and I fell back into our old routine like long-lost friends. But my usage was comparatively moderate and I wasn't shooting up. Yet.

Coke made me nuts, but in kind of a harmless way. Susan had a studio at Thirty-third and Third. One night she had crashed in her bed and I stayed up snorting shitloads of cocaine. With my partner-in-crime asleep, I decided to thank her for hosting by undertaking a few household chores. First, I took her toothbrush and used it to clean out part of her hair dryer. Her toothbrush. I was so pleased with my own industriousness that I crept over to Susan's bed and whispered in her ear, "I'm using your toothbrush to clean your hair dryer." She groaned and rolled over. So much for gratitude.

Soon the hair dryer was good as new, though it seemed that Susan would need a new toothbrush. But I was on to my next task. The tiles on her kitchen floor were chipped, and that night I noticed some new tiles stacked in her closet. I'd made an ashtray when I popped into rehab as a teen. I knew a thing or two about tiling. So naturally, I decided it would be a fine idea to retile her kitchen in the middle of the night. I got a steak knife and started prying up the worn tiles. This time when I whispered my plan in Susan's ear, she said, "Are you fucking crazy?"

Well, that night I pulled up half of her kitchen floor with no idea how to fix it. It cost a thousand dollars to have the floor retiled.

I felt kinda bad about the retiling incident, so I decided it was time to rent my own apartment. I found a gorgeous loft in Gramercy Park and besmirched it with silly decor. There was an electric-blue futon, giant stuffed animals, and from Think Big! a fetish store for giants: a human-size toothbrush and a massive can opener. Good thing the ceilings were twenty-five feet tall. I put a life jacket that I'd stolen from an airplane around the neck of the toothbrush and a Greek fisherman's cap on its bristly head. If I'd thought about it, maybe I'd have seen that it was an apartment that screamed, "I'm out of place! I don't fit in this world." But I just saw it as a playhouse.

By this time Val and Eddie Van Halen were married. Val called to say that they were in town and I invited them over for champagne. It was very civilized. I had some blow, but Valerie didn't know that, and I planned to keep it that way. I didn't mean to deceive Val, but I didn't want it to get back to the powers that be at *One Day at a Time*. Up in the apartment, it turned out Eddie had secrets of his own. He whispered, "Don't tell Val," then went into the bathroom and proceeded to hoover up most of my coke. In the elevator on our way out, Eddie dropped his smokes. When he leaned over to pick them up, about fifteen Quaaludes fell out of his pocket. Val was pissed. But we must have taken them, or at least I did, because I don't remember the rest of the evening. So much for being discreet around Val.

Some of the "little" incidents that happened in that time were big—or they should have been—but my perspective had warped, thanks to the coke. Retiling projects loomed large, and criminal abductions were odd mishaps. One night I went by myself to an after-hours club wearing Susan's floor-length sable coat and one of the best little black dresses of all time. And it was really little, since the coke had reduced my weight in a matter of weeks to about four pounds. The dress was organza, short-sleeved, with raw silk around the sleeves. It glittered all over. It sounds tacky, but it was beautiful.

One of the many dangers of drug culture is that it's common to hang out with people you don't know, to start a night with friends and end up in the wee hours at an unfamiliar apartment with a group of newly discovered fellow users who either have drugs or are going to get drugs or think there is some remote chance that they might eventually be able to score.

This time I picked the wrong group of strangers. Somehow they drugged me. I was on coke already, yes, but this was like being roofied. One minute I was leaving the club, drink in hand. Next thing I knew I woke up in a strange place with strange people and, most disturbing, I was wearing sweatpants. My dress, Susan's fur coat, and my stockings and heels were gone.

I had no idea where the fuck I was. When I went for the door, one of the guys said, in broken English, "You stay with us now."

I said, "What do you mean 'stay with you'? I don't know you."

A couple of guys pulled me away from the door, saying, "You're with us now."

I said, "You can't keep me here." I squirmed out of their grasp and went for the door. It was locked. I looked around. Six men and women stood staring at me.

They said, "You can't get out, so we *can* keep you here and we will." I ran back to the door again and started pounding on it, calling for help.

The same two guys pulled me back and told me to shut up. I had no way out. I had been kidnapped.

I was there for days. The food must have been drugged—I was foggy the whole time. I remember watching a fish tank, talking to the fish, watching them swim by, slow and melty.

And then, after five or six quietly terrifying days passed, there was a pounding on the door, someone saying, "Open up, open up!" Next thing I knew, the door flew open and Big Sal was standing there. Big Sal, my dad's friend, was an Italian guy who wore a leather blazer and turtleneck and had helmet hair. He was brawny, and now he stood filling up the entire door frame, brandishing a big silver gun. Sal yelled, "She's coming with me. Give her to me. Give me her shit. I'll fucking kill you." He pulled me out the door and, with my clothes and Susan's fur coat in a ball under his arm, led me to a limo and took me home. As we drove over the Verrazano-Narrows Bridge, I finally learned where I'd been all that time. Staten Island.

Kidnapped. It almost seems like it didn't happen. But I was there. And then it was over, so I let it go.

Bad things happen when you live the way I was living. Those bad things didn't affect me as they probably would have someone else—I didn't have the wherewithal to react properly. My father, as always, somehow had the power to save me—in this case through Big Sal. No matter how unavailable he was, or how he had violated the boundary between fathers and daughters, he did have the instinct to protect me. But I was down the rabbit hole again, my job was on the line, and when he wasn't saving me, my father was right there with me in the hole, racing me down.

19

I was at the edge of self-destruction, but I didn't know that, and there was nothing to stop me from falling in love. Love and addiction are bitter partners, in a power struggle from the start. But addicts still fall in love, and lovers fall addicted, and their lives converge and carry on, a dark stream meandering its way down.

The New Mamas & the Papas were rehearsing and recording in New York. We were looking for a new guitar player and Mick Ronson, a brilliant guitarist, who had most famously played for David Bowie, came in to play for us. He brought a young man with him with the stage name Shane Fontayne, but his real name was also Mick. Mick Barakan. The two Micks had a band called the Yanquis. They came into the studio pushing a road case with guitars in it. I looked at Mick Barakan. He had long, black curly hair and was wearing black eyeliner and mascara. He was almost Asian looking (I would later find out that he was half Burmese). I couldn't take my eyes off him. I thought, *That is the most beautiful man I've ever seen in my life. How am I gonna get that man?* I was in lust from the moment I saw him. Then he opened his mouth. He was British, soft-spoken, warm. Swoon.

Mick Ronson quickly saw that the New Mamas & the Papas gig wasn't for him. He had small children whom he didn't want to leave for long stretches of time. So my father hired my Mick. I said to Dad, "Oh my God, I love that guy, he's so beautiful."

Dad said, "Get him. That's the man for you."

Mick joined the band and started touring with us. He was gentle and funny. I found out that he was married, but that the marriage wasn't going well. After a while we started spending all of our time together. We'd sit and talk all night . . . and eventually we didn't leave the hotel room except to go onstage. Room service carts lined up in the hall outside our room. We were enmeshed. We were in love. Mick called me "my darling Lala" or, less seductively, "the Onion Queen," because I cooked great onions. He'd write me love notes, even when we were right next to each other. We felt connected.

I was no stranger to the enraged estranged wife, but Mick's wife, Karen, put Betsy Asher to shame. She sent me threatening letters with the edges of the paper burnt away. She called my hotel rooms in the middle of the night. Once she showed up at my hotel room and attacked me. There were other people in the room who held her back. I didn't blame her for being mad, for hating me, for trying to save her marriage. But the attack was really going too far.

When I first came back from New York my drug use was easy to hide. I thought I could just do a little—because every addict is doomed to travel that particular path of delusion. Not surprisingly, I started using more and more. I came back to *One Day at a Time* tellingly thin, which probably pleased Alan Rafkin—until it didn't. Julie had been pregnant on the show and had given birth to twins. (Or she had given birth to a baby who was played by twins. Must I really be held responsible for this kind of information?) I hated wearing the pregnancy belly because, as had been made all too clear, I was already chubby enough. But thanks to the coke, Julie got her pre-baby body back in no time.

Returning to the show was a second chance, an opportunity for me to redeem myself, and I fully intended to do so, but my actions spoke otherwise. Even though I was under contract only as a recurring character, not as a regular, it soon became hard for people to work with me. I was so thin that they had me wearing fanny pads so I could fit in the wardrobe. They couldn't do close-up shots of me because my face was too skeletal. Later, on Howard Stern, Alan Rafkin would call my face a road map. And I can only guess how using was affecting my behavior on the set. I was given a warning to remind me that when I signed the contracts for my return to the show, there was a clause that allowed the producers to subject me to a drug test at any given time. It was shape up or ship out.

A few weeks after I was given the warning at *One Day at a Time*, I was napping on the couch during lunch hour. Patricia Palmer shook me awake. "Mack, wake up, Mack. We're going to take you to the doctor for a urinalysis."

I'd been given a second chance, and I'd blown it. I'd tried to fix myself, and I'd failed. I didn't know why I couldn't do it. It was bewildering and, above all, humiliating. I didn't really know what sobriety was, but it was starting to seem like something that only made sense for other people.

I said to Patricia, "If you do it tomorrow, everything will be fine. Can you wait a day?"

She said, "No, honey, no we can't." I told her not to bother and she asked me to leave quietly. I picked up and left. That was it. That was the end. I didn't see anyone from the show for a long time.

Being fired the second time was much harder for me, but when I told Mick I'd been fired, he said he was glad because now there wouldn't be so much money for drugs. Later, Bonnie Franklin would say essentially the same thing—that it seemed like the most responsible thing to do was to stop the paycheck that was funding the drugs. I know she wasn't the only one at the show who saw it that way. People had no idea what to do. They just wanted me to survive. I thought about Norman Lear, how kind he'd been to me. I knew how disappointed he must have been. My respect and love for him never flagged, but later, years later, after I was clean, whenever I saw Norman, I felt a distance between us that I knew came from umpteen broken promises on my part.

After I lost my job, I couldn't find other work. I had been blacklisted in Hollywood again, and this time I wouldn't have acting work for many years.

I'd lost my job, but I still had Mick. When Mick quit the New Mamas & the Papas to start working with other musicians, he moved in with me in L.A. We found a beautiful apartment on Norton Avenue in West Hollywood that had belonged to Marlene Dietrich. It was an art deco palace with custom beveled mirrors everywhere. I went to Harvey's Tropical and bought beautiful original deco rattan furniture—authentic versions of the knockoffs I'd shipped to the New Jersey house I had shared with Spanky. Mick and I had a great time together. We laughed a lot. We had close friends like Randy and Suzi VanWarmer. Randy was a Nashville songwriter—he wrote and sang "Just When I Needed You Most." He and Suzi were funny and quirky. The four of us had great chemistry.

Mick had a hard time with the domestic aspect of our lives from the start. He's an organized, neat person who was accustomed to living a clean, ordered life. I, on the other hand, was a total slob. I grew up with let-it-fall-where-it-may chaos, and I brought that philosophy to every aspect of my life. Without acting work, I was living beyond my Mamas & the Papas income and my bank account dried up fast. I charged all our food on credit cards at Arrow Market, the specialty market near our house, and ran up huge balances.

There were weird people coming and going at all hours, and under-the-influence arguments and crises. Once, I had been up for many days. Mick and I made love, then I started freaking out, telling Mick I was in love with our friend, a coke dealer.

As I told him this I interrupted myself. "Your hair looks blue," I told him. Mick started freaking out that he was going to lose me. He put me in the shower to "wash the love back into me."

Mick, beautiful Mick, Mick who was the great love of my life, Mick was infinitely kind and patient and forgiving. Mick knew I'd been fired. He knew about the drugs, the constant use and oblivion. But Mick had no idea what was now going on between me and my father. For all the hundreds of ways and hundreds of reasons we would never be able to be together forever, I alone knew that I had crossed a line that people don't cross, and it made me different, and it made it impossible for me to have an honest, real relationship. I was a fragment of a person, and my secret isolated me. I had to destroy my relationship with Mick for the same reasons I had to destroy myself. It was impossible to live with who I was.

When my father and I went through rehab together, the headline on the cover of *People* called us "John and Mackenzie Phillips," as if we were married. It made me uncomfortable. It was wrong; it hit too close to home.

This is what happened; there is no other way to explain it: one night after a Mamas & the Papas gig, a night like any other drug-drenched post-performance night at any hotel in any city, I woke up in my father's hotel room with my pants down at my ankles. I woke up, in that state, with no memory of how I'd gotten there or what had happened the night before. Had I been so wasted that I undressed myself? Had my father touched me? I didn't know the truth, and I was scared to find out. My father was asleep on the bed next to me. A girl who grew up pulling at her father's pants leg, waiting for him, longing for him. A man who had no boundaries, who knew no rules, whose own pleasure was his highest priority in life. I went to my room, showered, and called Mick wherever he was on tour to tell him I loved him.

It was a night that I wanted to purge from memory, but instead that night became one of many nights. Waking up in Dad's room with my pants around my ankles became regular. Not normal, never normal, but regular. Every night after we performed I would go over to my father's hotel room and ask for Placidyl, a strong sedative that we were into. Dad would pull out his drug bag—I called it his "Bagdad"—which was full of pills and powders and paraphernalia. He'd go through an act, pretending he didn't know what he might find in his bottomless bag. "What have we here?" he'd ask, rooting through the bag with a devious smile while I waited for my fix.

No matter how long Dad pretended to search, he always found exactly two "greenies," the big Placidyl pills that promised us a night of oblivion. Placidyl was a downer prescribed to people for insomnia that came in the form of a liquigel. Before I swallowed the pills, I'd poke holes in them with safety pins so the high would come on faster. Almost immediately after I took a pill a chemical odor would rise from my skin. Then came euphoria, a kind of high where I could feel the air that my body was displacing. I knew I was in "the window," the twenty-minute period before walking and talking became nearly impossible. Placidyl made us happy zombies. It also caused blackouts. Every single time I took it there was a period of the night that was completely obliterated from my memory. And this was a welcome side effect, because then . . . then there were the moments of awareness that I was having sex with my father.

Why did I keep coming back? The idea was as repulsive and wrong to me as it would be to anyone. But I can't exactly say my father repeatedly raped me. Nor can I say that I wanted or intended to have sex with him. I returned to his room for more pills with the knowledge of what might happen. I wasn't unconscious while we had sex. But it was never a tangible desire or deliberate decision that took place in the present moment. It was always a fact that only emerged after it had happened. I kept waking up in my father's room, indisposed, with the sickening knowledge that what took place wasn't just a recurring bad dream. It was a series of twisted, blurry memories that I had no desire to see by the light of day.

20

Years passed after I left *One Day at a Time* and continued on the road with the New Mamas & the Papas. Every junkie's story has this in common: there are periods of time when the drugs just win. After the seduction of that first high, after the honeymoon when drugs enhance a functioning life—after all that comes submission and demolition. My life went on, but I wasn't living it. Days whirled by in a jerky blur like a malfunctioning carnival ride.

Not long after I got fired, Mick landed a gig with a popular local cowpunk band called Lone Justice. This was a real break for him. He saw a chance at success and a real career. When Mick joined Lone Justice I became a liability. Here he was, a young, gorgeous, talented up-and-coming guitar player. I was recognizable, visible, and very fucked up. If he took me out with him, who knew what I was going to do. I might be ridiculously drunk and inappropriate. I might fall over, pass out. I was so over the top. So Mick would go out and ask me not to come along. Seven years earlier I'd left Peter Asher because I felt that he treated me like a piece of furniture. It was demoralizing. Mick was different. Mick was dedicated to me, but he was also careful about his life, professionally and personally. Even when he used cocaine, it was never completely out of control. When he decided to stop, he stopped, and it was over. Mick put up with plenty of crap from me over the years. He was always loving, a truly decent human being, loyal beyond what anyone would hope for or expect. Through all that, he also tried to preserve his career and himself. We both saw the life we could have had, and it was incredible, but neither of us was in good enough shape to live it.

We weren't exactly formally broken up, but Mick started building a separate life and I was really upset. Now I see that he was protecting himself, but at the time I was pissed and hurt. I dealt with the rejection by getting and staying high, far and beyond what Mick knew I was doing.

In the spring of 1986, we left Marlene Dietrich's beautiful apartment. We would have had to move even if we hadn't separated—someone had bought the building. I packed up all my stuff and went to stay with my friend Amanda three miles away. Not long after we moved out, I saw the handcrafted built-ins, the etched mirrored walls, the closets from the thirties, all of it, sitting out on the curb, left for garbage. The guy who bought the building had gutted it. It was heart-wrenching to see the priceless fixings of the life Mick and I had shared uprooted and discarded, a blatant symbol of what we had lost.

My friend Amanda was also my drug dealer. Staying with her meant I never had to leave the house. I holed up and shot coke day and night. At some point I traded her my TV for cocaine. Then I realized I hadn't had my period for a while. Amanda thought she might be pregnant. I was almost certain that I was. We stood in front of the mirror with our shirts up, looking at our bellies. It was time to venture out of the apartment.

I always hated going to the gynecologist. I'd wear sunglasses during the exams, like a little child who hides behind her fingers, believing that if she can't see you, you can't see her. But on this visit, there wasn't time for shyness. The doctor did an ultrasound, and there it was. A tiny blip on the screen. A little heartbeat. I was pregnant. I'd been through an abortion, a miscarriage. I knew, as before, that I was in no shape to be a mother. But this time was different. I fell in love with that blip.

When we came home from the doctor, I called my on-again, off-again boyfriend Mick. I said, "This child is going to be born. This little person is ours." I was pregnant, and I wanted to have the baby.

A few weeks later I went for another ultrasound, this time with Mick. He was now busy with Lone Justice and our relationship was by no means solid, but from the very start he made it clear that he wanted to be a good father to this baby.

When we got in the examining room, I said, "Don't tell us the sex, just tell us if it's healthy." The doctor took his first look at the monitor and said, "Oh my God, look at that penis!" Couldn't he have said "Look at that adorable arm"? But we were elated. This was the baby. This was the one. My little man. I loved him before he was born.

And yet that didn't stop me from doing coke. With guilt and shame and terrible determination, I shot cocaine throughout my pregnancy. That in itself is a testament to the evil power of drugs, but the power of drugs is a given. The real questions are how far an individual goes, and why, and what, if anything, gives her the power to stop. Those were questions I wouldn't be able to answer for a long time.

I moved to a sweet apartment on Crescent Heights in Hollywood. I was living alone now, with Amanda and other drug dealer friends within a mile radius. In no time that charming apartment became a slum. You couldn't see the floor. It was littered with clothes, pizza boxes, and empty vodka bottles.

In November of 1986, around my twenty-seventh birthday, the New Mamas & the Papas had a three-week gig at a hotel in Las Vegas called the Four Queens. I was six months pregnant and this was to be my last gig before the baby. When I arrived in Vegas I went to a doctor, pretending to be sick just so I could steal a needle from him. Back in those days it was hard for your average junkie to get ahold of needles. Now, because of AIDS, needles are more available, but back in the day you'd use the same rig for months, sharpening the needle on a pack of matches. Those dull needles were nasty and left terrible scars. I stole needles from doctors many times before and after that.

I told people terrible lies to get them to sell me coke. Amanda, my dealer friend, was under the impression that I'd stopped shooting up when I got pregnant. Somehow, for her, that was a line that made selling coke to her pregnant friend okay. She flew up to visit me at the Four Queens and of course she brought a supply of coke to sell me. What are friends for? But hours later, when she found a bent spoon I had accidentally left in the bathroom, she was furious. She turned around and went straight back to L.A.

Amanda was angry at me for shooting coke and lying about it, but I would lie to her again and she would sell me coke again. People see what they want to see and believe what they need to believe. Lies often succeed when people want to be lied to. Did Dad and the rest of the band know what was going on with me? We played a cruise ship in the Caribbean, and I was shooting up the whole time. In order to hide my track marks I never wore short sleeves or a bathing suit. I had one shirt with three-quarter sleeves that I put on because it was the closest thing to short sleeves that I could pull off, but I couldn't lift my arms too high in the air for fear that the shirt would slide up my arm and reveal my damaged veins. I'd wave hello with my elbows pinned to my sides. Anyone in the world of users knows what long sleeves mean. So did Dad and the band know that I was pregnant and using? How could they not?

What went on in my apartment when I came home from Vegas still amazes me. I sat on the john with my big belly and shot up again and again. My calico cat, Thursday, watched me. She sat at my feet, staring into my eyes and howling. I knew she was trying to say, "You're killing the baby! You're killing yourself!" I agreed. It went through my head time after time: *I'm killing my baby but I can't stop.* I rationalized the problem the way any addict does, swearing to quit after the next shot, tomorrow, soon. Every shot came with a sour dose of shame, shame for my inability to control myself, shame for what I was doing to my unborn child. Twenty-three years later, it's still hard to reconcile that behavior with who I am.

Who knows what the neighbors thought. They knew I lived there and that there was something shady going on in the apartment. I hadn't slept for days, just shooting coke all day long, when there was a knock at the door. It was the building manager. (Oh, Schneider, where were you when I needed you for cheap laughs?) She knocked and knocked, and I got scared that she'd use a key to come in, so I yelled through the door, "Yes? Can I help you?"

"We're doing an inspection tour of the building," the woman said. I looked at the wreckage around me and thought fast.

"I'm sorry, it's a really bad time. My friend who lived with me committed suicide." Another lie.

"Is she in there?" the woman asked. Actually, given my circumstances, it was a reasonable question.

I said, "No, but everyone's upset."

"Is *everyone* in there?" the woman asked. Clearly, they thought I was insane, but what could I say?

"Yes," I said, "Everyone's in here and they're all upset."

Days and trouble added up. My car was an old Audi that kept overheating. Bernie—a friend who was living with me for a bit—borrowed it one day and it overheated. He parked it and I never saw it again. There were base pipes and torches on the table. Baking soda all over the kitchen and dishes that had really old food on them. I'd been reaching out to my mom for help. I didn't tell her what was really going on, just that I needed help cleaning my apartment, but Mom was distracted. She had met a man. Charles January was a tech consultant at ABC. My mother and Lenny had been divorced for six or seven years, and when Chuck's wife died he came to see my mother. He said, "Suzy, I've come a-courtin'." My mom and Chuck married, and they were very happy together, although they both drank a fair amount. Still, Chuck was a loving stepfather to me. I'll never forget a time when I was holed up at a drug dealer's house on Mulholland and he came up and said, "Give me my daughter," and brought me home. But this was the beginning of their courtship and Mom missed or didn't want to hear or couldn't grasp my desperation.

A month after the Vegas gig, my brother Jeffrey came to visit me at my apartment. I tried to clean up for him, but cleaning up when you're on coke is a challenge. You start to give the dogs a bath, but you stop in the middle to clean the grout in the shower. You want to put on makeup, but in the middle of doing it you change your clothes three times, feed the cat, and start to alphabetize your music collection. Being on coke, I felt like something huge and monumental was about to occur. I was on the verge of a great discovery.

Feel like you're on the verge of changing the world
You pick things up
You put things down
Feel like you're on the verge of changing the world.
Find something no one else has ever found.

I would start something; make a mess; have a better idea; get distracted; look out the window for an hour; weed through a drawer looking for what, I don't know; bug out; then crash.

I tried to convince my brother that I was fine, and I didn't shoot up in front of him, but it was very obvious what was going on. After Jeffrey had been there an hour, I was jonesing for a shot. I said, "I'm just going into my room for a minute." In my room the sheets were crusted with old food. I pushed them off the bed into a pile and sat down on the mattress. My only syringe was broken. In the middle of trying to fix it I passed out. When I failed to emerge, Jeffrey stuck his head in the room to tell me he was leaving. The needle was on the bed next to me. I woke with a start and yelled, "Wait! I'll be out in a minute." I didn't want him to see the needle and spoon.

Jeffrey saw that my life was in shambles. He knows me, and he knew I wouldn't live like that unless there was something horribly wrong. Plus I was pregnant. Given what happened next, I think he must have gone home that night and called my father.

The next morning I was over at a friend's—a drug dealer, all my best friends were drug dealers—and my dad called. I don't know how he got the number, but he did. He told my dealers, "Take my daughter to the airport. I'll have a ticket waiting there for her. Put her on the plane. Don't give her drugs. If you don't do this the police will be at your door." Dad's unerring instinct for when I was near bottom had kicked in again. Dad wanted to rescue me and if I wanted to be saved by anyone, it was my father.

My girlfriend Taylor met me at my disgusting apartment to help me pack, but I couldn't deal with the mess. Leaving Taylor in my apartment, I went down the hall to borrow my neighbor's phone—mine had been disconnected—and call my father. Dad was in Albany, New York. I talked to him for a long time, trying to arrange my trip back east. I thought Taylor knew where I'd gone, but apparently she didn't. When I came back to my apartment the door was locked. Taylor had left, I was locked out, and I was desperate for my next fix.

I had a shot waiting for me in the bathroom, pulling me toward it. With robotic compulsion, I climbed up the fire escape, just as I'd done when I was a teenager coming home from a night out in Tarzana. But now I was a six-months-pregnant shoeless cokehead. When I got to my floor, I realized that there were two feet of wall between the fire escape and the kitchen window. It was a louvered window with slats of glass. I stretched over the fire escape, reaching to pull out the slats one by one. Then I reached through, turned the latch, swung the window open, and crawled like Spiderwoman into my apartment and went straight for the shot.

Somehow I finally got myself to the airport for a red-eye east. The airline held the plane for me, the way they used to for high-profile passengers. I was wearing a hand-knit ensemble with nubbly gray leggings that were so long they bunched up around my ankles, black suede boots with skinny heels and snaps all the way up, a stop-sign red nubbly sweater that came to midthigh, and, wait for it . . . a six-foot-long scarf of the same nubbly material, but in royal blue. The scarf was wrapped around my neck a million times. To top it off I wore a black fisherman's cap. I was thin as a rail with a huge belly. A pregnant cokehead, a desecrated Uncle Sam. All the other passengers stared at me as I walked down the aisle, as if I were the strangest thing they'd ever seen. Maybe I was.

The plane arrived at Albany airport very early the next morning. I made my way off the plane, stepped out of the gate, and—there was no one there to meet me in spite of the arrangements I'd made with Dad. I waited . . . and waited. Waiting for Dad again. I was so tired. I'd been up for days and now the drugs were all gone. I made a few calls. After four hours of trying to reach Dad or anyone who might know where he was, I lay down on a bench and promptly fell asleep. I was pregnant, coming down, exhausted, and alone in upstate New York. But the nightmare was over.

21

When someone finally woke me up at the airport it wasn't my father. It was Dad's driver, who had instructions to take me to meet my father at a hospital in Glens Falls, New York. When I got to the hospital, my father wasn't there. He was out of town with his girlfriend Marci. I just cried and said I wanted to go to bed.

Since they didn't have a detox program, they put me in the psych ward of the hospital. I turned over my precious needle. As the cocaine cleared my system for the first time in ages, I felt melancholy descending on me. Coming down was the feeling that always made me want to go up again, made me crave more cocaine. And I also felt addicted to the needle, to the familiar ritual that meant a high was coming soon. I was sick from dehydration and malnutrition, throwing up and experiencing intense pains in my abdomen and back. I slept and wept and waited for Dad to come, because being alone just made it all worse. While I was in the hospital, Mick appeared on *Saturday Night Live* with Lone Justice. I tried to tell my fellow inmates in the psych ward that the rocker on-screen was my boyfriend, but they didn't believe me. I guess I wouldn't have believed me either. After I'd been there a while, Dad and Marci came with a bag of candy, soda, and chips. And a Kmart maternity outfit. 'Nuff said.

A nurse on the birthing floor of the hospital, Marie Capezutti, heard that there was a pregnant woman detoxing. She came down to my room, strapped a monitor around my belly, and told me the back pains I'd been having were Braxton Hicks contractions. I was so glad to have some attention, so relieved that the baby was okay. Marie had me moved up to the birthing ward, which was called the Snuggery. It was the antithesis of the squalor and depravity of the L.A. apartment I had fled.

When I met the head of the natal unit, Doug Provost, he looked at me and my track-marked arms and asked if I had considered adoption. I was appalled. How could he think that I didn't want this baby? Of course, it certainly seemed as if I'd done everything in my power to kill it. I was twenty-seven years old, pregnant, and had shot coke until my sixth month. Now I just felt very tired. Tired of running, tired of using, tired of lying and scamming, tired of living. But my desire to keep the child and be the best mother I could be never wavered. They told me my child might be stillborn, born prematurely, or mentally ill.

My dad and I had a long talk about where I should go to give birth and take care of the newborn. Dad wouldn't be around much—he was going on the road with the Mamas & the Papas—we'd dropped the "New" from our name. A woman named Laurie Beebe had been hired to fill in for me for the end of my pregnancy and the first couple months of the baby's life. Nonetheless, Dad said, "I know I haven't been there for you. But you're about to give birth to my grandson. Take as much time off from the band as you need. You're not going to lose your job. Stay here, near me." His words made me feel safe. Bolton Landing, where Dad and his girlfriend were living, was a small town outside Glens Falls, New York. It was far and protected from the toxicity of L.A. I decided to stay.

The house Dad found for me was an old log cabin, with Lake George right outside the window. It was Christmastime, and the icy force that swept across Lake George rattled the windows and pushed under the doorjambs. In town I made friends quickly, as I always have. A local attorney named Rolf lent me an old truck to get around in. A guy named Andy taught me how to build a fire. I didn't get high for the remainder of my pregnancy.

My friend Amanda came to visit. The first thing she did was

pull out a bindle and say she found it on the floor in a public bathroom. I emptied it into the fireplace. I was so proud of myself.

Mick was on the road with Lone Justice. They had a huge new gig, opening for U2 on the *Joshua Tree* tour. I missed him terribly. When the band had a break for the holidays, Mick went to pack up my foul L.A. apartment. He was shocked at what he found. Now he knew that needles were involved—the place was a junkie hangout. Still, Mick carefully, respectfully salvaged my treasured possessions from the wreckage. He put it all into storage, ran out on the rent, and came east to me.

On Christmas Day we went to a friend of Dad's for dinner. Halfway through the meal I started having contractions again. It was still too early for the baby to come. My dad drove us to the hospital. I lay in the backseat with my head on Mick's lap. At the hospital the docs put me on something called Brethine to stop my contractions. I stayed the night to be monitored, and Mick stayed on a little foldout bed next to me. Then they let me go home again. After Christmas Mick went back on the road with Lone Justice. I was in and out of the hospital with contractions. I very much wanted my child but I was scared to death. Scared of becoming a mom, scared of the baby coming out sick or unhealthy, just plain scared.

On the first of February, my doctor decided I was far enough along to be taken off the Brethine. The next day I was with my new friend Lucy at a bar, which may not be the appropriate place for a woman in labor, but it was a step up from the example I had been given: my stepmother giving birth to Bijou on the living room couch. At three in the afternoon I sat on a bar stool, timing contractions on the bar clock. It began to snow. I called Marie, the nurse, who had become a good friend. She said to wait a few more hours, so I went home. Around nine that night I started getting nervous. The snow was coming down hard now. There wasn't anyone around to take me to the hospital. What if I got stuck in the blizzard, gave birth alone in my car, and we both froze to death? I panicked, threw clothes in a bag and shoes on my feet, and jumped into Rolf's truck. The back window of the truck was broken and snow filled the backseat as I drove the twenty-five miles down the dark country highway in labor, in a snowstorm, to the hospital.

My son, Shane Barakan, was born at Glens Falls Hospital at 2:42 a.m. on February 3, 1987. He was jumpy from all the cocaine. The hospital knew my recent past. They could have taken him away from me, but they didn't. Instead, Marie taught me how to give him a bottle, how to burp him, and how to change his diapers. I took a class in infant CPR. I was so happy to be a mommy. I was so in love.

After a few days it became clear that I was going home to an empty house because Mick was stuck on the road for another eight days. Dr. Doug took pity on us and invited me and Shane to come live at his house until Mick got back. He moved me into his house with his wife and children.

The Provosts lived in a beautiful home in Glens Falls. They set me up in the guest room, and Shane slept beside me in a little bassinet that Doug's wife, Judy, set up for him. Judy gave me baby clothes and furniture, everything I needed but hadn't known or had the wherewithal to buy. I slept next to Shane with a hand on his precious shoulder. We stayed with the Provosts—such generous people—until Mick came home.

Mick was thirty-two years old. He had been a rock 'n' roll guitar player all his life. He had those long black locks and usually wore skintight jeans and pointy boots. He was beautiful and he had a heart of gold, but he had told me, over and over again, that he had no idea how to be a father. When his plane landed in Albany, he came straight to the Provosts' house to meet his son. I dressed Shane for his father in an awesome tie-dyed onesie with long sleeves. The hood of his bassinet was facing away from the door. Mick came in, and as he walked toward the bassinet it was as if he expected to see Rosemary's baby. But the minute he picked up Shane, his whole face changed. He was as in love as I was. Mick, that startled, scared rocker, was transformed into an amazing father.

Doug and Judy sent us away with a bottle of champagne, a changing table, a swing, and clothes for Shane. The three of us went home to our log cabin. No matter what I had done during my pregnancy, no matter how low I had fallen, there was this salvation: Shane, a perfect little baby boy, proof that I hadn't destroyed everything. I loved him, we loved him, I wanted the best for him from the moment I laid eyes on him. I wanted to give him the love my parents had always given me, the care they hadn't, the safety, protection, and parenting I had only begun to understand how much I missed. I wanted all these things for him and had no idea how badly I was about to blow it.

22

Mick helped me set up the house for Shane. The cabin was idyllic. Along the front was a long, screened-in porch, looking out on a picturesque marina. February wasn't porch weather—winter in the Adirondacks is long and brutal—but there was a big, cozy living room with a stone fireplace. We pushed the two sectional sofas together to create a fully enclosed king-size playpen where we could snuggle with Shane.

Mick stopped doing drugs the moment Shane was born. "We're parents now," he told me. "We can't keep living this way. We have this little life—it's our responsibility."

I said, "Yeah, oh, you're absolutely right." Then Mick had to go back out on the road. I drove him to the train station and cried my eyes out. With Mick on the road, I was lonely. Bolton Landing felt like Siberia. I tried really hard to stay clean, but not hard enough. In hindsight, I liked the *idea* of being clean, but I had no idea how to go about it. I didn't know about recovery as most people think of it now—a process that includes self-examination, therapy, and support. I didn't know I needed help. I thought that I just needed to stop taking drugs. Using willpower. And that I definitely didn't have.

The town had two bars, and I couldn't score anything good. My friend Lucy said she knew somewhere we could go for decent coke. It was hours away. I brought Shane, who slept soundly in the car as we drove through the night, getting lost on our desperate search. When we finally found the place, I went in carrying my sleeping infant in my arms. Do you take the baby into the crack house or do you leave him alone in the cold car? Even though I hadn't read the parenting books, I was pretty sure they didn't cover these decisions. The house was dark and creepy, with unsavory people lurking around. They were selling crack, and crack was not for me. It made me even more of a lunatic. We turned around and drove all the way back empty-handed. My innocent son had been to a crack house. It was yet another new low.

When Shane was two months old I went back on the road with the Mamas & the Papas. At the same time, Lone Justice was now opening for U2 on the European leg of the *Joshua Tree* tour. Mick came out to meet me at the Fairmont Hotel in San Francisco and collected Shane to bring him to Europe. That was the plan—we would both go on the road as needed, and we would trade off taking care of the baby.

I hated saying good-bye to Shane, but I knew he'd come back soon. His father adored him and had a right to spend time with him too. I handed Mick the baby, a sling to carry him, and a diaper bag, and my boys were off.

Mick boarded the plane to fly to Rome or someplace like that, with his long black hair, a little of the last night's makeup, and his guitar, looking every bit the band member that he was. Except he had tiny Shane snuggled up on his chest. Then he reached up to get something out of the overhead compartment and inadvertently banged Shane's head on the shelf above. Shane started wailing. People on the plane looked at Mick as if to say, "What have you done to that child?"

The first years of Shane's life, I was on the road more than half the year. Sometimes Shane was with me and sometimes he was with Mick. While Mick cared for Shane, I thought about my baby constantly. Whenever we sang the song "Dedicated to the One I Love," I dedicated it to Shane. When Bijou, who was seven, came to the show, she protested, saying, "Here I am, sitting in the audience, and you dedicate the song to a baby who isn't even here."

I was glad to be back at work, but on the road the craziness began again. I had someone FedExing me cocaine, and before long I brought this practice home. Mick still thought I was clean, so I'd wait until he went out of town to arrange a shipment. Then, when I was alone with Shane, I'd put him in the bathtub and play a game. I'd say, "No peeking," pop behind the shower curtain, and shoot up. Again, Mick had no idea this was going on. As I went downhill, Mick was trying to improve us both. He arranged for us to go to a hypnotist to stop smoking cigarettes. It was a group hypnotism during which I snuck out to the bathroom to do lines. Mick never smoked again. As for me, well, I'm pretty sure that being high doesn't exactly enhance hypnotism's success rate.

Things got very dark. FedExes came from my dealer in New York to hotels all over the country. They would arrive at the hotel before I did with "Hold for Arrival" written in familiar blue handwriting. I'd be on tour, alone in my hotel room, late to the stage. People would be knocking on the door and I'd be in the bathroom shooting up. Then I'd run out onstage. Shooting cocaine isn't anything like snorting cocaine. The rush of the drug hitting my bloodstream made the world seem like it wasn't a real place. I saw and heard things that weren't there. Shapes moved around me. It was frightening. I got to that point, but I still had to go onstage. I was hardwired to go onstage. I couldn't not go onstage.

At home, Mick lived my lies. Promises went unfulfilled. I said I would be somewhere and didn't show up. I said I would "be good" while he was on tour but went on a tear. Soon enough the pretense fell away. Mick became increasingly upset and concerned. He could see that I was going down, down. What he objected to above all was my behavior around Shane. He grew afraid to leave me alone with our son, who was by now four years old, and with good reason. I was not a good parent. When I came home from the road, I'd sleep for days. Then I'd tune out Shane and smoke or shoot coke in the room next to his. When

Mick had to go out of town and leave me alone with Shane, I wouldn't always take him to his daycare/preschool. I'd rent movies and sleep all day while poor little Shane had to fend for himself.

I always wanted to be a good parent. But I was doing the same thing to my family and child that had been done to me. I was committing the sins of the fathers. Shane wasn't in dirty diapers or unwashed or unfed. But I did what I wanted to do. I was pursuing my own interests. It's been hard to come to terms with that.

What caused the shift? Was it the drugs themselves, or was it the incest, which had escalated? It's a painful admission, but after Shane was born, when I went back on tour with the Mamas & the Papas, the incest became consensual.

The first time it had happened, back in Florida, I felt raped. That event stood alone. Many years passed before he touched me again. But as the isolated encounters added up, I could no longer tell myself that I was having sex with my father against my will. It was consensual, but not in the way one might imagine consensual sex. It didn't happen daily or weekly. It wasn't planned or discussed. And it most certainly wasn't romantic or real. We didn't walk around holding hands. Sex with my father was never anything but an occasional act of drug-fueled desperation, a hopeless grasp at comfort and security in a daze of hell.

When I woke up in the morning next to my father, my first thought was inevitably, *Oh, fuck. How am I going to do this day, this life, again? How can I function with what's going on in my life and my mind?* The sex with my father was like a runaway train. It took on a life of its own. It was a fact. It was happening. This was what I had become. And I felt like I had no power to do anything about it. My world was built around my father. He was my boss. He controlled my paycheck and therefore my drug supply. I was so fucked.

But now there was a new element. I didn't want it. I didn't

enjoy it. But at the same time—I did. I started feeling complicit, like I was just as much an instigator as he was.

Take a girl who has the daddy issues that I did, then throw huge amounts of drugs at the relationship—it's a toxic mix. And then there was the compelling, magnetic man who was my father. I knew him very well. We had been great friends for many years. We laughed and joked and had great talks. He felt more like a friend than a father.

Many years earlier, I'd been in New York at my father's apartment with my dad, Genevieve, and Mick Jagger. Dad and Genevieve went into the bathroom to shoot up. When they came out, Mick said, "Why do you do drugs in front of and with your kid?"

My father said, "I'm not going to hide anything from Max. We've been friends for too long." His twisted idea of the parent-child relationship was all I had known. But it was more complicated than that. For all I knew him, for all the time I'd spent with him in recent years, I hadn't let go of the child who was still waiting for him. I was desperate to connect. And here I was spending day in and day out with him. Dad—my charismatic, magnetic sorcerer father—was available to me. That—minus the sex—was the experience of John that all his children would have killed for. And it was happening to me. A route to him had presented itself, and it satisfied some part of me that was at war with the rest.

Incest is an abuse of privilege. It is an abuse of trust. It is abject manipulation. By making it consensual, I turned my anger and confusion inward and made it my fault. I thought, *This is a bad thing. Why am I letting this happen? Maybe Aunt Rosie was right. There must be something inherently wrong with me.* I felt dirty, I felt shameful, I felt completely and utterly alone. It brought out many fears—fear that people would find out, fear of my own thoughts. I felt like I couldn't trust myself. I knew it was wrong, but I didn't put a stop to it. I felt powerless to do so, and I blamed myself for that too. What I never wondered, never, not once, was, *How could he do this to me?* I couldn't question him. I couldn't hate him. So I hated myself. This kind of self-blame is classic, textbook in incestuous abuse, but I didn't know that at the time.

But this is important. My father abused me, but he wasn't a monster. He was a tortured man who led a tortured existence. I waited until he died to talk about this because I didn't want to put him through it. I had and have profound love and respect for him. This is hard for me to talk about, not so much because of how personal it is to me as because of what I'm doing to his memory—to the way other people remember him—his friends, his fans, his family and other children. My first instinct is to preserve his great legacy. He wasn't a good father, but he was a musical genius, and the truth about our relationship doesn't change that. But these are the reasons that people are silent about incest: Conflicted but deep love for the perpetrator. The desire to protect the family. The fear of what the revelation will do to one's own reputation. If nobody ever rocks the boat, if real stories of love and incest and survival are kept behind the closed doors of therapists' offices and judges' chambers, then current and future victims are destined to do what I did, to weather it alone, to blame themselves, to hide behind drugs or whatever other lies and oblivion they can find. It happens, it happened to me, and the desire to preserve my father's legacy is not reason enough for silence.

23

The Mamas & the Papas had several gigs in Hawaii, and Dad and I had adjoining rooms, but I don't think I went to my own room the whole time. Dad had brought tons of pills and I found us some coke. We were lying in bed, in a stupor, when Dad said, "We could just run away to a country where no one would look down on us. There are countries where this is an accepted practice. Maybe Fiji." Then he said, "We can take Bijou and Tam and Shane and raise them as our children." My father was completely delusional. He was fantasizing about living with me, as husband and wife, and raising my siblings, his children, and my son, his grandchild, as our children.

The moment he tried to make it romantic, I had a visceral reaction. *No,* I thought, *we're going to hell for this.* What had I wrought? Suddenly I was scared. I wanted to escape. I had to get out. I had a lot longer to be on this planet—I hoped—and finally, in that moment, I saw with certainty that my life was going really, really wrong. But how could I extract myself? He was my boss, my father, my drug supplier, my lifeline, and he was out of his mind. No part of me wanted that husband-wife life with my father, but neither did I have an alternate plan for our relationship or my future. I just played along with it as I went along with everything else.

God, this doesn't feel like my story. It seems so distant, as if it happened to another person in another life. I haven't broken from reality, but it's almost impossible to reconcile the person I was with the person I am. Sometimes I think that having lived the life I lived, I should be in paper slippers and a johnny coat, shuffling around a psych ward. I understand why my siblings have turned to humor, meditation, family, and recovery, why my son never thought of John as his grandfather. We all look for ways to survive. At one point Bijou, who like her parents is a singer, thought of calling her first album "Raised by Wolves." And she was right. It was like being reared by a beast. A gorilla. A narcissist, a Svengali, a megalomaniac. A charming, endearing rogue.

In 1990, soon after the Hawaii gig, Mick joined a band based in the Pocono Mountains of Pennsylvania, and he, Shane, and I moved to a beautiful old house with a hundred-year-old attached barn. With a little financial assistance from my parents, I was able to get all of my furniture and clothing out of storage in L.A. and ship it east. Here, after four years, were the boxes from the decrepit Crescent Heights apartment—the boxes that Mick had packed up for me when I fled to Albany as a six-months-pregnant cokehead. I spent days going through box after box of smelly, gross old stuff. All my vases and dishes were covered in grime. It took days to get everything clean.

After we'd been in our new home for a while, I came up pregnant.

This couldn't be happening. It shouldn't be happening. *Oh God, how could this be?*

I called Mick from a pay phone at the mall, where I was shopping. There wasn't much else to do in the mountains. I told Mick that I was pregnant, leaving him to assume it was his. But things between Mick and me weren't great, given my ongoing addiction. We barely saw each other, and our focus had become caring for our son. Mick said, "Oh my God, what are we going to do?"

I said, "We can't have another baby."

He said, "I agree." So I called Sue Blue, who was now Dad's girlfriend. When I told her that I was pregnant, she understood immediately what had to be done. Sue Blue made arrangements for an abortion. She met me at the Champ—our name for a pied-à-terre Dad kept in midtown New York. We went to the doctor and I had the procedure.

I loved Shane with all my heart. I simultaneously mourned the life that could have been and felt certain that it should never be. I was confident in the decision, but also tortured by the outcome, as I still am.

The abortion marked the end of the incest, and afterward the Mamas & the Papas began to unravel, mostly because of how far down Dad and I had slid. We continued to travel worldwide—to Brazil, England, Hong Kong, and so on—but Dad was drinking a lot and getting really fucked up. I'd wash his hair, iron his clothes, and put his makeup on for him. When it was time for the show I'd find him passed out and have to wake him up, drag him to the bathroom to splash cold water on his face, and make him pull it together to go onstage. I have no idea how I was able to help him, given my own sorry state.

Living on the road
Gave me a great excuse
For hiding out in hotel rooms
Seclusions self-induced
Forget about the outside world
Just sing and smile and dance
They won't know that you're half dead
Or bored and in a trance.

What for me had been the wonder and thrill of performing with the Mamas & the Papas was gone. I was a drugging, singing automaton. As the end neared, the road memories began to blend into a litany—a sordid list of times I used people to get what I wanted, times I tested people's patience and tolerance, times that were even more painful and humiliating to me than they look on paper. When you're bottoming out, there is no progression of thoughtfulness and realization. I didn't think about what I was doing, how it made me feel, or how it affected the people I cared about most. I was doing my best not to feel, not to see the damage, not to live. There is just more and more of the same, until it gives. This is how it gave.

New York. When traveling long distances it became my ritual to go into New York the night before the flight and stay at my dad's apartment. I'd always score and stay up all night till flight time.

Portugal. I went with the band to Portugal and again had sex with my dad. I only knew because he told me.

Vegas. It was a two-week gig at the Dunes Hotel. I looked up my old drug friends and found out that one of them was using needles. I got him to bring some over to me. During those two weeks I lost about twenty pounds. I hadn't been that small since before I was pregnant. I was so pleased to be thin again.

Puerto Rico. We finished a gig in San Juan, but instead of going home I stayed with a couple I'd met. The man was a jazz musician. I missed several planes, and the man raped me while his wife slept. When I finally got to the airport with no ticket, I told the check-in employee that my son had suffered a head injury and I had to be on that plane.

Miami. There was a show in Miami where I was too high to get to the venue. I spent days in an apartment with people I didn't really know.

Atlanta. I never thought I had blackouts during shows until I realized I couldn't remember the shows we played in Atlanta. We had a show at Chastain Park. Peter Al-

len, who wrote "Don't Cry Out Loud" and "Arthur's Theme (Best That You Can Do)" was opening for us, which was an odd lineup. Chastain Park was always a fun gig—backstage there was limitless wine and vodka, anything you might want. But Dad and I got so drunk and high that people booed us and asked for their money back. After the gig people wrote letters to the promoter, saying it was shameful and horrifying to see a father-daughter act where they were too wasted to talk or perform. It was an embarrassment to Chastain Park. We knew we would never be welcome there again.

Austria. I've always had this party trick—I have good leg extension and can kick really high, so I'd kick at people and come just short of their faces. Dad and I were in the hotel bar. I was very drunk, downing grappa and slamming the glass down on the table. I was wearing skinny jeans, a red sweater, and red lizard cowboy boots. I showed my high kick to a German guy at the bar and he said, "I have never seen such a dangerous girl."

Aunt Rosie's funeral. Rosie had been diabetic, with Bell's palsy, for years. She suffered a heart attack. Dad and Bijou were visiting us in Pennsylvania when we heard that Rosie was near death. I hadn't spoken to her in a while and hadn't seen her in even longer. We tried to fly to L.A. before she passed away, but for anyone who is that deeply into needles and drugs, getting in a car to go to the airport, in time to make a flight, is a difficult undertaking. Many a time I missed three flights in a row. By the time we made it to L.A., it was too late. Rosie was gone. At first Dad, Bijou, and I were staying together in a two-bedroom suite. Then Genevieve arrived and I moved into a hotel room of my own. I met up with Sugar Bear, our old family friend, who hooked me up with coke. Then I was back and forth from Hollywood, getting high and making connections.

At the funeral, I looked into the open casket and saw Aunt Rosie, with her midthigh-long hair up in its familiar bun, her blue and white bandana keeping it out of her face. But she had shaken off her mortal coil. That wasn't Rosie. She was gone, and with her went the glue that held the family together. Rosie had been there when Jeffrey and I were parentless and rootless. She was there for me every day on the set of One Day at a Time. *She was strong when Patty died. In her later years, Rosie had moved to Venice Beach. Her small apartment on Pacific became a haven for local neglected kids. Every day she made big pots of soup or stew and the ten- and eleven-year-olds whose parents were beach bums or Venice crazies would come to eat and to feel Rosie's force of love. She did her best to save them—and me.*

Rosie's death, every loss hit me so hard. I couldn't handle grief. I went on a binge that began with shooting up in the bathroom at the funeral home. My brother Tam, now twenty years old, climbed through the bathroom window to get me out. He'd seen far worse.

Greece. Rosie died in October 1991. I went to Greece with the Mamas & the Papas to play a New Year's Eve concert. It was a lost week for me. I ended up with a weird Greek flight attendant guy and other strange people, trying to find drugs.

Home to Pennsylvania. On the road my empty, shattered life was hidden behind the structure and habit of the tour. But when I came home with syringes in my purse, it was clear what had become of me. Mick was on tour, and it was my turn to care for Shane. I'd come to the point in my addiction where at night I'd make a breakfast tray for Shane with juice, cereal, and a pitcher of milk. I'd cover it with Saran Wrap and put it at the foot of his bed so in the morning I wouldn't have to get up and take care of my kid.

New York. Then I ran dry. I couldn't get needles so I was smoking base. I sat on the bedroom floor, scraping my pipes, hoping to collect residue, but when I gave up on that, the next logical move was to go to the city to score. Shane was at school and Mick was on the road. I called the babysitter and arranged for her to pick up Shane at school. I told her I'd be gone for a couple hours at most. I left all the paraphernalia out on the floor and took a limo to a druggie hangout in New York. I fully intended to be back home in several hours, but I stayed in New York all night smoking coke like a crazed fool. I didn't go home and didn't pick up the phone. When I finally called home the next afternoon, Mick answered. The sitter had tracked him down wherever he was on tour and he had rushed home to relieve her. Nobody had any idea where I was. Mick was understandably panicked and furious. I'd really done it this time.

Home again. Mick said that if I was to come home at all, I would have to live by his rules, and that meant no drugs. He said those words, and I spun back in time. I was Julie Cooper again, telling her mother she would only come home if she could live on her own terms. I was Rosie's niece Laura, promising to make curfew but going out again night after night. I was Laura, the twelve-year-old whose father told her to be sure to sleep at home at least once a week. Mick had the wrong girl. I was not somebody who lived by anyone else's rules. I never had, and I didn't see why I should. I called my father, the only person whom I knew would back me up. I told him Mick was trying to control me, that he wouldn't let me get high. The solution Dad proposed was exactly what he would have done. In fact, he had done it years earlier with Tam. He said, "Take Shane and get out of there."

I didn't always jump off the buildings Dad presented. Instead, I took a bus home. I hadn't agreed to Mick's edict, but there was no way he was going to keep me away from my kid. Mick and Shane came to the bus station to pick me up. Just before they arrived, I was in the port-a-san doing a hit of base. I got in the car and Mick just glared at me. When we got home I took the car out and drove around for a couple of hours so I could keep smoking. When I got home Mick was driving up in a friend's truck. He'd been out looking for me.

A huge fight ensued. Mick told me I was nothing but a disgusting drug addict. He said, "You're just like your father. Your son shouldn't be put through this. It's not fair to him and it's not fair to me." Mick, the most patient man alive, was like a lion protecting his cub. He was very, very angry and he said some really hurtful things. True or not, they hurt like crap.

I was on defense, saying, "You're so high and mighty. You're not perfect either. A couple years ago you were doing the same thing." But he hadn't been. Not on the same scale.

I'm sure Mick also said, "You need help; you can't keep living like this; you're going to die." He was scared. He loved me. Shane was our child. They needed me. He said all that stuff, the stuff that addicts learn to ignore.

After a while I ran out of arguments and all I could say was, "Fuck you. Fuck you."

The next day I set about planning my getaway. Shane and I would escape Mick's rules and accusations. I called Shane's school and told them to have him ready, that I was coming to pick him up because Mick had beaten me up. But when I tried to leave for the school, Mick and I fought for the car keys. I kicked him in the balls and he fell to the floor, rolling in pain. He grabbed the phone and called social services to tell them not to let me remove Shane from school. Carol, our landlady, who was also the mother of Mick's music partner, heard the commotion and came over to mediate. Finally, hours later, I admitted defeat and stomped upstairs. I put a note that said "leave me alone" on the bedroom door.

I sat on the bedroom floor and smoked more base.

In the middle of the night I was back in the kitchen smoking. Mick came downstairs and I threw a brush at him and we were at it again. He punched me in the stomach. I called the cops. While I was waiting for them to arrive, I punched myself a bunch of times to make my stomach look worse. When the cops came, I filed a complaint. But then they wanted to arrest Mick, and I wouldn't let them.

Shane is the love of my life, and failing to care for him properly meant I wasn't living. The writing had been on the wall since he was born, from the first moment I turned away from him toward drugs, since I took him with me to a crack house, since I couldn't wake up to make his breakfast. I couldn't raise a child as a junkie.

The next morning found me shooting up in the bathroom after having found an old rig in a shoebox. Shane was pounding on the door, calling, "Mommy! Mommy, come out!" I flashed back half a lifetime to when, as a teenager, I knocked on my father's door and he said, "Not now darling, Daddy's shooting up." Now I was doing the same to my son. I put down the shot I was preparing. *Oh God, Shane.*

I'd gotten to the point where I couldn't get high from cocaine no matter how much I put into my system. It was never enough. And there was nothing but more of the same coming. Death was definitely in the next shot. But saving myself had never been reason enough to stop. Shane was four, almost five years old. He was a little guy. He was full of curiosity and joy. As a three-year-old he looked in a bucket of water and said, "Mom, what if there's a parallel universe under the water? That would be cool." Once, when we were standing in the bathroom and he was trying to use the big-boy potty he said, "Mom, I cry for the future."

"Why?" I asked.

He said, "We don't know what's coming. Look what happened to the dinosaurs." At dinner parties Shane would talk about the planets, the universe, his theories about God. When I was a kid I'd take over a room by tap-dancing in the middle of it. Shane captivated people with his theological discourse. There was just so much he wanted to wonder about and understand.

That curious, wonderful little being needed me, and I wanted more than anything—anything!—to be his mother. He needed me and I wasn't there. I was in the bathroom busy with a needle. I was doing what my father had done to my siblings and me. I was perpetuating the cycle of neglect and abuse. And it was certainly abuse. I never left Shane alone or hit him or locked him in a closet or anything like that. That's not me. But I abused him through my self-absorption. No matter if he saw or understood what was going on, he was affected by the world I showed him, by the emotions, and by what was in the air. I wasn't a responsible parent. I wasn't available the way a parent should be. Shane distinctly remembers a before and after in his childhood, divided by when I stopped doing drugs. It shouldn't be the job of a three-year-old to worry about his mommy.

There was Shane pounding on that door, and I knew what I was doing to him all too well. I saw that if I wanted to redeem myself and the situation, I had to change. I knew there were sober people in the world, but I had never thought of myself as one of them. I meant to run it out till I died a tragic junkie. But that wasn't what I wanted for Shane. I had to fix his world, and the only way to do that was for me to quit drugs and to quit them absolutely. I had to quit them forever.

That night I used up my stash, knowing it was the end, desperate for the last high that would take away the fear and doom that went hand in hand with sobriety. I didn't know life without drugs. I didn't know how to be in my life. I grew up with drugs as a buffer between me and everyone and everything else. I relied on that buffer, and I couldn't conceive of facing each day without it.

In the morning I got up and dressed Shane for school. That afternoon when Mick approached me about getting help, I told him I would go into treatment. I called Mark Gold, the doctor who had helped my father get clean for a minute of his life and had saved him from jail. I said, "Doc, it's Mack. I need help. I'm going to lose my kid."

Dr. Gold said, "Thank God you're still alive." The people who weren't in my immediate circle had given me up for dead, which, given the circumstances, was a reasonable assumption. There were drugs before and after this call. Maybe even during the call. But for the first time in my life, I was ready.

I said, "I need to be in rehab by sundown," excess being the hallmark of the addict. Dr. Gold said that he would call me back.

Mick went to pick up Shane at school. While he was gone I lay in the bathtub, going into heavy withdrawal from Darvocet. I lay in the bath shaking, alternately hot and cold. I was afraid I was going to die right then and there. The phone rang and it was Doc Gold calling to say, "There's a place for you at Alina Lodge. It's for the 'reluctant to recover.' " Doc Gold told me where to go and what to do. I called a car company and arranged to be picked up.

By the time Mick came home with Shane, I had packed a small bag and was all ready to go. Mick said, "You mean you want to go tonight?" After all the talk about rehab over the last year or so, he couldn't process that it was actually happening. I was in the limo by nightfall with a bottle of Courvoisier and a pocketful of Xanax.

I was in detox for two weeks. I had Mick bring me extra clothes and every day I wore a flashy outfit, like tie-dyed harem pants with a matching silk shirt. I'd always been afraid that sobriety would take away the fun, that all the color would go out of my life. So I treated detox like a fashion show. But playing dress-up was a poor substitution for getting high. I called a dealer and had him bring me some cocaine. He delivered it right away. *To a detox center.* Business is business, I guess.

I wanted to shoot the cocaine, but of course I didn't have any gear. So during a nursing shift change I snuck out of my room and found a crash cart that seemed like it might have a syringe. This was a joint psych ward and detox ward, and they knew how desperate their patients could get. The crash cart had impenetrable plastic locks. But somehow, maybe it was the Librium or whatever I was on for withdrawal, I summoned the superhuman strength required to break into the crash cart. I found an IV tube with a needle attached, but there was no syringe. I'd have to make do.

My roommate was an old hard-core alcoholic with missing teeth and wild, unclean hair. We had a small room with twin beds and a shared bathroom. She had the DTs (delirium tremens). She was crying and hallucinating. I thought she was freaky, but what I was about to do was far worse. I went into the bathroom. I mixed the cocaine with water and cotton and sucked it through the needle into the IV tube. I tied off. With its long tube attached, I put the IV needle into a vein. Then I tried to blow the mixture through the tube into my vein. This did not work. Blood sprayed everywhere. The bathroom was a crime scene, horrifying enough to represent all I'd done, all I'd become. I was bleeding, crying, royally fucked. The incomprehensible demoralization of that moment—I thought the stain of it would quench any future desire to return to drugs. I thought that was the last time I would ever try to use cocaine. For fifteen years it was.

PART FIVE

THE ROCK

24

It was January of 1992. I was thirty-two. I'd been introduced to drugs at eleven. I'd been heavily using cocaine for thirteen years, except for one clean drunken year in New Jersey. I arrived at Alina Lodge in Blairstown, New Jersey, in a white stretch limo, wearing a multicolored patchwork button-down shirt tucked into suede shorts, with forest green tights and the same black suede snap-up boots that I'd been wearing when I flew to Albany, six months pregnant.

I had no idea what to expect from the Lodge. I'd been to other rehab programs, but most of them were twenty-eight days long. The Lodge lasted until you were clean and sober and determined to stay that way. I didn't yet know that smoking wasn't allowed, but I still puffed away in the car as if it were my last pack of cigarettes. When the driver opened the door, clouds of smoke poured out, and there I stood, in a curtain of smoke, in my outlandish outfit, with open sores on my arms. Oh, they were going to have a field day with me.

I walked into a great room where, I'd soon learn, all the meals were served. The ceilings were very high. There were long institutional tables surrounded by metal chairs. A pot of flowers attempted to cheer up each table. At the far end of the room was a platform stage with a podium on it. All around the sides of the stage were posters with guidelines for behavior. We weren't allowed to leave the grounds, to use the telephone, to talk to the opposite sex, nor, damn them, to smoke. There were stark black-and-white signs with slogans like "Live and let live," "Let go and let God," and "Think think think." I saw one that read, simply, "One day at a time," and I thought, *They knew I was coming and they put up a sign for me*. What an idiot I was.

The first order of business was to meet with the eighty-five-year-old founder of the Lodge, Geraldine Owen Delaney. She had her initials, "G.O.D.," on her license plate, and as soon as she saw me she lit into me: "I don't care who you think you are. You sit down and shut up. You don't know anything. You are lower than worm sweat. I wouldn't wipe my feet on the cleanest part of you. You are a moral leper." Nobody had ever spoken to me that way. Why did this woman I'd never met before hate me? I didn't understand. But out of shock, I complied. I shut up. For a few minutes. Then I decided my time-out must be over and started talking again. Mrs. Delaney stood up and pinned a zipper on my jacket. She said, "You don't know how to listen. You're too busy trying to figure out what you're going to say next. Shut. Up." The approach was called ego deflation, and the idea was to tear down my ego and rebuild me a new and improved sense of self.

The philosophy at the Lodge was that by using drugs, screwing up our lives, and hurting those around us, we'd relinquished our rights as humans. I had to ask permission to start eating. I had to ask permission to stand up and walk out of a room. I wasn't supposed to read anything but approved materials. Long hair—mine was down to my elbows—had to be swept into a bun; skirts were to be worn below the knee. And I wasn't allowed to speak in public spaces—at meetings or meals—for three months so I could learn to hear what others were saying. That's what the zipper on my jacket signified.

We communicated through writing. If we had a request, such as wanting razors to shave, we had to write it down and hand it to a staff member. If it was approved, Mrs. Delaney would initial the note, called a "write-it," and give it back. It was Victorian boarding school meets boot camp.

The staff also used write-its to communicate with us. One

day I received one that said, "Your father is undergoing a liver transplant." I immediately wrote one back: "Can I call him?" My request was not approved. The response was simply, "We'll give you another write-it when we know more."

I had been on the road with the band for ten years. Before that I'd been on a top-ten TV show for seven years. I had always had total freedom. Now I was completely at the mercy of the staff of this facility. My father was having surgery. Mick was playing guitar for Bruce Springsteen. Shane was in the care of Pat the Boy Nanny, as we called him, and I was about to miss his fifth birthday. I was stuck in rehab missing everything, missing everybody, and feeling sorry for myself. I couldn't stand it. Finally I wrote a note: "I'm putting in my seventy-two-hour notice." That was the policy. The contract I signed when I entered the Lodge stated that I would give seventy-two hours' notice if I wanted to leave. I fully intended to go home. But the Lodge kept close contact with the families of its patients. Soon after I wrote that note, and each time I wrote one of the similar ones that followed, I'd get a note back from Mick saying, "Get well, then come home. If you try to come home now, there will be no place for you." So what could I do? I stayed.

The only way to achieve more freedom was to earn it back. Soon enough I decided to embrace the opportunity and to follow all the rules.

Dear Mrs. Delaney, here is a list of the rules I have broken:

1. *I have gone back to bed in the afternoon.*
2. *I have showered for longer than three minutes.*
3. *I had a nonretractable pen.*
4. *I smiled at DL.*
5. *I left my closet light on and did not write myself up.*
6. *I have gossiped.*
7. *I have washed my hair more than once a week.*

As I succumbed to the program, I started to change. I had never been sober for such a prolonged period. The fog had time to clear. It felt like the first time I had been chemically free, away from my junkie lifestyle, and continually educated in a new way of thinking. Gradually, with work, my true self started to emerge. When I told my mom I was being brainwashed, she said, "Good."

At the Lodge I finally started to examine the life I had lived and the role drugs had played in it. I covered page after page of loose-leaf paper with confessions: I would do almost anything for drugs. I left my child alone in the middle of the night to go out for drugs. I let strange people live in my home because they had easy access to drugs. I befriended total strangers for no apparent reason, except not to be alone. I stole pills and cocaine from my father and then lied and lied about it. I used openly in front of my brother Tam, who was eight or nine at the time. The lists went on and on.

As I looked closely at my life, new realizations came pouring out. I faced my true emotions—especially the anger—some legitimate, some shallow, that I'd never let come to the surface. Every last bit of the anger that I'd masked with drugs. Anger at my father; my mother; my ex-stepfather, Lenny; my ex-husband, Jeff; Genevieve; Hollywood Professional School for throwing me out; Mark Gold and Fair Oaks Hospital for telling me it was okay to drink the first time I got clean; Valerie for being pious; even Chynna for thriving despite our shared parentage.

I came to understand that being high wasn't something I did for fun, as I'd always insisted. It wasn't a cool, alternative choice that other people didn't understand. Even if it had been fun at one point, now my relationship with drugs was different. It was an escape, the only way I knew to deal with emotional pain.

At the Lodge I learned that to stay sober I would have to change myself. I would have to change the way I dressed, the way I lived, the way I saw myself. I wasn't a countercultural rebel who was going to run it out till I dropped, dying a tragic junkie. I developed a new, sober identity for myself. No more cowboy boots or tight jeans. When the video loop of unresolved events from my past played in my head, I just ignored it.

My brother came all the way from San Francisco to New Jersey for Family Week. Jeffrey had been clean for three years. He had a thriving business as a mortgage broker. He was married to a research scientist named Gail, and they had a young daughter, Lauren. Jeffrey and I had shared so much, and I had missed these major events in his now sober life. But he was here for me now, as he'd always been, and he was as happy as I'd ever seen him. He said, "I'm so glad you got clean. I was preparing myself for the phone call that you'd been found dead."

When news finally came from my father after his operation, it was in the form of a postcard. He wrote, "Hey Max, the logjam is finally broken. Heard you're about to poke your head out of the nest. Heard you're doing great. Let's never go to Greece again." Dad was back to his cryptic self, but there was one thing I knew for sure. I wasn't going back to Greece or any other place with the Mamas & the Papas. I was done with the band.

When the day came to leave the Lodge, I was absolutely ready. My bag was packed, my room was clean, and my life story, handwritten on pages of loose-leaf paper, was stuffed in a plastic bag in my suitcase. As I waited for the limo to pick me up, I felt scared of everything. Of people, of having sex with Mick, of aspirin. I had gained fifty pounds and felt uncomfortable in my own skin. I was used to being a tall, skinny witch. But for the first time in a long time, I felt hope. I was clean for the first time in my adult life and I planned to stay that way. I was no longer a broken kid. Cheesy as it sounds, I had been reborn. I was a woman, and I thought of myself as someone who was meant to be a sober, functioning member of society. I was going to make it. I was going to be okay. After the initial fear and panic, the world seemed clear and bright, as if the eye doctor had clicked from the wrong lens to the correct one, or as if the September rains had washed the L.A. smog off everything.

25

I went back to the barnhouse that Mick and I shared near Stroudsburg, Pennsylvania, and did what I'd been longing to do every minute of my time at the Lodge. I immersed myself in raising Shane. I hadn't seen my boy for nine long months. When I walked in the front door, Shane came running to me and threw himself into my arms. He had long blond hair with funny bangs, missing teeth, and was wearing his Batman pajamas with the attached cape. He was the cutest thing I'd seen in my life, and I held him for as long as he'd let me.

Starting the next day, I took Shane to school every day. I drove him to karate, soccer, playdates, birthday parties. Mick and I read him every Roald Dahl children's book ever published. I put on Spandex and went to aerobics to burn off the rehab weight. I got into cooking and hosted a Tupperware-type party for moms, friends, and neighbors. I loved my newfound sobriety and was careful to preserve it. Stroudsburg was a small town with a strong recovery community. I surrounded myself with other clean former users. I didn't put anything chemical in my mouth, not even aspirin. I was a new person, not just because I wasn't using. I dressed differently. I spent my time differently. I lived in the country, surrounded by trees and streams and frogs and snow, far from the palm trees, cars, and people of Los Angeles. I had done what I thought was necessary to stay sober—I changed everything about myself and it was incredible. Being a mom made me very happy.

Playing wife didn't come as easily to me. When I came out

of the Lodge, it was the first time Mick had known me sober. In truth, it was the first time I had known myself sober. When one member of a couple gets sober and the other doesn't need to, it's as if you are navigating a whole new relationship. Mick and I tried to make our relationship work, we really did. But we were on different paths. Mick had fallen in love with me and all my quirkiness. He'd always been quiet, soft-spoken, and spiritual. After our son was born he'd grown up a lot—he stopped smoking, drinking, and using. Mick stuck with me through my addiction, but now that I was sober, my true self was evident. I'm always talking, singing, making jokes. This wasn't a huge change, but it started to grate on him. He got cranky. Cliché as it sounds, Mick and I were growing apart. We were great friends, and we were completely in love with our son. But the romance was gone. After several years of trying to make it work, we decided to let go of what wasn't working—the romance—and to keep what was: the friendship and the parenting.

Maybe this is true for everyone, but I've found that once I love somebody, it doesn't really go away. As I said, I even loved Jeff Sessler as we went through a horrid and painful divorce. Just because the relationship doesn't work, the love doesn't disappear. It just becomes a different type of love. I've stayed friends with pretty much all of my exes, but especially Mick, who was and is a perfect, lovely partner in raising our son. He calls me "Ma" and I call him "Pa." But even now there's only so much of me he can take at a time. I see a curtain come across his eyes and I say, "I love you, Pa, but I'm going to leave you alone now."

At some point Mick and I decided we wanted to get Shane a British passport to match his father's. It was an opportunity for him to move freely in the world. We petitioned the Crown, but they wouldn't issue the passport unless Mick and I were married. So—even though we were no longer a couple—we got married.

Although it was meant to be a perfunctory ceremony in our living room, Shane wanted to dress up, so he put on his Cub Scouts uniform. I wore a minidress with boots. We took a ring I was already wearing (as I had done for my wedding to Jeff Sessler) and put it on a couch pillow so Shane could be the ring bearer. Our dear friends Randy and Suzi VanWarmer flew in from Nashville. A local guy from who-knows-what ministry performed the ceremony wearing a fire engine red shirt, a black tie, and a black jacket. When he was done I expected him to segue straight into his Vegas act.

After the quick ceremony I noticed that there were matchbooks lying around the tables. A closer look revealed that they said "Mick & Laura" with the date. There were also Mick & Laura napkins, and a Mick & Laura wedding snow globe music box. Leave it to Randy and Suzi not to come empty-handed. Once we were official, Mick presented me with a huge box. Inside were ten enormous photo albums. Mick had gathered all the photos we'd taken over the years—from the day we met to Shane's birth, millions of them—and put them together in those ten huge photo albums. Mick had worked on it for weeks and weeks. It was my wedding present.

Mick and I stayed married for many years. We were very close. Whenever anything good or bad happened, Mick was the first person I'd call. But eventually we found that the kind of intimacy we shared—we talked on the phone many times a day—wasn't fair to our partners. It was tough on our relationships and we had to back off for their sakes, but we will always be family.

After a couple years of living in the mountains of Pennsylvania, I found myself sitting in our house, listening to my sister Chynna's new album, crying. Wilson Phillips, Chynna's group with Carnie and Wendy Wilson, was at the height of their success. I played the cassette tape and thought how beautiful Chynna's voice sounded, and how happy I was for her. Chynna and I have always had a complicated relationship, and it was particularly so at that point. I couldn't help comparing where we were in our lives and thinking, *Look what I've done to myself, all my wasted opportunities.*

Our rural existence was idyllic, but something was missing. Then I realized, *Wait a minute. I'm an actress.* I started yearning to work again. The question was whether the industry that had watched me crash and burn would take me back.

In 1994 I went to L.A. and had a meeting with an agent at the big Hollywood agency William Morris. The agent I met with listened to me for a few minutes, then said, "You know what, Mackenzie? Don't even bother. Go back to Pennsylvania, raise your kid, and forget about Hollywood." He didn't think there was a soul who would hire me. But I loved acting, and I owed it to myself to try again, to return to a piece of my former life, but to do it right this time. I called Pat McQueeney, my beloved manager whom I'd fired on the advice of my father. To my great relief and delight, she accepted my apology. Pat told me she knew the woman who was perfect for me: Arlene Dayton, a veteran Hollywood manager. Arlene took me on and with single-minded determination set about reestablishing my career. Arlene was on a mission.

In later years, Arlene told me she'd promised herself she'd never fall in love with another client, but then I came along. She was like a mother to me; I loved her so. She was my manager until her death.

With Arlene's help I started making the rounds. Soon I landed my first part as a clean and sober actress: in a wink-wink casting decision, I was to play an intervention counselor on *Beverly Hills 90210,* running an intervention on Luke Perry's character.

A lot of what holds former child stars back is an inflated idea of status. They won't read. They won't audition. But—especially if there's been a gap in your work, and especially if that gap existed because you were publicly and embarrassingly fired from a major sitcom—you *have* to audition. I pounded the pavement, man, and just started booking stuff. *NYPD Blue; ER; Walker,*

Texas Ranger; Melrose Place. I didn't care that I was a day player. It was amazing to be working.

I rented a house with my old friend Sue Blue—she's one of my best friends to this day—up the street from my mother's condo. Soon after we moved in, Shane came to spend the summer with me. When it came time for him to go back to Pennsylvania—school was starting soon—I talked to Mick on the phone as I packed. I said, "Look, here's his little underwear. And his little socks." His clothes made me cry. I didn't want him to go back, but his school, his home, were in Pennsylvania. He needed to go back. But that summer I knew I wanted to create a home for him, and the following year he came to stay.

Every morning I got up at six, took Shane to school, went to work, and came home in time to make dinner. To be self-supporting after the life I'd lived made me feel fulfilled and good. There was nothing in my mind that could ever make me pick up another drug again. I was a working mom. Who would give that up? Why would I give it up? There wasn't a chance.

Getting clean was a chance for me to return to some of the people I'd lost over my years of addiction. Valerie has had the same phone number for twenty-five years, a number that she has managed to keep no matter where she moved, and I've never forgotten it. When I moved back to L.A., I called that number. An answering machine picked up, and I left a message: "Hey Val, it's Mack. I'm just thinking of you. I love you. I'm six months clean. You don't have to call me back but here's my number. I love you." Val didn't call back. A while later I left another message: "Hey Val, it's Mack. I'm eight months clean . . ." This went on for close to a year. I just kept leaving messages. I never wondered why she wasn't calling me back. I'd done damage and I knew it. Val is a reserved, private person. I knew it wouldn't be easy for her to just pick up the phone, but one day the phone rang and it was Valerie.

I apologized and Val was very gracious. We started being buddies again. I brought Shane over to play with her son, Wolfie, while Val and I sat on the couch drinking coffee, petting her cats, and talking about the old days. Val said, "Mack, I was always frightened for you. I'm so proud of you." Another time she invited me to her beach house in Malibu. It was a spectacular home that she had purchased with *One Day at a Time* money long ago, even before she married Ed. At least one of us was smart with her money. A couple of her other girlfriends came, and Alex Van Halen, Eddie's brother. Val, her girlfriends, and I climbed onto a big, deep couch and talked about girl stuff: breakups, dating, our bodies. We talked about being mothers, and Val and I couldn't help musing on how we'd played children and now we were the parents.

We weren't the only ones who found this mildly amusing, at the very least. Val and I went to the mall once and as we wandered through the makeup section of a department store, I saw people recognizing us. They noticed me, then whipped around, not sure if they'd just seen Val a few makeup stations away. The looks on their faces said, "Does she know the other one is here?" Wherever we went, people seemed somewhat flummoxed at seeing us together as grown women instead of the teenagers we once were and played on TV. I wasn't so confused by it, but I was amazed and grateful for the renewed friendship with Val.

Another unexpected friendship seemed to emerge fully formed. Peter Tork, formerly of the Monkees, asked me to sing a song on his album *Stranger Things Have Happened* alongside Owen Elliot, the daughter of Mama Cass. Owen and I had crossed paths many times over the years. Her first memory of me is at Chynna's eleventh birthday party. I was one of the grownups chauffeuring the younger guests to On the Rox, the small bar above the Roxy. Owen climbed into the backseat of the TV star's red Mercedes convertible, with no idea that we would one day be best friends.

Now, as we recorded a song called "Giant Step," we felt a

kinship—her mother and my father were a Mama and a Papa—and that connection ran deeper than we might have anticipated. We were both part of a strange little family. From the day we met we were comfortable saying anything to each other. There was a bond between us that felt like it had always been there.

Years passed during which I lived in L.A., building a life outside of my drug world. I worked with more joy and fulfillment than I'd ever known, took care of my sweet little man, developed friendships that weren't inspired or defined by drugs, and spent time with loved ones. Those are years that I cherish more than any others in my life, but what makes them the best is also what makes them less interesting to tell. When I was high I had always feared the boredom of sobriety. Happiness was mind-blowing excess and hyperstimulated decadence. But when I was in the midst of a normal life, I saw that the quietness of real life in the real world was a kind of joy and happiness I'd never felt before. It was sweet and solid and familiar and comfortable—a rocking chair, a temperate day, a good view.

As I watched Shane grow up, I often reflected on my youth and the radically different world I'd known. I already knew my childhood was crazy and didn't necessarily produce healthy people. But I started to see my youth on Shane's time line. When Shane was five, I looked at him and thought that I must have been that innocent and vulnerable at his age. But I was in the Virgin Islands, wandering around and talking to sailors. How could someone let me run around alone? I mean, Shane spent his early years living in the country. He ran around pretending to be a Jedi warrior or catching frogs with a pack of kids in the woods near our house, but there were parents all around. Sober parents. We knew where the kids were. I never would have allowed him to tramp off alone.

This went on through all the stages of Shane's life. When Shane was around seven or eight, he came home one day and said, "I want to be an actor." Our next-door neighbor's son Jesse was a couple of years older than Shane. He was an actor, and I guess that put the idea in Shane's head. My agent had been urging me to let Shane do a movie.

"Just one!" she'd beg.

I said to Shane, "Okay, you know how this works, right? You come home from school, clean up, and go to auditions. You're home by five, then you have dinner, do your homework, and go to bed. I was on the set eight hours a day when I was fourteen. That's what your days are like if you're a working actor." Shane usually came home from school, rode his bike, ran around, chased the cat, got dirty.

He said, "You mean I can't play when I get home from school?"

I said, "Not on days you have auditions. Not if you have a gig. Acting is a job. It's work."

Shane said, "Oh, forget it." He jumped on his bike and went down the block to the library. I smiled and watched as he rode away. I wanted him to have a childhood. I wanted him to look back and say, "I had a blast as a kid."

In fifth grade Shane started at Highland Hall, the same Waldorf school that I had attended and loved. I had hitchhiked to school, often on acid, with a ready supply of signed excuses from my father. My son was dropped off and picked up right outside the school entrance by his mother, then brought home and served dinner.

When I left Highland Hall I went to high school in an office in the *One Day at a Time* studio. I never experienced all those great feelings of companionship—the camaraderie of high school, college—so I don't miss them. But I saw them through Shane.

• • •

Every morning I stood at the kitchen counter, packing his lunch, the light in the kitchen reminding me of another season passing, another year of school for him, a child growing in time. I helped him with his homework, knew the names of his friends, and chatted with their mothers on campus and at school events. Shane was my little person. My primary purpose on this planet was to be there for him. I had lost that ability for a while, but it came naturally to me now.

As a parent you try to keep your child safe. It's a gargantuan responsibility. With my new role as a parent, I couldn't help but reflect on my father. Time and distance usually lessen anger and resentment toward others, but now, looking at my life with a mother's perspective, from a sober, family-oriented angle, I was shocked at the kind of parent Dad was. What was he thinking? *What could he have been thinking?* I knew firsthand that drugs destroy parenting instincts, but—for me—those instincts and the desire to be a good parent were what gave me the strength to kick drugs. My father actively, enthusiastically guided me down his treacherous path. Why? Maybe for my father to be a parent, he himself would have had to grow up. It was impossible for him to impose rules on us because he refused to do it for himself. You can't draw lines and set limits if you believe in hedonism. Hedonism is infinity.

Once I was sober, I put distance between myself and Dad. At first, I had tried to save Dad from himself. I was a convert to sobriety, and I wanted to proselytize. I said, "How can you not see that this is killing you?"

Dad wouldn't hear it. He said, "Get down off your high horse and leave me alone. I'm fine. I'm not like you. I'm an old hand at this. Don't expect me to change." Dad was not an old dog you could teach new tricks. He was a stubborn hound. Eventually I gave up.

Dad and I were now living on different planes of existence, and it was hard, if not impossible, to make the transition from the unhealthily intense bond we had had to a warm, loving, meet-you-for-brunch relationship. I didn't want to sever ties with him completely. I still needed him in my life. Nor did I see myself as a victim of incest. I held my father responsible, but I also had my part in what went on between us, and I never believed that Dad deliberately set out to hurt me. He was in his own reality, and I was vulnerable. But one thing I knew for sure was that I was never going to put myself in that position again, not with Dad, not with anybody. Sobriety was my protection. He was never going to touch me again. And he never did.

So I still saw Dad frequently. There were family weekends in Palm Springs. Chynna's wedding. And I never stopped loving him. He was my father. I loved him very much. But I had changed.

26

When I first moved to L.A. to rekindle my acting career, I stayed in my mother's condo, in my childhood bedroom. Over the past few years Shane and I had been making regular visits to see my mother and Chuck. Chuck was like a grandfather to Shane, playing on the floor with him, and those visits were a happy time for all of us.

The Northridge earthquake struck on January 17, 1994, and I was in the exact place I'd been twenty-three years earlier, for the last big earthquake. This one was even worse—the whole world was shaking apart—and when I emerged from my room I saw that the floor was covered with broken china and glass. I went to the laundry room to get the broom and found the door blocked by an enormous metal tool cabinet that had fallen. I found adrenaline-fueled superhuman strength to lift it, and felt that I'd been put there to help my mother and Chuck pick up the pieces.

They had to move out of the apartment for a year, and during that time it became clear that Chuck had Alzheimer's. Chuck was the sweetest man. He loved Shane like a grandson. But now he started behaving unpredictably. He lined up all of his shoes as if they were about to march out the front door. He threw away the fake Christmas tree that my mother had used every Christmas for ten years. He'd say, "What do you mean, Chuck? My name is Richard!" There were tales of him leaving the house and walking for hours. He had walked all the way from Tarzana to the Van Nuys airport, about seven miles. The cops would pick him up, check his ID, and say, "Mr. January, we're going to bring you home." One day we were sitting in the living room and he was making a funny clicking sound he liked to make. Out of nowhere he looked at me and said, "I should probably just walk out in front of a bus because I'm losing everything and I know I'm losing it." Then he went back to making his funny sound.

Poor Chuck. My mom kept him home, but the stress of his decline took its toll on her. I was in New York making a low-budget indie film and staying with my friend Grainger when my mother started calling at all hours of the night to tell me that I was a little bitch, a horrible daughter, and that she was going to disown me. When I came back to L.A., she'd call and ask me to bring her some vodka, and when I refused, she told me I didn't love her anymore. She'd roll up to the door three sheets to the wind, drunk and mean in front of her grandson. I understood—I knew my mother, and I knew that she wasn't a horrible woman. She couldn't face the pain of her life, and it was driving her to destroy herself. She was an alcoholic. I understood, but it was hurtful. Eventually I had to stop answering the phone.

The only benefit to the Alzheimer's was that most of the time Chuck forgot to drink. He forgot he was an alcoholic. But he still had his moments. Just as I was packing my bags to go on the road for the musical *Grease*, I got a call from the hospital saying my mother and Chuck had both been admitted. Apparently, on a routine trip to the grocery store, a drunk Chuck backed into my mother with the car. When I got the news, I zoomed to the ER to see if my mother was okay. She was getting stitches in her arm and I smelled the booze on her breath. I said, "Mom? Have you been drinking?"

She said, "No!" Then, "Why—can you smell it?"

Chuck died right before Christmas of 1998. I was worried about what would happen to my mother. But mere days after his funeral, on December 27, 1998, my boyfriend D. and I walked into my mother's condo. I'll never forget that moment.

My mother asked if we were going to a meeting for recovered addicts. We said that we were. She said she wanted to come. At that meeting, she fell in love with sobriety. This was a woman in her sixties. She had *lived* to drink. It was a miracle to watch her change. But all those years of booze had taken their toll. Now Mom's sober, but she's a bit toasty. She'll call on my birthday and say, "Honey, my little snowflake, I just called to wish you a Happy New Year."

Not long after Chuck died and my mom got sober, I was acting in an episode of *Chicago Hope* when a script for a show called *So Weird* came to me. The name of the main character was so close to my own that it jumped out at me. It was Molly Phillips. She was a rock star and a mother whose teenage daughter had paranormal encounters. I couldn't imagine a better part. I'd been out of the business for so long, but during that time I had acquired two legal, legitimate skills—the ability to sing and knowing how to be a mom. Now I had a chance to bring both to TV.

When I found out that I landed the part, it dawned on me almost immediately that I was famous for being a daughter, and now I was going to be a mom. I was famous for being a druggie, and now I was working for Disney. I was determined to make the rest of my experience on *So Weird* similarly black and white.

We were shooting the pilot in Vancouver. I got up early to make sure I made it to the plane on time, but as I was opening the cat food, I gouged my finger with the can opener. My flight was in two hours and my finger was sushi. I thought, Okay, I can be the fuckup who misses the plane, or I can try to bandage my finger and make the plane. I wrapped my throbbing finger in several paper towels and used rubber bands to hold them in place.

A few hours later I disembarked, went through immigration

in Vancouver with my still painful finger held high, waited in line for my work permit, then went straight to a doctor and got six stitches. In the photo shoots we did that afternoon, I held my wounded paw behind my back. Whatever happened on this show, I was not going to be the problem child.

I loved that job. The show was so well written. The cast was lovely and felt like a family. Molly Phillips's tour bus even had my real initials emblazoned on it. What more could I want? I found a beautiful apartment near Stanley Park in Vancouver and made a real home for myself, but every Friday I flew home to spend the weekend with Shane. I did that for all three seasons of the show. It was stressful, but I couldn't imagine not seeing my boy.

I had blown my chance to redeem myself on *One Day at a Time,* but by being a model actor on *So Weird* I felt like I was cleaning up my mess, little by little.

While I was working on *So Weird*, Owen's daughter was born. Luckily, I was in town, so I was able to come straight to the hospital to meet one-day-old Zoe. There I found Owen in bed holding the baby. She was flanked by her husband, Jack, and Jack's brother, Fritz. They all looked stricken—frozen in the same wonder and fear that I must have had on my face in the first days of Shane's life. Zoe was crying, and Owen was patting her back tentatively. Owen said, "She won't stop."

I said, "Give me that baby." I put Zoe on my shoulder, let her feel my heartbeat, and burped her. She calmed immediately.

Soon after Zoe was born, Owen told me she had something for me. She came over to my house and put a big box down on my floor. "Can you keep these for me?" she asked. Owen explained that her in-laws, who were observant Jews, had laid down the law. They wanted their granddaughter, and any future grandchildren for that matter, raised strictly Jewish, which meant no Christmas tree. No Christmas tree meant no ornaments. I looked in the box. In it were all of Owen's Christmas decorations, some of which had belonged to her mother, Cass, who died when Owen was seven. There was a black Santa, a Wonder Woman wearing a Christmas hat, a black baby grand piano, ornate Victorian ornaments that Cass had collected, and ornaments that Owen had made when she was little. I knew how much they meant to her, and I knew that asking me to keep them meant she was as certain as I was that we would always be friends. She would be welcome to bring her children over to decorate the tree with me anytime. Owen and I will be part of each other's lives when we are old.

Three years later, when Owen's son, Noah, was born, she called me when she went into labor. Her close friend Carnie Wilson and I arrived at the hospital right after the birth. Owen and I laughed about how different the vibe in the room was with Noah. Now that she was having her second child, everyone was a lot more relaxed. I said to her, "I'm so glad you're having a boy, because boys are for their moms. Just wait. This is going to be the biggest love affair of your life. The first time he puts his arms around your neck and says 'I love you Mommy' you're going to melt, and you will keep on melting."

The next year, still working on *So Weird,* I skipped one of my precious weekends with Shane to celebrate Valerie's fortieth birthday. She planned a girls' weekend in Vegas. There were moms from her son's school and other friends from her life. It was a great weekend of amazing meals and massages and pedicures. Her birthday dinner was on a balcony of the Bellagio. There were about twenty of us at dinner. There were moving toasts for Val, saying what a wonderful mother and friend she was. I held up my glass of water, and I was happy for her. But as I looked out at the dancing fountains, I felt a part of the group and apart from it at the same time. After all these years, it was still hard for me to have a true, steady sense of self. My father was a crazy hippie. My mother was an aristocratic eastern seaboard socialite drunk. For all of my childhood I'd been bounced between those worlds. At *One Day at a Time*, I was a hardworking young actor, and a partying rock 'n' roll chick at night. Then came the drugs, obscuring my transformation into an adult. There is a part of me that will always be a chameleon, shifting to try to fit into a world where I don't really feel like I belong. This was Val's big night. She was an old, dear friend, but I felt strangely lonely. Everyone seemed so wholesome and so complete. I had a dream job. I had a wonderful family. But for all I had outwardly achieved, I didn't have the same level of peace that these women seemed to; I was still quietly enduring the unhealed internal wounds of my past. And I didn't see any hope of that changing. I thought of that past—the pain, the anger, the issues that led to the drugs, and the addiction itself—as the monster. That monster was still inside me. It hadn't gone anywhere. The monster was sleeping.

27

I used my Mickey Mouse money to buy a house for Shane and me. We'd been renting for years, first near my mother, then nearby in Woodland Hills. When I came home for weekends with Shane, we always spent a little time house hunting. Then we walked into an old Spanish house that I fell in love with on the spot. Shane sat down on the floor in one of the empty bedrooms and said, "This is my room." The house was a little beyond our budget, but we found a way to make it work, and I was proud. I had owned many houses as a teenager, but they didn't count. This was my first house as a responsible adult.

In mid-February of 2001, a month after we moved, I was driving down Santa Monica Boulevard in West Hollywood and got a call from Dad's manager. He said, "Your father is very ill. He's in an ambulance on the way to the UCLA Medical Center. Can you call everybody?" Shaking, I called my siblings, pulled Shane out of school, and drove with him straight to the hospital.

Dad was obviously very ill. Not surprisingly, there was something wrong with his new liver. (A photo of him drinking had appeared in the *National Enquirer* mere months after the successful transplant. On the Howard Stern show he claimed he was just trying to "break in" the new liver.) Dad's belly was distended; there was dried black blood on his teeth; his hands were like claws. Dad, the smooth-talking, high-rolling drug-rock legend was writhing on the bed, sick and fragile and fallen. Shane, now an eighth grader, tugged my hand and I took him out of the room. He sat down in the hallway with his backpack and said, "Look, Mom, that guy in there? He's not my grandfather. Chuck was my grandfather. That guy is a bad guy. I don't need to see him. I don't even know him. I don't want to know him." Fair enough. There were hundreds of photos of Shane playing with Chuck, but maybe five of him with my father. We'd kept our distance—in part at the will of Dad's current wife, Farnaz—but also, Shane knew what had gone on between me and Dad. He was just fourteen and, unlike me, there *was* much he hadn't seen. I'd spared him the details, but he knew enough.

With Dad in the hospital, I stopped going to my addicts' support group. Dad had an album coming out and his "team" didn't want anyone to know he was sick. I didn't see how I could go to meetings without talking about his condition, so I stopped going regularly. Instead, I went to visit Dad in the hospital every day. I drove over Beverly Glen to UCLA, driving right past 414 St. Pierre Road, half out of nostalgia and half because it was a traffic-free shortcut. I flew over the hill as I listened to the Coldplay song "Trouble," about being tangled, twisting and turning, in the middle of a spiderweb.

Late one night at the end of February, I was in the kitchen having tea with Mick when a nurse from the ICU called and said, "Your father wants to talk to you."

Dad came on the line and said, "The doctor is insane. The nurses are having sex on the floor under my bed. They're trying to kill me. I need you to get me out of here. You've got to come over." Dad was losing it. Outside, it was pouring rain.

Mick said, "You don't have to go."

I replied, "How can I not go? He asked for me. He called me." Reduced in an instant to a five-year-old, under his spell, I drove over the hill to the hospital and hurried to his bed. When I opened the door in the dim light I saw his quiet form. He was fast asleep. I kissed him on the forehead, squeezed the rain out of my hair, and went home.

No matter how remote Dad had been, during his weeks of

illness the whole band of loopy siblings kept chatty, spirited vigil at his bedside. Dad wasn't talking much. Mostly he wanted to be well enough to be wheeled out into the courtyard to see his pug, Monty. Sometimes he'd ask for a paper and pen and write lines and slashes, hieroglyphics as mysterious and frustrating as the man himself.

When I finally found myself alone with him, I said, "Dad, I want to talk to you." For all our past together, I felt timid. My dad could cut you with a sentence, making you feel worthless. Just the day before, I had put my head on his chest and said, "I love you so much, Dad." He'd grunted, "Enough, Max."

Now I steeled myself for his likely dismissal and said, "You know, we've been through a lot. You know what I'm talking about: good times, weird times, bad times, scary times. I would not be the woman I am had I not been your daughter. So I want you to know that I forgive you, and I love you very, very much."

Dad had never said "I'm sorry" or "I was wrong." He never even acted like any of it was regrettable. For so long that was what I thought I wanted from him in order to move on, get on with my life, and exorcise that particular demon. But now I realized I didn't need him to say anything. I had the power to close that chapter for us. He was reaching his end and would never apologize, because that was not who he was. But I could let that go and forgive him, and love him, which is what I'd really needed to do all along.

Dad looked up at me. As I expected, he didn't say anything; he just sighed and put his head on my shoulder. That was the moment, our moment. The weight of it was even and bearable—welcomed by us both. All that had passed between us was spoken and unspoken. We both knew the scope of it all, and neither of us wanted to reduce the complexity of our relationship to fault and blame. Words and apologies were smaller than what we told each other with our eyes. We were human, and we made mistakes, and we lived with them, and he was dying with them. At the end of his life, where we were standing, the most important emotion was love, in a simpler form now than it had ever been between us. We sat quietly, and it was one of those moments in life when the past washes away and you feel clean and new.

I'd been invited to Aspen for the 2001 Comedy Festival for a tribute to *American Graffiti*. I agonized about going—I knew the end was near for Dad—but I decided to honor my commitment. On my last visit to the hospital before the trip I said, "Look, Dad, I have to go out of town."

He said, "Fuck you."

We'd made our peace, and I wanted to keep it. Which meant I wasn't going to let him get away with that. I said, "No, you're not going to do this again. The time for you to rule my emotions is over. You can't destroy me with a word or a look. Not anymore. What I want you to say is, 'I love you, Max. Have a good trip.' "

He looked at me with his tired eyes and said, "I love you, Max. Have a good trip," a little like a reluctant teenager obeying his parent.

I said, "That's more like it Pops." I kissed him and turned to leave.

Then he said, "Hey Laura-bug, you dropped your bag on the floor. Don't forget it." There was nothing to the words themselves, but in his voice—in the tone and the way he said it—there was an apology, the regret and love I'd always known was there but had so desperately needed to hear. Shane and I went to Aspen for five days. We went skiing and snowboarding, saw comedy shows, and met cool people. We had a great time. By the time we came back Dad had taken a turn for the worse. He was intubated and unable to speak. He never spoke another word.

At the end, Dad was suffering enough that my brother and I asked the doctors to up his morphine. Even though he was so out of it that he couldn't talk, we were reasonably sure that if anyone should go out under the influence of an opiate, it was Dad.

I sat with him for a couple hours. He wasn't conscious, but I told him stories. I said, "Remember when we were on the road and we had that food fight and you used the clear plastic food dome as a shield over your head?" And "Remember when the band got stuck in the Lincoln Tunnel and you made us sing 'The Teddy Bears' Picnic' in four-part harmony for hours?" And "Remember in Norway when you were holding Shane and you slipped in the snow, but Shane didn't get a scratch on him?" I sang songs we'd written together. I knew it was over and I just stayed, holding his hand, loving him.

Watching Dad slowly dying was like watching a great tree fall. A beautiful, old, majestic, noble oak with tree rot and disease spreading through him. His core was tainted and you could see it in his eyes. He was so sad and so sick and so isolated, by design. I thought about his life and his body of work—his potential had been limitless, but after a certain point the production was a bunch of crap. What a waste. I could spend time being furious and damaged, but what was the point? My father didn't get that he was connected to others, that the harmful stuff he did to himself was harmful to other people. Harmful, in some small way, to the universe.

That night, as I walked out of UCLA, I passed a chapel. I detoured in and picked up a prayer card and a little orange pencil. I wrote, "Please take my father, tonight if possible." I folded it, put it in the box, sat there and cried for a while, then went home.

At five the next morning Farnaz called. She told me it was the end. I tore ass over the hill, listening to Coldplay, frantically dialing Bijou, Chynna, Jeffrey, and Tam. Nobody was answering the goddamn phone. When the phone rings at five a.m.—*that's* when you're supposed to take the call. Bijou later told me that she knew exactly why I was calling and couldn't bear to hear it.

By the time I got to the hospital, Dad's eyes were fixed. As

I stood at his bedside, I watched Dad's heart rate drop all the way down to three. Farnaz screamed, "John! Don't leave me, John!" His heart rate shot up and slowly started falling back down. Farnaz screamed again and his heart rate went back up. This was going on and on. Farnaz was screaming and crying on her knees. Remembering how Dad had silenced Genevieve at his mother's bedside, I said, "Can you shut the fuck up and let him die already?" If I could let him go, she could let him go. Farnaz quieted and Dad flatlined. He was gone. I called Mick. Dear Mick got in his car, drove to the hospital, and played his guitar and sang to my dad's body. It was a Monday. *Monday, Monday, can't trust that day.*

Owen Elliot worked with Lou Adler, my dad's longtime producer, to organize the memorial service. It was held at the Roxy, one of my old Sunset Strip hangouts. It was open to the public and the marquee on Sunset Boulevard said "All the leaves are brown."

The place was packed with friends, family, musicians, celebrities, and fans, including Denny and Michelle, the surviving members of the original Mamas & the Papas; Scott McKenzie; Spanky; my siblings: Jeffrey, Bijou and her then-boyfriend Sean Lennon, and Tam; Mick and Shane; Tim Curry; Warren Beatty; and Ed Begley Jr. Chynna was not at the memorial service. She had already committed to performing at a Brian Wilson event, so she didn't come. Hanging on either side of the stage were poster-size photos of my father. One showed him in what he had worn for his *Wolf King of L.A.* album cover—he was standing at the ocean's edge, with long hair and a beard, wearing a raccoon fur coat, skintight stovepipe jeans, and a silver silk top hat with a rhinestone hatband that Leon Russell had given him. The other poster was the author photo from my father's book, *Papa*

John. It showed him clean and sanitized, the dad who never quite was.

After a video tribute, the live-music portion of the program started. Shane, who was just learning guitar and had never performed onstage before, sang a song by Silverchair called "Miss You Love." "I'm not too sure how I'm supposed to feel or what I'm supposed to say," he sang, and I thought, *That's my boy.*

When my turn came I sang a song Dad wrote about me called "Fairytale Girl." In the middle of the song, one of the photos of my father fell down. I picked it up and walked around the stage, carrying it and singing the song.

> *Once upon a time I knew a fairytale girl.*
> *She flew her plane all around the world.*
> *It all went well until she couldn't find a place to land.*

Jeffrey joined me and others up onstage to sing "Monday, Monday" and "California Dreamin'." Dad's light shone in that room, the powerful words and music that drew us all to him, and the imposing, large-as-life presence that made us want to be part of his world.

Two weeks after my father's funeral, Shane and I walked into a pet store at the Northridge Mall and I saw a pug puppy. I said, "Look, Shane, it's Max." Shane said, "You're right." It turned out that Max had been born on January 15, 2001, the day I bought our house. He was meant to live there. We brought him home. The same day, unbeknownst to me, Bijou went out and bought two dogs.

Max was my first dog, and he was exactly what I needed right then. I'd kneel on the floor next to my bed and say, "Max, I feel so sad and lonely and scared and my dad is dead." Max's buggy eyes looked up at me with that unconditional dog love that replenishes the soul.

When Max was still a tiny puppy, I got a card from a guy

named Lee Allan, who asked if I remembered him from acting class. Of course I did. Lee was tall and athletic—a devoted beach volleyball player. He was bright and extremely funny—a working comedian. In acting class we'd had a scene together in which we were supposed to kiss. When the moment came, we started kissing and didn't stop. The acting coach tried to interrupt: "Ahem . . . you guys?" Lee was in a relationship at the time, so that kiss stood alone, but soon after my father's memorial Lee's condolence note arrived. It started, "Dear Fairtytale Girl . . ." It gave his phone number, and we started dating. Little Max was like our child. We raised him, and Freddie—another pug I got as a companion for Max—together. It looked like I was moving on.

During this time I was invited to perform in a production of Eve Ensler's *Vagina Monologues* in L.A. The producer asked if I had any ideas for women to perform with me. I knew not to suggest Valerie—she would never say the word "cunt." I suggested Michelle, and she signed on. We did the show together every night for a month. Our dressing tables were right next to each other. Our makeup was done side by side. We were onstage together for the whole performance. Michelle was always a presence in my life. Over the years we talked on the phone and spent time together with the family, at dinner parties, going to premieres, but now it was amazing for me to sit with her as two adult women, to have the opportunity to become girlfriends.

One day I asked her to teach me how to dress like a lady. I wasn't a slob, but I had always been a bit of a tomboy, wearing boots and jeans. Michelle took me to Beverly Hills and had me buy stockings and garters and ladylike dresses. More than thirty years earlier she'd been like a mother to me, spoiling me with Beverly Hills finery, and now we were dressing me for an entirely different stage of life.

The age difference between us was not great, but any woman can learn a lot from Michelle. She is beautiful, ballsy, and bright. She raised a wonderful daughter. She is the last surviving member of the Mamas & the Papas. Years ago, when the band briefly threw her out, she said, "I'll bury you all," and she did, and I was not surprised. Michelle is a force of nature. She endures. I, on the other hand, was, underneath it all, weightless and exposed, soon to fall prey to an unexpected wind.

For so many years I thought I was meant for a junkie life. That was who I was. It was just live it and do it and screw it. When I got sober I learned not to think that way anymore. I was in the world; I was functional; I thrived. The moment that my father and I had in the hospital—when I told him he was no longer the ruler of my emotions—that moment was important. I've never been good at defending myself. I turn my anger inward or act out with drugs. But I did it. I stood up for myself. I assumed my power and said good-bye. It was the closure that pointed to a future life of sober joy.

But for all the healing, for all the stability, for all the trappings of a functional life, I wasn't the pillar of sobriety that I appeared to be and that I thought I was. My father was gone, but the monster, the sleeping addict within me, was yawning and stretching.

28

When I first went to Alina Lodge, I noticed that clean, sober graduates of the program would visit and sit with the program's founder, Mrs. Delaney, at her big table. I thought, *One day I'm going to sit at that table with my car keys and my purse—the accessories of a sober life—and I'll have lunch with her.* It came to pass. Day after day of not doing drugs. Week after week of not wanting drugs. Month after month of not even thinking about drugs. Year after year of living a normal life. I lunched with Mrs. Delaney. She became my friend. I joined the Lodge's board of trustees. Eventually I celebrated being sober for ten years.

I had reentered the world, rebuilt my life, rewired my brain, and even though I still went to support groups, I had a life in which I stopped thinking of myself as an addict. The past faded. The idea that there were people in dark rooms shooting cocaine became foreign. Who would do that? Why would anyone want to live like that? It was disgusting. I wasn't that kind of person, and it was hard to imagine I ever had been that kind of person. I could never be there again. I was so sure that the monster inside me was dead and gone. But that complacency, that arrogance would be my downfall.

Back in 1999, when I was on hiatus from *So Weird,* I'd had cosmetic eye surgery. I'd always thought that one of my eyes looked like a puffball compared to the other. It was particularly obvious to me when I saw myself on *Hollywood Squares* at age eighteen. Now the asymmetry was compounded by age. I had my upper and lower eyelids done, and I was happy with the results. I was a working actor, and staying youthful was part of the job. Along with the surgery came pain medication. I took it as prescribed. At the appropriate time, I stopped using it. No problem.

A couple years later, not long after Dad died, I decided that I wanted to have liposuction on my thighs. And I figured that while I was doing it I might as well get my breasts done. The thigh and breast surgeries were for me. Nobody was having trouble photographing me, but I wanted to stem the tide of aging.

I delayed the surgery for a week to play for charity on the quiz show *The Weakest Link*. I was playing for Children of the Night, a charity that helps child prostitutes get off the streets. I knew firsthand how quickly and easily a kid might find herself willing to do anything for drugs. During the years I was clean and sober, I spoke all over the country to thousands of people about addiction. My focus wasn't just the addicts but their family, friends, and colleagues. Obviously, my father would never have considered warning me about drugs. But all those other people who cared about me, worried about me, and wanted to help me—and there were many of them—had no idea how to intervene. I told my story to thousands of people. I talked about the signs of addiction. I did anything and everything I could think of to help those who might be as lost as I had been.

Now I was fighting for street kids, and I was on a roll. When the nutty English host-lady of *The Weakest Link* chided me about my "checkered past," I said, "That's all different now." The audience cheered. In a dramatic contrast to the fucked-up eighteen-year-old who couldn't do a spelling test on *David Letterman*, I answered all the questions right until everyone had been eliminated except me and one other girl. I lost on the last question. I was the weakest link. Good-bye.

The silicone breast implants were more painful than I expected. I was bruised purple. It was agonizing. The sleepy monster opened an eye. I think about that moment when I made the decision to have the surgery, and I wonder what was really going on. Cosmetic surgery is painful. It usually requires narcotic pain medication. But I had long before lost my right to take pain medication. Had my ability to handle the medications they gave me for eye surgery made me think I could do it? Or did the eye surgery make me want to have more surgery so I could get more pills? I don't know the answer. But it soon became a chicken-and-egg question, one I couldn't answer and one I hope I won't have to face again. The fucked-up result was that my doctor, a family friend, gave me Thorazine, Demerol, Vicodin, Xanax, and Valium.

Mick came over to see Shane. He took one look at me and said, "You're high."

I said, "I'm in pain."

He said, "I've known you forever. You are high." I was on opiates, and Mick could see that I wasn't myself. I wasn't getting out of bed. I wasn't happy. When I ran out of medication, I was sick.

My beautiful little sister Bijou was twenty-two. She had been a crazy wild-child in New York, dancing on tables, allegedly almost cutting off the tip of someone's finger with a cigar cutter, fake raping someone with a dildo on the dance floor. She was on Page Six of the *Post* several times a week. I knew why she acted out—born into madness and raised by wolves—and I spent hours and days talking her through various dramas. She looked to me as a mother, or a big sister at the very least. Now she was a hot model, dating a guy named James, still living a high life, but not such a wild one.

Knowing that I was on pills for pain, Bijou teased me, offering me ecstasy, saying, "Come on, roll with me."

I said, "No, I don't do that stuff."

• • •

I assumed that the pain from surgery would diminish, I'd stop taking pills, and I'd resume my life. Instead, I started having unbelievable pain in my neck, my lower back, and my joints. I've always had problems with my spine—I had scoliosis as a teenager and wore a back brace for two years. But this was different. My knees, wrists, hips, every joint was on fire.

I went to doctor after doctor and was diagnosed with brain vasculitis, lupus, carpal tunnel, scoliosis. All of the above.

I was desperate for relief. James and Bijou were into a pill called Norco, which was like Vicodin but much stronger. James had huge bottles of them. I arranged to get one, but when I went over to pick it up, Bijou tried to intervene. She'd invited someone sober to confront me about taking Norco. I was the stable one. I was the one she could count on. For all her teasing and trying to get me to party with her, Bijou wanted, needed me to stay sober. But my enormous pain was my excuse and I stood by it.

At first I had real pain and used pain medication exactly as it was prescribed to me. But the monster was stirring. In rehab they tell you that if you ever use a drug again you'll immediately be right back where you left off. I know people who may be clean—but if they go out and use, they are on their knees within a week. That's what you see on TV too. It wasn't the case for me. The pain pills I was taking for the surgeries were so strong that my addict drive kicked in. By the time I switched to Norco, I was already on the path to hell. But I still functioned really well for years—until I didn't.

When I finally started the inevitable slide, my family noticed right away. In January of 2005 I went to the Sundance Film Festival for the premiere of *The Jacket,* a movie I was in starring Adrien Brody and Keira Knightley. I had a martini at the screening. Then Bijou and I walked the red carpet together, doing our thing. The next day I got a text from her. She said, "I know you're drinking. I smelled it on your breath. You have to stop. You're going to die."

Back home Owen told Bijou that I was wearing the Fentanyl Patch, the same narcotic that had been Dad's drug of choice. We'd all lost Dad. This was more than Bijou could take. She came over to my house and went apeshit. She burst through the door, yelling, "You can't do this. What's wrong with you? You can't be on this medication."

People were talking about me. Mack was taking pills. Mack was drinking. Mack was using narcotics. I was pissed. I had legitimate pain—nobody seemed to get that. The pain was intense, and the doctors were saying to me, "Just imagine if you weren't on painkillers. How could you function?" My doctors wrote me multiple prescriptions for the same pills and told me to fill them at different pharmacies. My doctors put me on so much Fentanyl that it's amazing I didn't go into a coma. These are what they call "rock docs," doctors who are essentially legal dealers. You don't actually have to be in pain to get prescriptions from them. But I was. I was in so much pain that I had to walk with a cane. I tried acupuncture, a shaman herbalist, kinesiology, irradiology. I truly thought I was going to end up in a wheelchair. I didn't see any way out, and now the people I loved were trying to take away the only relief I had.

At the same time, though I'd forgotten it, I was an addict at heart, now and forever. Feeling pressured and being angry and in denial came with the territory.

It wasn't just the pain meds that awakened the monster and caused my relapse. My father's death should have provided closure. Instead, it came bundled with new issues and new anger. First, the secrecy. We were never allowed to talk about his illness. He'd gotten a liver transplant, and the fact that he had been using and drinking ever since he got the new liver was a family secret. Dad was not a stupid man. He was brilliant. But he had chosen this horrible death. How could he think that with someone else's liver in him he could continue to drink the way he did and not die? Fuck him. I was heartbroken and pissed off. But the official story was that he died of heart failure. Well, sure. We all die of heart failure.

When he was alive, I couldn't talk about Dad's illness at recovery meetings, so I'd tapered off my attendance. Now that he was dead, I couldn't talk about my anger and pain, and holding it in was impossible. So I stopped going altogether. And after a while, it was, *Okay, I'm out of the program. I'm already doing OxyContin. Why not do cocaine?*

My father's death also stirred unresolved issues. There was always a component of my sobriety that had to do with my father, an unacknowledged desire to show him that I could live a different life than the one he modeled for me, to prove to him that he too could do it, to save him. Dad never bought it, not for a minute. When he died, although it was far from so, it was almost like I had one less reason to be clean. I'd gotten sober to flip Dad off. Staying sober was a fuck-you to him. Now he was dead and I was using to flip him off again. In a world of logic and perspective, my son Shane is more than enough reason to stay sober, but the loss of my father threw me far and away from reason.

There was more. Someone close to me, let's call her M., had confided in me before Dad died. Knowing that he had abused me, she told me that he had done similarly inappropriate things to her when she was quite young. The idea that Dad had taken advantage of a teenager was horrifying. What happened between us was something I thought I had processed, but when I imagined the same thing happening to someone I loved, it seemed far worse. It made him into a real monster.

The fact that the same behavior seemed criminal to me when practiced on another was in itself a matter for the self-esteem police, but after Dad died it got even more twisted. M. came to me and said, "I have something I need to talk to you about. My husband has been bugging me to set the record straight. I'm sorry, but all that stuff I said about your father—I made it up." M. told me that she had lied because she wanted to be closer to me. My jaw hit my chest. He was gone. The man was dead. She had made me see him as a real monster. Now he had died falsely convicted. In my eyes. If she was telling the truth. My world was spinning, full of needs and questions. I played the Stevie Nicks song "I Miss You" over and over.

Well I miss you now
I have so many questions
About love and about pain
About strained relationships
About fame as only he could explain it to me

Seems like yesterday
I think about how much I
Wish that you were here with me now
The invisible girl that was my name
She walks in and walks out
And I'm sorry now
I'm sorry now

Although we'd made our peace, the overarching feeling was that I needed answers that only my father could give, and now he never would.

I was an angry half orphan. I was wrecked, physically and mentally. I didn't think I had a future. The monster was awake, and it was hungry, and I was fucked.

29

When I went on the road for the thirtieth anniversary production of the musical *Annie* in 2006, I was still on the Fentanyl Patch, which meant there was a constant stream of narcotic medication running through my body. I was also drinking.

Ten years earlier, soon after I moved to L.A., when I'd played Rizzo in *Grease,* first on Broadway and then on the road for almost a year, physically I felt very strong, fit, and capable. And being on the road with the cast, I felt the same, longed-for sense of community that I'd felt when I went roller skating with the other kids after the '71 earthquake. It was a little like what I imagined college might have been: sitting around talking, ordering pizza. I may have felt that in the early days of the Mamas & the Papas, but eventually we were too fucked up to have that idyllic sense of a united purpose and friendship.

When the tour brought *Grease* to New York, Owen happened to be there. She stayed with me in my tiny apartment on the Upper East Side. I turned her on to Cocoa Puffs and Aquafresh toothpaste, and she's been obsessed with Cocoa Puffs ever since—mandating all the more tooth-brushing with Aquafresh. I loved walking in the city, but Owen was not so big on walking. It was cold. At some point she said, "My legs are killing me and my ears are going to break off." I called her a pussy, but we jumped in a cab. We just had a blast.

During *Grease* I became especially close to the conductor of the orchestra, Keith Levenson, a goofy guy with glasses and a beard. We didn't have a sexual relationship—he had a fiancée—but at that point we certainly had an intellectual love affair.

Now, ten years later, on *Annie,* I was romantically involved—actually engaged to—and sharing a hotel room with Keith Levenson. But it wasn't to be the same good times I'd had on *Grease.* I played Lily St. Regis, the "Easy Street"–singing conwoman who wants to get rich off Annie. The show was two and a half hours of singing and dancing. It played to an audience of three thousand people every night. Between the work and the meds, I was zonked. I slept all day. At night I wanted to stay home and watch movies instead of going out with the cast and crew to restaurants or bars. Keith got fed up. He didn't know how to live with a drug addict. I was a person who never stopped loving anyone, but with Keith it got nasty at the end. He turned stone cold. I wanted him to love me again. We had huge fights like none I'd ever had before. One day he packed his bag and said, "This is it. I'm out of here." He walked out the door and, I presume, went to the front desk to switch hotel rooms.

I had gotten very thin, and the patches I was wearing were way too strong for my diminished body weight. Then I missed my entrance cue after a fight with Keith. I ran onstage and picked up the scene as best I could. The producers gave me a leave of absence.

A leave of absence. With my history. This time I didn't get a haircut and pretend to be better the way I had back on *One Day at a Time.* This time I went straight from the road to detox. I knew I was in trouble, but even as I entered detox I hid behind the belief that I was using drugs for legitimate pain. Besides that, I was focused on my relationship with Keith. I wanted to win him back, and I thought detoxing was the ticket.

I had been to rehab at a place called Crossroads the year before but it hadn't taken. It lingered in my memory as a beautiful vacation in Antigua where Bijou, her boyfriend Sean Lennon, and my boyfriend Lee had come for family week and partied. They were yachting, swimming, and snorkeling while I was stuck in rehab. Every night Lee and Sean would go out drinking, then come back in the morning to participate in the family program. During the group sessions, Sean started talking about losing his father. Needless to say, his audience was rapt. I just sat quietly, wondering how exactly this would help me recover. I wanted my loved ones there, but I was tired of having a family so colorful that their presence outshone everything else. Everyone at Crossroads was having family week, but mine had to be spectacular and sensationalized.

After I graduated from the program and Sean and Bijou left, Lee and I rented a little house right above Crossroads. We spent a few days kicking around, dancing on the beach, having a romantic time. And every night Lee would drink. I was one day out of rehab. I'd say "I don't mind, it's fine," but it sucked. I know if I'd said something, Lee would have listened. He was and is one of my dearest friends and had shown his devotion by fishing a piece of chicken out of my throat when I was choking to death after overdosing on Soma. Come to think of it, Lee had more than earned those drinks.

Lee and I flew home from Crossroads separately. I arrived at my house knowing with every ounce of my being that there was a Norco, a single Norco, in my closet underneath a sweater. I walked into the house, went straight to the Norco, and took it. I came downstairs and ordered Mexican food with Shane and his friends. It was fun; we all hung out. The next morning I went back to the doctor and got a new prescription for Norco.

This time, when I left *Annie,* I went to a detox in Florida called Summer House. I wasn't thinking about sobriety. My physical pain was so great that I didn't think I'd ever be able to stop opiates, or so the monster told me. But I knew that detox would get my dosage back down so the meds would work better. In most states it's illegal to help narcotic addicts detox by slowly reducing their dosage. Instead, they give you Librium, which is a nasty detox. You shake and sweat and have hellish diarrhea. You have involuntary leg kicks—which is why it's called "kicking" the habit. The unbearable illness of withdrawal was a significant barrier to rehab. Narcotic reduction was a much gentler path to sobriety, and Florida was the only state where it was legal.

At Summer House I befriended Wyatt, a gorgeous successful businessman. He was tall—six foot seven—with hair down to his butt. At Summer House they were accustomed to treating chronic pain patients who wanted to bring their dosage down to a manageable level. I left Summer House on a reduced dosage and went back to L.A. before returning to *Annie*. Wyatt came to town for a convention and we made plans to have lunch. When he parked his red convertible Mustang in front of my house, I ran to him and gave him a big hug. I adored this man.

After lunch we were chatting on my front porch when my phone rang. It was my agent. She said, "I'm sorry to have to tell you this, but you won't be going back on the road with *Annie*." I'd been fired, and I knew why.

My now ex-fiancé, Keith, had a long history with *Annie*. He had brought me on board so that we could be together. Now he wanted nothing to do with me ever again. I knew he was behind this news. I was so pissed off and so hurt when I got that call. Wyatt comforted me until he had to go.

A few weeks later I went to New York to visit my old friend Susan. Wyatt and I went to dinner and afterward came home to his apartment. There was some flirting going on, but I wasn't sure what to want or expect. He was thirteen years younger than I was. That night he slept on the couch in his living room and I slept in his bed. The bed had excellent sheets. I smelled the pillow. It smelled good. When I went through the living room to the bathroom, I snuck a peek at him sleeping. He was beautiful.

The next morning it was on. And the next time I came to New York to see him, I up and decided to move to New York.

• • •

Moving to New York was an impulsive decision, and drugs were at the heart of it. When I came home from Summer House, my pain had returned. I had to walk with a cane. *See?* As I'd tried to explain to everyone, my pain was real. Detoxing off the pain pills had caused it to return in full force. I went back on the Patch and pain pills. Then, that second time I went to New York to see Wyatt, he had OxyContin. We took it and started getting high together. I moved to New York because I thought I wanted to be with Wyatt. Only later was it clear that leaving L.A. was my way of running away from all the friends and family who were trying to save me.

Shane was almost twenty years old. He had been talking about moving in with friends, so when I left, he did too, and we rented out our empty house for nine months. I'd found an apartment in Queens, a few blocks from Wyatt. It was a two-bedroom apartment, much smaller than my house. In a frenzy, I gave away my refrigerator, my washer, my dryer, my fax machine. I hired a retired drummer who used to play with Buckcherry to pack up everything I didn't give away.

I sent my pugs cross-country by car so they wouldn't have to endure the plane trip. Wyatt came to L.A. to fly back to New York with me and my cats, Moley and Rupert. We sat in business class with the cats meowing quietly under our seats. The plane landed, and everyone stood up to deplane. Then I heard a voice call out, "Laura!" Whenever I hear that name, I know I'm going to see a face from my past. I looked over and there, directly across the aisle from me, was Peter Asher. He and I practically dove across the aisles to hug each other.

In the airport, Wyatt also ran into someone he recognized, so Peter and I strolled a little by ourselves, catching up. Three years earlier, he had produced a Wilson Phillips album with my sister Chynna. When the band had a big show at the Santa Monica Pier, I had expected to run into Peter, but we never crossed paths. After that I'd called to say hi, but he never responded. Now, as we walked along, I said, "Peter, why didn't you call me back?"

He said, "Because I've never stopped being completely in love with you." My heart jumped. Two years after I'd left Peter, he married a girl named Wende Worth, who had been my assistant. They had a child, and as far as I knew they were still happily married. But part of me was still in love with him, in love with him and in love with the memory of being in love with him, the same way I was forever in love with everyone I'd ever loved. I craved attachment, and once I found it, I never let go. But he was married, and I wasn't messing with that. Peter and I made plans to have lunch in the city, but I knew it wouldn't and shouldn't happen. How could I imagine how differently I would feel and behave—how fucked up I would be—the next time I ran into Peter?

I lived in New York for almost a year, most of which I spent at Wyatt's, feeding outrageous amounts of money to my raging addiction to OxyContin. Soon enough, Wyatt and I were ugly and desperate, fighting about money, fighting over drugs.

I flew back to L.A. for a short trip to host a luncheon for the hilarious and charming Motion Picture Mothers, a social group my mother belongs to that does charity work. I'm an honorary member. I wore the expected ladies' attire at the luncheon—a hat and gloves. Then I went back to my diabetic mom's, found her syringes, and started shooting coke.

I was supposed to be gone for three days, but I didn't go back to New York. And suddenly I understood all too well exactly how and why my father and Genevieve had left their children at 414 St. Pierre Road for a weekend trip to New York and then vanished.

Being a junkie again was, well, to tell the truth it was excellent. I called up Josh and Lisa, two dear old friends, lovely people—truly—who happened to be drug dealers. We'd been the best of friends back in the day, but I'd steered clear of them when I was clean. Now I said, "Hey, I haven't seen you in ages."

As we caught up it came out that they were in a tough spot. The apartment they'd been renting forever was going to be sold, and they had to leave. But they couldn't pass a credit check for a new apartment. Such are the struggles of career drug dealers. I said, "Why don't you guys just come and live with me?"

It's true: I was moving my drug dealers right into the guest bedroom of the dream house I'd bought for me and Shane. But Josh and Lisa aren't street people. I've known them for years. I had and still have a genuine love for them. They are really good people with a really bad problem. Now we lived that bad problem together.

But no matter what needs they had and what reasons I gave, the truth is that I moved the drug dealers into my house so that I could have a constant stream of access without having to leave the house. If I ran out of coke at four a.m., I could just go downstairs and get more.

For a good while it was deceptively fun. We were like a family—it was all almost normal except that they smoked heroin and I shot coke and there was no clock. Time was immaterial. Josh and Lisa had lived that way for a long time, and I fell right into the routine of timelessness. We cooked dinner together—it was five a.m. but the food was delicious. Lisa and I cleaned the house—it was two in the morning and we'd been up for three days straight, but at least the house was clean. We all took the dogs for walks—at midnight, but we all had a nice moonlit stroll. There was no difference between four in the morning and four in the afternoon except that the sun was either up or down.

If you took drugs out of the equation, it was a fantasy life. The three of us were roommates. We cooked, we cleaned, we took care of the animals. And then we cleaned some more. With two women on cocaine, the house was spotless. There was a certain comfort and serenity that I felt knowing that Josh and Lisa were downstairs in the guest room. Sometimes I'd even fall asleep at the foot of their bed like a puppy.

I said being a junkie was excellent because when you first start, the drugs enhance reality, and it's cool and enlightening and appealing. But over time the drugs take over reality until they create your reality for you. They own you. That's when you've crossed over, and if you're using needles, it's guaranteed to happen. Anyone who picks up a needle isn't a recreational drug user.

My doctor had prescribed Opana, an opiate twice as strong as OxyContin, for my pain. On top of that, I'd started shooting cocaine. Every time I went to my rock doc to get my prescriptions renewed, I worried that he would do labs—drawing blood from me—and he or the nurse would see my junkie arms. But for some deluded reason I didn't anticipate his reaction when I mentioned in a conversational, "Isn't *he* fucked up?" way that my boyfriend Wyatt was back in detox in Florida for OxyContin. The doctor said, "Oh, in that case we're going to do a urine on you today." I sat in stunned silence. A urine test for drugs. I had shot cocaine just before I walked in the door. I was done for.

I peed in the cup—what else could I do? Moments later, the doctor came in and said, "Your test shows positive for cocaine."

I said, "That's impossible! I haven't used cocaine in fifteen years." I was a middle-aged mother, indignant and outraged.

He said, "I'm going to give you your prescription, but if this comes back positive from the lab, we're going to have to talk." Those rock docs. Always game to fill one last prescription.

I left the doctor's office and went to the pharmacy to fill my prescription. But I knew what the lab results for my urine test would show. Even this doctor was semi-ethical enough to stop prescribing Opana after I tested positive for coke. After this round of pills ran out, what was I going to do?

Josh and Lisa smoked heroin all the time. It's called chasing the dragon. You put tar heroin in foil, light a flame under it, and with a straw, you suck up the smoke, chasing it down the foil. When I was down to two Opana and facing a gruesome withdrawal, a lightbulb went on in my head. Heroin. If I smoked heroin, I wouldn't go through withdrawal. Plus, it would take care of the pain. A perfect solution. If you are out of your fucking mind.

Lisa gave me a tutorial in how to chase the dragon and I smoked heroin for a couple weeks. The heroin erased any and all pain, physical, emotional, imaginary. It brought abject euphoria. It was an amazing high. When Wyatt next came to visit, we smoked heroin together. But then he found an old needle on the floor in my bedroom and said, "We should shoot this stuff. That'll be a better high." I had no plans to shoot tar, and when Wyatt suggested it, I wanted to and didn't want to at the same time. I knew that if we shot heroin, we'd be crossing into extremely dangerous territory. Even my faithful drug dealers never used needles. Wyatt and I discussed it, and you'd think that pausing to reconsider would lead anyone to decide, *No, this is a bad idea.* But I just thought, *What the fuck? At this point what the fuck do I have to lose?*

Wyatt and I shot heroin for the first time together.

I went first, and the feeling was so intense I thought I was going to die. I couldn't speak I was so high. But that didn't stop me. I don't blame Wyatt—I'm sure I would have figured it out eventually—but from that moment, things got bad fast. Wyatt left, and I had endless access to heroin. I started FedExing it to Wyatt, and night after night we stayed on the phone for eight to ten hours, shooting up together.

Once I started, once my brain experienced the engineered pleasure of opiates in my bloodstream, it did not want that feeling to go away. Ever. If I went too long between shots, I immediately started to feel like shit—pissed, tired, ravenous for more. Withdrawal was so intensely unpleasant, such a direct contrast to the intense euphoria, that it would've compelled me to keep using even if I'd wanted to quit. Which I didn't.

Nonetheless, heroin was not my perfect drug. It made me too fucked up to do anything but sit in a blissed-out daze. I liked to do stuff, to talk, to hang out, to keep the house in order, to feel like I was living some kind of life. Then it occurred to me. *Wait a minute—if I mix coke and heroin together, it'll wake me up and put me down at the same time.* When I started speed-balling, there was no turning back.

I can't blame my relapse on my father, nor can I blame it on his death. I was a mother, a sister, a daughter, a homeowner. I'd been trying to be everything to everyone. I came out of the Lodge trying to be Superwoman. I took on infinite responsibilities but forgot who I was and what I needed. I ignored the video loop of my past, that haunted reminder that I was still afraid, in denial, unable to face parts of my life. I tried to fold myself like a square of origami paper into as many different shapes as I could. For all the years of my sobriety I had been the matriarch of the family. Christmas and Thanksgiving were at my house. I always made a huge turkey and served Martinelli sparkling apple juice. I'm twenty years older than Bijou and I was the one she talked to about boys, sex, life. She called me if she was upset about a boyfriend, or needed help running lines for an audition, or needed a last-minute dog-sitter. I was available to her day and night, like a mother. I was the rock.

Then my father died, and it rained hard, and the rock turned out not to be a rock after all. It was a square of gray paper, folded into the shape of a rock. When it rained, the rock all but disintegrated. I was just a thin, folded paper pretending to be a person.

I lied to everyone for a long time. My brother, who had seen everything before, accused me of getting high. He said, "I've lost my respect for you as a human being." I told him he was crazy and an asshole. At least denying it meant that I still felt some shame, some guilt about what I was doing. But pretty soon even that went away, and eventually I was like, "Yeah, I'm not sober, but I'm not going to get sober. Sober's boring. I'm not going to do it."

Bijou had once teased me with drugs. When she saw that what she had thought was impossible was now a reality, she was vehemently determined to stop me. But I wouldn't listen. I said, "Fuck you, I'm fine, go away." I changed my cell phone rings for Bijou and Mick to a loud alarm that blared *Danger, danger, danger!* The phone would ring and I wouldn't answer it. They were no longer my beloved sister and my old friend. Now all they were was a threat to my happy needle time.

The only person I never pushed away or wanted to go away was Shane. I had gone to great lengths to explain to Shane that he came from a long line of addicts and alcoholics. His decision to pick up a hard drug could change his life forever. I had taken such pride in raising a son in a dry house. Now it wasn't a dry house by any definition. I channeled my shame into pulling myself together as best I could for Shane, but the shame was infinite. I buried the excess the same way I did everything and everyone else.

I upheld other responsibilities, minimally. For instance, I made myself visit my mother, who had moved into assisted living and needed me. When I first came back from living in New York with Wyatt, I had stayed with her in her house—the same condo where I'd grown up. We had an amazing time during the day together, even though come nighttime I was upstairs in my old childhood bedroom, shooting up nonstop.

My mother had been taking care of herself for a long time, but when I visited, I cooked for her and gave her insulin injections (and stole her syringes). She could let go a little, so she did. Once I left, Mom fell apart. Over a three-week period she went from being competent and refined to a disoriented and frightened person. Jeffrey and I decided she would do better in an assisted living facility, and she did. Now she dressed for dinner every night, in diamonds and pristine St. John Knits and matching bags and shoes. Her makeup was always perfect. It was as if she'd returned to her finishing school, to the Club of the Three Wise Monkeys. I saw her as often as possible and she believed me when I said that I was clean.

Genevieve, always bonkers, had her own past and her own advice for me. She didn't share her daughter Bijou's concern. Instead, she came to my door one day when I was using. She said, "You know, your brothers and sisters are worried about you." I thought I knew what was coming next. She was going to tell me they all loved me and I needed to get help. But no. In the high-pitched voice that Bijou imitates hilariously, Genevieve continued: "Maybe you should lie and tell them you're sober. It will make them feel better. Then they can stop bugging you and you can do whatever you want." Leave it to Genevieve.

On Christmas Eve of 2006 it dawned on me that I had no Christmas presents for anybody in my family. It's true that I've always been a last-minute Christmas shopper, but I love Christmas. My mother had always made it a special time. Every year she had a fifteen-foot white-flocked Christmas tree, first with Lenny, then with Chuck. As children, Jeffrey and I left out cookies and milk for Santa. My mother would go down, break the cookies, and leave some crumbs. Every year she'd sneak into our rooms and leave us new robes, pajamas, and slippers. We'd wake up Christmas morning, put on our Christmas PJs, go downstairs, and tear into the gifts.

I loved researching what Shane wanted, loved picking presents, loved wrapping them. Mick would come over in the morning so the two of us could creep into Shane's room and wake him up together. I remember watching him unwrap presents, smiling an impossibly huge grin. There were always far too many presents: instruments, books, every video game on the planet. We all loved it.

Mom had passed the Christmas torch to me. I always bought a nine-foot tree, moving furniture around to accommodate it, and played corny Christmas music from Thanksgiving to New Year's. After Mick and I had our morning with Shane, the whole family would gather at my house. As we opened presents, the music would be playing ("Not Perry Como again!"), the coffee would be brewing, and I had bagels, toast, and Marmite to sustain us through the present exchange.

After the presents, Mick and Shane would go to Mick's house so Shane could have Christmas with his family on Mick's side. At my house the cooking would start. My mother and I always made the turkey, and we'd spend all day cooking, watching football, setting a beautiful table for sixteen with china and silver. In addition to family, I always took in strays. Christmas was an open house for anyone who didn't have a place to go, like my homeless friend and sometime garage resident, Greg. For a time my friends Steven, a musician, and his wife, Marion, a painter—wonderful people I'd known for thirty years—joined the motley crew living at my house and enjoyed the Christmas festivities. It was always a lively cast of characters.

But for the last couple years I'd stopped hosting Christmas. And this year I had done nothing. I hadn't bought a single present. I didn't have the strength.

Now Christmas was upon me. Everyone was coming over to my house the next day, and I had nothing to give them. I thought, *Holy fuck, what am I going to do?* So at three in the morning on Christmas Eve I went to a drugstore to do my Christmas shopping. I was thinking to myself, *You are in so much trouble on so many levels,* when a song came on the store's sound system. It was "California Dreamin'."

Dad's songs are ubiquitous. It's inevitable that I hear them, but it seems that ever since he passed away, at crucial moments in my life, when I'm in despair, bereft, he appears—on the radio or on TV—as if to say, *I'm here for you. With you. Finally.* After all those years of waiting for my father, now that he is gone, I don't have to wait anymore. But I'll stop short of saying that it gives me true comfort. Dad left a huge hole in the family when he died. I'd much rather be waiting for him alive than accompanied by whatever spirit I feel.

Still, on Christmas Eve in the drugstore, "California Dreamin' " felt like a message from my dad. He was trying to say, "I know what you're going through, and I'm here, and I'm sorry."

I said, "Thanks Dad, I know. I know, man, I know."

I hurried through the store, buying Chia Pets, candy, candles, phone cards. I must have spent four hundred dollars in CVS that night. Merry fucking Christmas.

30

One day Josh and Lisa had to go out of town on business. I was left alone in the house with the dogs, shooting up. This wasn't a casual matter of shooting dope every once in a while. I was injecting myself every fifteen to twenty minutes unless I was asleep. That was just what I did.

Shortly after Josh and Lisa left, I did a shot. I woke up later—how much later I don't know—on the floor with a table on top of me. This had happened before. I'd shoot up, pass out, come crashing down, and wake up on the floor with a needle in my arm. More than once I woke up slumped on the toilet with a needle sticking out of my foot. The syringe had dropped out of my hand before I could do the shot and stuck where it fell. I'd pull it out of my foot and stick it in my arm.

Left on my own, I'd stay up for three days straight, then sleep for the next three. Most junkies wake up when they start to go through withdrawal, but I often couldn't get up to deal with preparing a shot. I'd fall back asleep and another day would go by. I'd enter withdrawal in my sleep and wake up the next day, drenched in sweat. The sheets would be soaked. The dogs would be wet from sleeping next to me. Three days into withdrawal, a heroin junkie is horribly sick, and I got there all the time, with the spoon, syringes, and drugs resting on the table two feet away. It was a form of self-punishment.

This time I woke up and slowly crawled out from under the table. I shuffled around, looking for my glasses. I hadn't been able to get it together to order new contact lenses, so I'd been wearing reading glasses for months. I had at least thirty pairs of reading glasses, but, inevitably, the pair I found had a missing lens or a broken ear thingie. With blurry half-vision, I felt my way to do the shot.

When I was done, I dropped the used syringe into a cup and looked around the room. There were fifty or sixty syringes in cups lined up on the floor like soldiers. There was blood on the ceiling, and one of my dogs was licking drops of fresh blood off the floor. Dirty dishes had accumulated on all surfaces. I was starting to feel better and it was time to clean.

I brought a Rubbermaid tub up from the kitchen, filled it with crusty dishes, and brought it back downstairs. I took the cardboard boxes that I'd filled with used syringes out of the bathtub Jacuzzi that I now used as a trash can. There were hundreds and hundreds of syringes in those boxes. I sealed them shut, wrapping silver duct tape around and around the boxes. I wrote "biohazard" all over the boxes with a black Sharpie pen. This was what I called my "bad trash." The last thing I wanted was for a trash guy to grab a bag or a box and prick himself with a needle. So I drove to a dumpster five miles away and pitched my load of bad trash in.

I came home from the dump and did another shot. Then the paranoia hit me. Extreme paranoia is universal with cocaine. Even if I told myself that there was nobody in the house, nobody in the shower, nobody in the closet, nobody at the window, the minute the drug hit my bloodstream, *bam!* There was someone in the closet, someone in the trees, someone looking for me, someone trying to get me. When I was on the road with the Mamas & the Papas, I'd be in my hotel room shooting coke, and I'd spend half the time lying on the floor, looking through the crack under the door for hours. Even if I was on the fortieth floor of a hotel, I'd still think there was someone right outside my window. Shitloads of drugs will do that to you. Reality is warped. You can't even believe the notes your sober self left for your high self, the sticky notes pasted everywhere to remind you that it's just a psychotic fantasy. As soon as you're high, the notes are just part of the conspiracy.

Now I turned off all the lights in my house and crept around, looking out every window. I got the binoculars to see if anyone was in the trees. I lived in silent darkness like a maniac for the ten long days that Josh and Lisa were gone. That emptiness, the loneliness—it was like the days I spent in my father's flat on Glebe Place, forgotten by my dad and losing my grip on reality. When Josh and Lisa came home, I was happy as a puppy, thrilled to be safe at last. With my best friends and drug dealers.

Money was a growing concern. The heroin I bought from Josh and Lisa was far cheaper than the prescription pills I'd been buying, but now I was doing a couple hundred dollars' worth a day, plus an eighth of coke. So when I got invited by some rich guy to be flown first class to his huge birthday party and paid five thousand dollars to schmooze with the other celebs and guests, I accepted.

Of course I missed my plane. And the next plane. When I finally got to the party, the first person I saw was Peter Asher. Peter was in his sixties by then, but he looked the same to me, with his bright red hair and black glasses. He and his old music partner Gordon had gotten back together to do a tour. As part of that, they'd been invited to this party.

I was late as fuck, and now that I'd arrived I was supposed to circulate and meet all the guests, and then sit down at my assigned seat a table away from Peter. Instead, I sat down right next to him to talk.

Peter was the one who got away. I don't know how else to say it. I know I was only eighteen, and we were living a wild life, and I spontaneously dumped him to marry Jeff Sessler on a cocaine-fueled impulse. It wasn't exactly Romeo and Juliet. But when we talked, it was like there was nobody else at the table. I asked after his wife and daughter, but I soon dropped the small talk. I said, “So what’s going on with you? What’s your relationship with Wende like?”

He said, “It’s really good. We’ve been together a long time. We have our lifestyle,” and so on and so forth.

Cutting to the chase, I said, “Well, do you fuck around?”

He said, “Look, I know what you’re getting at. I’ll put it this way—whether I fuck around or not is beside the point. I can’t with you because it would mean way too much. I don’t think I’d be able to have just a fling with you.” And that was that. Once we got past that matter it was a great night. Our conversation flowed as it always had. We had known each other so well once upon a time.

Peter and I made plans to have breakfast together the next morning, but I was late. Forty-five minutes late, to be exact, because I’d been up all night shooting up. I found Peter waiting with Gordon in the conference room, where breakfast was set out. We all had planes to catch.

The night before, Peter had asked me, “Do you still get high?”

I had said, “I do now,” and he had looked concerned. Peter could see that I was in trouble. Now, when I walked back to my room, Peter came with me.

He followed me through the door and said, “Look. I don’t think that you are meant to do drugs. There aren’t many people I would say that about. I have liberal views on drugs. But I just don’t think that this is good for you.” Then he kissed me. It was electric. I started crying.

He said, “I loved you so much, and I’m so worried about you.” We were in a cheesy bittersweet romance movie, but it was my life and he had no idea how bad it was. I turned away to the window. He stayed at the door. I looked back. He blew me a kiss. And then he left. I sat on the windowsill and cried my eyes out for love and missed opportunities and my wasted, lost life.

• • •

As a junkie, I purged my life of most obligations, but when Val and I were invited to present an award at the TV Land Awards in 2008, I decided it sounded fun. Before we left, I preloaded a couple shots and brought them with me in my bag. I looked like shit, but I convinced myself I was pulling it off. We were backstage, waiting for our turn to present, and I slipped into the bathroom to shoot a speedball. Suddenly I heard Valerie's voice. She was knocking on the door, saying, "Mack, Mack, it's time. We have to go onstage." I wiped the blood off my arm and hurried out of the bathroom. Val looked at me and I thought, *Oh God. She knows.*

What I was no longer hiding from my family was now impossible to hide from my friends. Valerie, Peter, these were the people who'd known me the first time around. That life had passed, but now here they were again, and here I was with a needle in my arm. I had never expected to pass this way again. I was an adult. I'd had the experience of living a drug-free life, and yet I was making the same mistakes all over again. How did it happen? I'd been sober so long that I'd grown complacent. I thought I didn't need to actively fight my addiction. But in the last couple of years things had fallen so far so fast that I didn't know if I could ever come back. My relationships were crumbling. I was lying to my son. My dog Max was dying. I missed my father and was full of regret about his life and death. I loathed myself. The only way out was the cheap way out—making all feeling go away.

When I landed back in L.A. after seeing Peter, I called Josh and Lisa from the limo. I said, "Make sure you have some dark for me." Dark is the tar heroin I used. Arriving at my house, I ran in the door and straight to the office with my hand out. They gave me coke and heroin and I went right upstairs to start all over again.

31

I was in the worst shape of my life. There were only two possible endings: death or sobriety, and the smart money was on death.

At first I had shot up in my big closet, hiding what I was doing from the people, the dogs, the furniture, myself. Then I moved to the bathroom, because that was easy to clean. But I felt vulnerable in the bathroom, so I went back to the closet for a while. Finally, I moved to the vanity in my bedroom—the one that fell on me while Josh and Lisa were out of town. A sweet little wooden rocking chair lived next to the vanity, and that was my place. I sat there day after day. It was not the most comfortable place to sit, much less to sit and shoot and slump and sleep for hours and days and weeks. But many and long were the nights I spent in that chair, that incidental armless rocking chair that was made for some other house, some other woman, some other life.

The chair had no arms to prop me up, so when I nodded out I'd slump sideways in the chair. One time I slept that way for sixteen hours. I was in that chair for so long that when I woke up, my body was stuck in the slump. I was crooked and couldn't straighten myself. I didn't stand up straight for three weeks.

Wyatt had gotten sober. I didn't want him to visit because I knew it would jeopardize his sobriety, so instead we talked on the phone every day. We watched movies together as long-distance date nights. Wyatt was terrified that I was going to die. He wanted to chase Josh and Lisa away with a shotgun. Mick knew something was terribly wrong, and he backed off. I know now that he was trying to protect himself. Bijou was militant about rehab. She'd say, "I know you're using. Show me your arms."

I just said, "I'm not going to dignify that request." I tried to convince everyone that though I wasn't sober, I wasn't doing anything bad. I know Shane, more than anyone, wanted to believe that I was okay, but to look at me was to know that I was in bad shape. I could feel the walls—the family—closing in on me. I tried to go cold turkey more than once, but it never worked. I got so sick that I started using again. I was lost. I didn't know what the fuck to do. I hoped I'd stay alive long enough to change, but I couldn't imagine how it would happen. It seemed too complicated. It was easier to do nothing.

Waking up in the morning, barely able to walk because I needed to be high. Thinking, *Oh my God, I am so fucked.* Creaking out of bed: *This is bad, I'm dying, why am I doing this, what is the matter with me?* Making my way to the chair, because the only way to rid myself of the self-loathing and fear was to do a shot, but this, I promised myself, would be the last shot, the one that would make me feel better enough to change, to fix everything, to stop. Doing the shot: *I'm so fucked, I'm so fucked,* then the drug hit my bloodstream and . . . *Oh, it's not so bad. I'm not that fucked. It's going to be okay.*

The needle keeps the demons at bay. You want to function? If your body is addicted to drugs, the easiest, best way to function, the only way you can see to get through the day, is to never come down. And there is no way to be objective, to decide that suffering withdrawal, the physical and mental illness of withdrawal, is better than being hooked for life. Because when you're in that scene, there is no objectivity.

The fun part was over, because it never lasts, because there is no fair battle between reality and the drugs that enhance it. Drugs always win. They beat me, as they had before, and the spoils they claimed were my will, my spirit, my values, my valuables, my relationships, my safety, my body and soul, and, almost, my life.

• • •

Salvation came in the form of my worst nightmare come true. It started with something harmless: a request to tape the Rachael Ray show that would air on September 10, 2008. Apparently, *One Day at a Time* was Rachael Ray's favorite show. For her fortieth birthday the cast of *One Day at a Time* was going to surprise her, appearing on a re-creation of the show's set. All my former costars were going, and I didn't want to miss it.

In the couple of years I'd been shooting up, I'd had many appearances that required me to be on TV, traveling from here to there. A year earlier I'd appeared on the *Today* show for a *One Day at a Time* reunion celebrating the publication of Val's book. I flew to New York with my two-day supply of drugs without incident. Making it to the airport in time for the plane was a challenge, but otherwise, being a jet-setting junkie wasn't a big deal. I always brought my drugs and my needles, did the show, and came back home without incident. When I agreed to appear on Rachael Ray, I truly didn't see any risk.

The day before the trip, I was in my room, trying to figure out what to wear on the air. Josh came upstairs and into my room with a little package for me. It had four grams of cocaine and one and a half grams of heroin. He said, "Look, Laura, make sure you take the foil off the heroin. It won't set off the alarm, but if you get wanded they'll find it."

My flight was early the next morning and I was running late, as always. I did a little of Josh's package while the limo waited out front. Then I stuffed the rest of the drugs in the pocket of my pants. I was wearing an amazing new pair of pants. They were cotton pants with a beautiful dragon embroidered on one leg. The other leg had a cargo pocket with a buckle. I put some cash in the pocket along with the drugs and hurried into the car.

On the way to LAX I was on the phone with a guy at the Rachael Ray show, doing a standard pre-interview to give them an idea of what sort of stuff I might talk about the next day. He said, "Thanks, Mackenzie, this is going to be great," and we hung up. I chatted and joked with the limo driver, and we soon arrived at the airport.

At the airport, I checked my bag and got in line for security. I made a couple phone calls and chatted with the people next to me in line. Then I went through the metal detector and it beeped. I said, "I don't have anything in my pockets." I knew the foil—which, contrary to Josh's instructions, I'd left wrapped around the heroin—wouldn't set off the metal detector. I didn't think of the metal buckle on my cargo pants. The security monitor asked me to go through again. The alarm went off again.

The guard waved me into the corral for people who were going to get wanded. I stood there thinking, *Wow, I'm really in trouble here. Fuck.* I put my hand in the pocket and felt the bag of drugs. A tiny bag of destruction. I turned the bag over in my fingers. The package was so small, so seemingly harmless. It wasn't a gun. It wasn't intended to harm anyone. But this was it. This was going to be my downfall. This small bag that I needed to live.

Glancing around nervously, I slipped the cash and the drugs out of the pocket. I put the cash back in and put the drugs in my waistband, senselessly, hopelessly.

A female security guard gestured me forward. I stood rigid and silent on the footprint marks on the floor. For all the horror I had created in my life, this was the nightmare that I feared more than anything. I knew what getting caught meant. I'd seen it happen to my father. It changed everything, and I didn't think I wanted anything to change. But time was marching forward. The next sequence of events had been planned and executed a million times, all over the world, a routine as familiar as setting a mouse trap, catching the mouse, disposing of it. A small, unpleasant task, memorable but not significant. Unless you're the mouse. And now I was the mouse.

As the wand passed over my underwear, it beeped. I had

no plan. I couldn't think. I said, "I have a buckle on my underwear." It was obviously a lie.

The security guard said, "I have to do my job."

I panicked. I was beyond panicked. I lost it. I started saying, "Please don't bust me. Please don't bust me. I'm someone's mother. My son doesn't know." I was quietly begging. Begging, I thought, for my life.

She said, "I'm sorry, Ms. Phillips. Please go over there and sit down." She waved me toward the chair where you're supposed to take off your shoes. I took a few steps in that direction and was standing in front of the chair when I felt the package drop from the band of my underwear down through my pants leg. It landed on the floor. I put my foot on it. Now I was stuck. I couldn't walk away and leave the drugs on the floor. How in hell was I going to get out of this without being taken away in handcuffs?

The nice security people had receded, back to their task of separating the criminals from the travelers. In their place stepped six cops, including a giant woman. She got in my face, yelling, "You're gonna get honest with us. Are you holding? Are you gonna tell us the truth?"

The giant woman ordered me to sit down. I was terrified. Without lifting my foot off the drugs, I turned and sat. The woman pointed to my foot. The corner of the package was sticking out. There, for anyone to see, was a bag of cocaine. It was time to face reality.

"Yeah, yeah, I'm holding," I said. I cannot express the deep fear and dread that I felt. I was powerless, about to be shuttled through the system like the criminal that I was. But it was hard to feel like a criminal when I only did drugs in the privacy of my bedroom. When—in my selfish view—the only person I was actively destroying was myself. "Please, please, please don't arrest me."

The overprivileged celebrity brat in me hoped I would get away with it. One time when Tatum O'Neal and I were coming home from a party, she was driving behind me on the Pacific Coast Highway at four in the morning. I got pulled over, and Tatum pulled up behind me. The cop informed me that I had been driving too slowly. I had a two-gram vial of coke burning a hole in my jeans pocket.

I said, "I'm sorry, Officer. I'm on my way to Tatum's house. She's in the car behind me."

It was not long after I'd been arrested with enough Quaaludes in my system to "kill a horse." He glanced back at her car and said, "You've had enough trouble. I'm not going to add to it. Go a little faster, but not too fast." I must have been let off the hook like that at least a dozen times in my youth. I drove without a driver's license for ten years. With the exception of that one infamous arrest, the cops always just told me to go home.

When I was an adult, on tour with the Mamas & the Papas, I was stopped by U.S. Customs in Amsterdam. They were going through our stuff when a young customs officer unzipped my Carlos Falchi phone book and pulled out a block of hash the size of a cookie. He looked at me, then down at the hash. He slid it back in, zipped my book shut, and sent me on my way.

After all those free passes, all those blind eyes, I felt immune, and part of me still believed that I could get out of anything, that if I was just polite and friendly enough, they would let me go. But at LAX that late summer day, I'd finally stepped over the line.

The giant woman cop stooped down to pick up the bag of drugs. She said, "We're not going to arrest you. We just want to talk to you." She walked me over to another cop. This one—a Latin-American woman—had a sweet, warm manner. She said, "I'm really sorry, Ms. Phillips. You have the right to remain silent." She cuffed me behind my back.

Busted.

• • •

As they drove me to the airport police lockup, as they moved me to a police station they called Prospect for processing, as they locked my handcuffs to a bench, as the passing cops stared at me, as my kind cops decided to take me to a farther, safer police station, one close to my house, as we sat jammed in bumper-to-bumper traffic, I just kept weeping: "Shane, Shane, Shane, I'm sorry, Shane."

The drive took forever as the cops tried to find a jail for me. I'd been crying in the back of the police car, crying for what seemed like hours, getting sicker by the minute as the drugs left my system, when I looked over at the Latin-American woman cop. She had tears in her eyes. Finally, when we checked into the Van Nuys station, the cops who had escorted me on that long ride from the airport were ready to leave. The woman cop came to my cell and said, "I want to thank you for being respectful and cooperative." I said, "Thank you for being so kind."

At the Van Nuys police station they strip-searched me. I had hidden my arms from everyone except Wyatt for two years. I never descended the stairs of my house wearing anything less than full-length sleeves. There were open sores all over my forearms, bug sores from picking at the coke bugs I hallucinated crawling on me—junkie pox, we call them. There were black dead veins on each arm.

As instructed, I took off every article of clothing, turned around, and spread my cheeks in front of two female cops. I said, "Please don't look at my arms."

The cops didn't respond to that. One of them just said, "Sweetie, I've been watching you for years. You're going to be okay. I'm going to make sure you're safe and nobody's going to bother you."

As a cop was photographing the evidence—my drugs—he told me, "You're number two on TMZ. Dr. Dre beat you out." Someone had alerted the tabloids. The news was out. There were fifty photographers waiting outside the jail. That morning

I had woken up in my bed. I was on my way to surprise Rachael Ray. Now I was in police custody facing drug charges and a media storm. I worried that Shane would find out where I was and what had happened through the press. I thought about Bonnie, Val, and Pat, in New York for what was supposed to be a fun reunion, having to deal with another mess that Mack had made. Twenty-five years later and I was putting them in the exact same position. The cop swiveled his computer to show me the TMZ website. There it was, "Mackenzie Phillips Busted." Above it I saw the top story. Dr. Dre's son had died. A father was suffering, I was sure. I looked away from the computer screen.

Now I was in custody. The handcuffs came off and I was led to a cell. In it there was a Naugahyde cot with a plastic pillow. Beside it, a toilet with no lid. And there were bars. It crossed my mind that this would make a good jail set. And then it crossed my mind that any jail would probably make a good jail set. But this wasn't a set and I wasn't acting. I was actually behind bars. And if I still doubted it—or maybe it enhanced the feeling of playacting—I was soon offered the standard phone call, the chance to get a family member or friend to come pay my bail. I declined. This was really happening, and it would be my undoing. I hoped I would die that day and never have to see anybody ever again.

A few hours later a cop came to my cell and said, "Ms. Phillips, someone's here to see you."

I was led to a room with a glass booth and a phone or speaker. Bijou was there, looking spectacularly Bijou. Her perfect blond ringlets were up in a clip. She wore a yellow tank top and blue jeans. She was like a ray of sun shining into a cave. Bijou saw that I was holding a carton of milk and a burrito and said, "Look at your jail food!" Then she observed, "Mack, you're in jail."

I shook my burrito at her. "I know!"

She said, "You have to go to rehab."

I said, "You can't manipulate me! Fuck you!" I couldn't conceive of the future. I was starting to get sick and in that moment all I knew was that I needed to get out of there and I needed drugs. I shook my burrito at her again. "You can't make me go to rehab!" If she wanted me to promise to go to rehab, well, I guessed I would just stay right where I was.

I went back to my cell and fell asleep. The next day when Bijou came back to see me, all my cockiness and burrito shaking were gone. I staggered out to the visiting room. Withdrawal was kicking in and it was brutal. Bijou started weeping. I leaned on the counter and groaned, "Fuck you."

Bijou said, "I can't take this anymore. I'm bailing you out. Shane says I'm weak and I should leave you in jail, but I'm bailing you out. You have to go to Narconon." She had flown in the director of Narconon Louisiana. He was waiting with Owen in the car outside—Owen, who for the last several years had felt me disappearing and known that I was suffering, but who had always believed me and insisted to my family that I wasn't messed up, I wasn't this, I wasn't that. She thinks she was naive, but I think she wanted to believe the good. Owen is the best friend a girl could ask for. She loved me no matter what. I didn't purposely play on her naïveté, but my priorities were screwed-up enough that I let her defend my lies.

Now that I was so sick, leaving with Bijou and Owen seemed like my best option. There were drugs in my house that would make me better. I said, "Fine, I'll come, but I want to go home and see my dogs before I go away." I had to get to my drugs, and I didn't care if the director of Narconon had to wait while I did them. He was welcome to sleep on my couch.

Slipping past the cameramen yelling "Mackenzie, Mackenzie," I ducked into the car with Owen, Bijou, and the Narconon guy. Three short miles and I was home. I went to the back of the house and crawled into Josh and Lisa's bed as if they were my parents, the ones who would protect me and keep me safe.

As soon as I told Josh what had happened, he started collecting all the drugs that were in the house and throwing them into his briefcase.

I said, "You've got to get me some cocaine and some heroin right now."

He said, "You've got to go to rehab." I knew he was right, and I was going, but not yet. I needed one more shot. Josh took his briefcase, full of drugs, and carried it out to his car. Then he came back into the house, past the Narconon director, past Bijou, her assistant, and Owen. He walked into the bedroom and gave me a bag of coke. He refused to give me heroin. The bad day was about to get worse.

I went upstairs to my bathroom and shot up until the bag was empty, but I wasn't high enough. I went downstairs, ignoring the growing retinue of people in the living room, to get more coke. Back and forth I went, every twenty minutes, getting another last bag of coke from Josh and bringing it up to the safety of my bathroom. I had just been arrested for carrying drugs, and now I was bingeing while my loved ones waited for me to agree to go to rehab.

Finally, I came out of my bathroom to find that everyone had assembled in my bedroom. In addition to Bijou, Owen, and Jeff Lukas from Narconon, there was now Lee, my friend Grainger—a family friend who has a child with Michelle—and Shane, my Shane, holding a bouquet of tuberoses, my favorite flowers.

They said, "It's time to go, Mack." Bijou had gotten us a flight leaving that day.

I said, "Fine. Let's go. Right now." I knew it was over. I was going to rehab. But still, even then, I wanted to do as much coke as I could before I left. Like having a sundae before starting a diet. But much worse.

So although I said "Right now," I had a different definition of that than a sober person. I had run out of syringes upstairs, so I excused myself and went downstairs to get some of my diabetic dog's syringes. I went into the kitchen and rifled through the drawer where I kept his supplies. I grabbed a ten-pack of dog syringes, then turned to see my son standing there looking at me. Shane.

I put the syringes back, closed the drawer, and said, "Okay, let's go."

32

One of the first letters I wrote from Narconon was to Patricia Palmer, the onetime executive producer of *One Day at a Time*. She was the one who had woken me up and told me they wanted to do a urine test. And she was the one who had fired me from the show for the last time. Patricia had sent a note to my house in L.A. saying, "I'm sending you a big hug. Can you feel it?" Now I wrote back to her. I asked her to tell Bonnie, Val, and Pat Harrington that I knew I had put them in an uncomfortable position . . . once again. I asked her to apologize on my behalf and to let them know that I was working hard to change my life.

A reply came sooner than I expected. Patricia wrote something like, "I remember watching you wait for your dad to come to the show. I understood your need to be with him and to have his approval. When I lost my father it was difficult for me and I turned to what I know—hard work and doing what's expected. You did exactly the same thing. You turned to what you know."

Afterward, I heard from Pat Harrington, and Bonnie sent me a funny picture of the two of us from some event for TV moms and the people who played their kids. In the shot it looked like we were kissing on the lips. She wrote, "Thought you'd enjoy seeing our lesbian love kiss. Ha, ha. Love, Bonnie." I didn't hear from Val, but I understood. I know her. After my arrest, the press had swarmed around these people, unpleasantly, I suspect, but all their words were full of unwavering love and support. Valerie said, "We love Mack. She's a light. We just love her." I know, no matter how much time passes before we speak again, that she feels that way. If I was the black sheep of that otherwise functional family, they never stopped loving me and hoping I would come back to the fold.

I threw myself into rehabilitation with the same zeal I had had for shooting cocaine. The Lodge believed in stripping you down to worthlessness and then rebuilding your ego. Various rehab programs I had done always taught that I was powerless over drugs and alcohol. I know these approaches work for many addicts—they worked for me for years—but ultimately they were almost an excuse not to fight so hard. Narconon had a different philosophy. It was a simple, practical, unemotional approach to healing and growing. Instead of relinquishing my power, I now reclaimed my will, I fed and nurtured it, I decided to rely on it. If my father had left me with unanswered questions. I would find the answers within myself. At Narconon I learned to use my own strength to make good choices.

It's not that I don't believe in God, but there are a million ways to get to the top of the mountain. Yes, there is a higher power. Yes, I pray for help. But for me, succumbing to powerlessness means behaving instinctively, and if I followed my instincts then every time I encountered difficulty in my life, I'd get high.

Alina Lodge saved my life, no question, but there were issues left unresolved. Maybe that's always true—once you're formed, there are some fundamental elements you can never reshape—but the fact stood that I had relapsed, so by definition it wasn't a real recovery. Certainly my complacency was in part to blame, but maybe what I'd also gotten wrong was that I couldn't throw away who I was to be clean. It sounds corny, but what I realized at Narconon was that I could still be my quirky left-of-center self without doing drugs.

It wasn't just my cowboy boots and my tight jeans that I'd

left behind at the Lodge. The real problem was that being the Superwoman I learned to be in sobriety didn't leave room for me to be as adrift and lost as I was when my father died. I wasn't prepared when the monster stirred.

There wasn't one single reason that I relapsed. Would my father's death alone have awakened the monster? Did I seek out cosmetic surgery to dull the pain of losing him? Or was it a perfect storm of prescription pain medications and a hard emotional time? All I know is that I needed to find my way away from the drugs, this time without feeling like I was trying to be someone I was not.

At Narconon I was allowed to listen to my iPod. During breaks and free time I plugged myself in to Shane's music. My friend Lee likes to say that Shane got all the talent of my father without the darkness. He is a brilliant singer, songwriter, and musician. Shane has recorded a couple hundred songs with his father. When I listened to his sweet voice it gave me strength to know that I was on the path—home to my son.

After three months at Narconon, Shane picked me up from the airport. He had moved back home to take care of his mother. He brought me back to my house, to the scene of my downfall. Josh and Lisa were gone. While I was at Narconon, with my court date looming, I'd been terrified that the court would discover that drug dealers were still in my house. I tried to impress this upon Josh and Lisa. If they didn't leave, I risked losing everything. They were still in their mellow heroin scene—they just thought I was being mean and cruel. I loved them, but I wasn't prepared to sacrifice my whole world for their convenience. It took awhile to convince them I was serious—I was on probation and wouldn't set foot in my own house while they were still there—but they finally found an apartment on the beach and moved out.

I was home. I was clean. The monster was dormant, comatose, and I was safe, but never again complacent. I knew, intellectually, that this was good. I wasn't scared, as I had been coming out of Alina Lodge. I had confronted my past in a whole new way, and I no longer had to ignore the video loop of times past. It had no power over me anymore. But I still felt tentative, as if a blindfold that had long been on my eyes had been removed and, eager as I was to see again, the sun was too bright and the assault of color and movement—and life!—was overwhelming. The challenge was not how to get through each day without drugs. The challenge was how to live. I didn't emerge from so many years of active addiction and drug abuse without some battle scars: The old habits of a drug-warped lifestyle. The dysfunctional personality that led me to do drugs in the first place. And a pair of scarred, pocked forearms I still went to great lengths to hide from everyone.

It may sound melodramatic, but from where I stood, the world as it was seemed complicated. People, dogs, cleaning the house, doing laundry. Little things felt big. A junkie scrapes by, exerting the least possible amount of effort. After so many years of that life, of going to bed at four in the morning one day and starting your day at four in the morning the next, it's hard to adjust. Eliminating drugs doesn't change that you were that person, living that life. Nothing changes overnight. For a while it feels strange to just be alive.

Bijou and Owen had cleared all the old needles out of my bedroom and bathroom (the last "bad trash"). And Shane had tried to clean up. But in the months I was away my once clean house had fallen into disrepair. I had to face the bedroom that had become my shooting gallery, the garage that was crowded with Josh and Lisa's abandoned boxes, the driveway that held their broken-down car. The garden was overgrown. The pool needed repair. There were dishes in the sink. There was dog shit and trash everywhere. My house was destroyed. And the damage wasn't just superficial. Poor Max, my beloved but diabetic and very high-maintenance pug, was half dead.

Ten days after I came home from rehab was Christmas Eve. Bijou wanted the whole family together, and Bijou is a force, so all five kids—Jeffrey, me, Chynna, Tamerlane, and Bijou—gathered with husbands and wives and children and significant others at Bijou and her boyfriend Danny's house. It was the first time in I don't know how long that all five kids were together. The next day, Christmas Day, we all met at a Chinese restaurant in West L.A. and all three moms—my mother, Michelle, and Genevieve—were together with their families.

I can't think of a better way to come home from rehab. I was met by nothing but love and support. A chorus of voices saying, "We're so proud of you, you look amazing, we love you."

It was also my chance to apologize. When I was a young addict, I did whatever it took to get drugs. I lied to people. I was late. I was manipulative and self-righteous. When I relapsed, I tried not to hurt anyone. My father took others down with him—wives, girlfriends, me. I didn't want to do that. Instead, I withdrew. I barely left the house.

But now, in daylight, I saw the pain I'd caused. There were the castmates I'd let down by getting arrested when I should have been taping the Rachael Ray show with them.

There was my mother. On top of worrying about me, the publicity surrounding my arrest had been hard on her. The news spread through her assisted living community like wildfire, and my poor mother locked herself in her apartment for a couple days to avoid the stares and whispers.

There was the rest of my family, all of whom had been profoundly worried about me. At some point Bijou had said to Danny, "My sister's gonna die and I'm going to flip out. Don't touch me, don't tell me everything's going to be okay, because it won't be okay. Just leave me alone. Don't try to comfort me. I'm not going to be okay." To have someone I love so much tell me she was expecting me to die was a strange and painful thing to hear. As I said, when I was arrested, I didn't *feel* like a criminal because my crime was committed in the privacy of my own bedroom, but if crime is inflicting pain and suffering on others, then I was guilty. I had hurt the people who mattered most.

Most of all there was Shane, who deserved a sane, constant mother, and who had faced my very public arrest, though when I asked if he'd been embarrassed in front of his friends, he dismissed me, saying, "My friends are your friends. They love you."

My father damaged the people around him. He failed to see how all our lives were entwined. My father, my mother, Jeffrey, me, Michelle, Chynna, Genevieve, Tam, Bijou, Cass, Owen, Denny, Spanky, Rosie, Nancy, Patty, Sue, and on and on. Lives are connected, and we cause one another joy and pain. We love one another. We carry one another. We create and destroy one another. Drugs manipulate these relationships. The actions of someone whose life is drugs aren't a fair portrait of who she is and how she intends to treat those most important to her. That is why I try to let go of anger, bitterness, spite, grudges—these distance us from the people we love. I forgave my father, and now it was my turn to ask for forgiveness.

That Christmas I saw that the relief of having me back was greater than the pain of enduring my behavior. What could be a stronger force to keep me clean? And it was Christmas. I sat back and looked around me. There were candles everywhere, beautiful food, and a Christmas tree with tons of presents under it. Chynna sang songs from her soon-to-be-released Christian album. Shane played guitar and sang for everyone. The whole family jammed together. All those years of hosting Christmas were behind me. Bijou had found her path. She had turned from a wild child into one of the most stable people I know. She would soon get engaged. It was time to pass the torch.

My relationship with Wyatt died a quiet death. We were both clean, but we lived far away from each other and had no time or place to remeet and rediscover each other as clean companions. I still love him, because I never stop, but it was over.

As my drug-free days added up, I started to notice something. The drugs had left my system, but with them, amazingly, miraculously, unbelievably, had gone the physical pain. The racking, constant pain that had thrust me toward painkillers as a means of survival. Now I could jump out of bed, chase the dogs around the house, dance for hours on end. Shane said, "The fact that you don't have physical pain astounds me." He reminded me that just moving used to make me cry out in pain. He used to have to help me get up. He said, "How did you manifest this miracle?"

But was it a miracle? Or did I create the pain in order to justify my behavior? Was I that mentally fucked up? Or was it a sorry, sad coping mechanism? I don't know. All I know is that I am now drug free and pain free, and I am certain that there was a correlation between my addiction and my pain.

Several months after I came home, I got a call from a pharmacy. The guy on the phone told me it was time to refill my prescription for Soma, a muscle relaxant I had abused. I said, "Please take me off your list. I don't take medication of any kind."

The pharmacy rep said, "You have to refill. If you don't refill I'll be fired."

I was surprised to hear such a forceful sales pitch for a prescription medication. I said, "I'm sorry, but I'm not going to refill my prescription."

He said, "Please. Just thirty pills. I'll lose my job! I have a family to support." Now I was getting pissed. Who was this guy, the devil?

I said, "Leave me alone. If I take those drugs I'll die."

He said, "If you don't take them, I'll die!" And that's when I hung up. If this was the job he was hired to do, then I didn't care if he was fired.

When I was a young addict, I had lived in squalor. But during my relapse, when I was getting high as an adult, my house was spotless. Cocaine makes you clean obsessively. I had so much energy that I'd do the floors in my room every day. I ran loads of laundry ceaselessly. Now that I was clean, I didn't have that kind of energy anymore, but I still had dear Max, a sick, blind, and often-incontinent dog. The thought of my increasingly filthy bedroom weighed on me, the daunting reminder that I didn't have it together, that chaos was encroaching, that I might not ever manage to clean that goddamn room. But one day I just did it. I woke up in the morning, went out, and bought cleaning supplies. I vacuumed and mopped the floors. I scrubbed the bathroom on my hands and knees. I swept out the laundry room and cleaned the kitchen. Such a simple day, a small accomplishment, but once it was done, I felt much better. It was only a step, but every decision in the direction of the rest of my life made me feel stronger. My life skills were starting to reemerge.

Now I was ready, but for what? My life on drugs had a built-in purpose: to do more drugs. Now the holes in my life made themselves apparent. My bank account was drained from the drugs, the rehab, the lawyer. My relationships were damaged. My father was gone. I had dug a huge, deep ditch and it was going to take several years to get out of it.

• • •

I'm nearly fifty. I'm watching my son become a man. And for the first time I'm starting to see that the old ideas I have about myself don't have to be true forever. I thought I couldn't clean my house. I thought I couldn't drive a stick shift. I thought I would always carry the ghost of my father on my back. I thought I could never stay clean.

And so it is that I'm getting back into the swing. When I first got home from Narconon, every morning I woke up and thought, *Oh, man, this is hard.* Now when I wake up, I pause, expecting to feel the weight of the day descend on me, but it doesn't. Relieved, I stand up, relishing my newfound lightness. I feed the dogs, I make my coffee, I sing bits of the Neil Young song "Old Man": "Old man look at my life / I'm a lot like you were." I'm back to being the mom who takes care of the house. I cook for my son; he cooks for me.

My support comes from friends and family: Owen, Lee, Shane, my mother, my brothers and sisters, my friends from Narconon. I attend an ongoing recovery program. My spiritual practice reaffirms everything that I know about myself.

I visit my mother once a week in assisted living. When she left her three-bedroom house in the Valley and moved to a one-bedroom apartment, she brought her house-size collection of holiday decorations with her. As every holiday passes we put up and take down the appropriate ornaments: the candles, cupids, Easter egg tree, fake mini-Christmas trees, Santas. And nearly every time I visit she has inadvertently managed to switch her TV to closed-caption subtitles, with no volume. I fix it for her, then we go down to the dining room, sit with her lady friends, order dinner, hang out, and laugh. It was unexpectedly hard on her when I was away at Narconon, so now we both slow down to enjoy our time together as mother and daughter.

Through all the years and both our struggles, my mother never stopped being my mother. We were so close, always, no matter what, but once she stopped drinking, our relationship reverted to what it was meant to be. Through my years of recovery and abstinence, though my raising Shane, she was a constant, beloved presence, a wacky, perfect grandma who picked Shane up at school and took him to McDonald's. Now, as she ages, our roles are reversed and in many ways I'm a support for her. But at the same time I need her. My mom's belief in me helps me believe in myself.

Work is slow—and by slow I mean nonexistent. I'm not surprised. This isn't my first rodeo, and I'm all too aware that getting busted at LAX isn't exactly a résumé-builder. People need to get used to me, to see me doing well, to learn to trust me again. It takes time. I can't force it. I can only make an example of myself—to myself and to other people. I try to be a force for good. Maybe not on a daily basis, but in how I conduct myself and what I do.

I'm clean and it shows. The other day I was in a phone store buying a new cell phone charger when a woman came up to me. I hadn't seen her since back in the days of Rodney Bingenheimer's when I was fourteen. She'd borrowed my platform boots one day and returned them a year later. As we spoke in the phone store she told me that she was sober and asked how I was doing. I said, "I'm ten months back." She looked me right in the eye and said, "I can tell that you're done."

I appeared on the reality show *Celebrity Rehab,* and a psychic came to talk to the group. She took one look at me and said, "You—of all the people here—you're finished with drugs."

At Bijou's Christmas Eve bash I saw my longtime friend Courtney. She said, "I've never seen someone ten days out of rehab so composed, so clearly on a path that works." Shane has told me more than once, "It's so great to have you back. Your body and your mind are here with me." I know what is in my heart and mind, but it is comforting and affirming to hear it from both new people and people who've known me forever.

I don't look like a boy anymore. I was a skinny, cadaverous creature for so long, and whenever I gained weight and started to feel like a woman, I panicked. I was so focused on size zero. But I'm a grown woman, and I've started to feel comfortable having a woman's body. Many years ago I wrote,

There is a woman
She lives inside of me
Although I love the child I be
There is a woman who lives inside of me

I saw myself as a child, not a fully formed being. But I finally feel formed. Not complete, maybe never complete, but formed. I am at home in my body for the first time, loving to be the woman that I am.

Because the jobs aren't exactly rolling in these days, I spend a lot of time sitting on my front porch. I love my neighborhood and my neighbors—the people from the veterinary clinic who walk this route with their patients, the toddler next door who likes to visit my dogs, my sober friend who has two pugs. I chat with all who pass—isn't that what front porches are for? And when the street is quiet I can sit for hours out there, watching the familiar, changing world.

I don't feel like an addict. I don't fight an urge to use drugs. My monster is a quiet sleeper. But I don't ever forget who I am. As for what will become of me, well, my needs are simple. I am and always will be Shane's parent, and that is all I really want. To be a good mother and sister and friend. To live in my house, stay drug-free, take care of my family, my dogs, myself. To work in my chosen profession. To be humble and happy in the precious life I nearly lost so many times. I am amazed to be alive, and I am wildly in love with this great life.

AFTERWORD

MACK

My earliest memory is of my father. I was wearing a diaper and nothing else. My dad motioned to me. I wobbled over to him and he put a daisy in my belly button. Later, when I was about four years old, I was on a private plane with the Mamas & the Papas and, at my father's behest, the pilot did a nosedive that made us all go weightless. Everyone else was strapped in, but I was on my dad's lap. For maybe half a minute I floated in the air while the Mamas & the Papas tossed me back and forth. I wish all the subsequent memories were innocent flower-child bucolics.

If my father set out to raise a drug addict, he did everything right. He modeled the behavior; he introduced and encouraged drugs; he was unavailable and then abusive. He was a friend but not a father. He was compelling but not safe.

I was desperate to be close to my father, and that informed everything I did. Everything. When you want someone to love you badly enough, you do what he does, you say what he says. You imitate to flatter. For instance: I have never, ever heard my son swear. I'm sure he does swear around his friends, and I've been cursing around my kid for as long as I can remember. But when I asked him, "Why have I never heard you say the word 'fuck'?" he said, "I'm just not a swearing-in-front-of-the-parents kind of guy." Shane doesn't imitate me. He's not trying to be close to me, because he already is. He can have me for anything, for whatever he needs: emotional support, advice, affection. He knows he doesn't have to do anything to get me. I'm there. I didn't feel that way about my father.

When I look back on it, I see that the hero worship I had for my father led to the incest, and that the incest went hand in hand with the drug-induced oblivion that helped me survive it. My father was responsible for his behavior, but I don't want him reviled for it. It has passed. I'm still here, and I'm a good parent and friend, sister and daughter. I see myself as blessed and lucky, not just by virtue of still being alive, but because of all the good and bad that has shaped me. I have to work to steer clear of anesthetizing my pain, but alongside and in spite of that pain I am hardwired to love the life I was given and the one I am still creating.

It was, as I've said, a hard decision to reveal the sordid side of my relationship with my father. But these are the complex, painful, heart-wrenching truths that infiltrate lives, many lives, not just mine. I can't be the only one. And I needed to tell that part of the story because I wanted to earn the right to talk about forgiveness.

That moment I had in the hospital at my father's deathbed, the moment when I forgave him, was one of the most important moments of my life. Although I went on to relapse, I firmly believe that if I hadn't had that opportunity, I might not have made it. Fathers die, usually before their children. It can be hard to forgive, because along with sexual abuse come other abuses—physical, emotional. Sometimes stuff can't be forgiven. But what I found was that without forgiveness you end up in the same cage you were in when you were suffering the abuse. I didn't forgive my father for his benefit, although I know it brought him comfort. I did it because it was genuine. But I also did it because he was dying and if we had never spoken of it again, it would have been almost impossible for me to put it to rest. That is what I want to say to those who relate to my experience: Forgiveness is not to give the other person peace. Forgiveness is for you. Take the opportunity.

When Dad died I thought that was it. I was free. I thought his death would be the changing force. At last my life would blossom and change. What I see clearly now is that it wasn't my father's existence that kept me stuck. It was me and how I dealt with what came up in my life. The letter Patricia Palmer wrote reminded me that when my father died I went to what I knew: self-destruction. But it's not like I thought, *Oh, I'm self-destructing.* It took years to realize that my way of dealing with life was going to kill me. I wasn't free. I was still trapped in me. I wish I'd learned that before he passed away.

When I was still adjusting my eyes to the real world, I went to San Francisco to see a movie of Bijou's, *Wake,* premiere at the Cinequest Film Festival in San Jose. I stayed at my brother Jeffrey's house, with him, his wife, and their cute dogs and kids.

Jeffrey was such a fuckup as a kid. He was constantly getting into trouble. But he has made a good life for himself. His wife, Gail, works on the cutting edge of breast cancer research. They now have three kids and a beautiful home in San Carlos. He meditates six hours a day. I'm not being cruel when I say that you never would have expected that from the Jeffrey I knew and loved as a child. He doesn't speak much about those years we spent with Dad. They were painful for him. But Jeffrey is proof and reminder that the past is over and that we can all rise above it.

My relationship with my brother had been strained during my relapse. We hadn't spent any time alone together since I'd been arrested. Now we took the time to sit and talk, to meditate together. It was nice. We were everything to each other growing up. We're both middle-aged now. I wasn't afraid to look right at him, right into his eyes. I wasn't hiding anything anymore.

My brother Tam said that if he had been publicly humiliated as I was at my arrest, he would never leave his apartment again. It's true that at first I thought, *There's no way I can come back from this. I could be going to jail. How am I going to do this?*

How am I going to face people on the street? You just do it. If you have a sense of humor about it, you can make other people laugh about it too. I feel brave about going out into the world and owning who I am. If I let the past define me, I would live in shame and regret. Instead, like my brother Jeffrey, I live in what is happening. I'm finally free of the negative effects of my past.

Telling all of this, out loud, in print, for the public, makes it real and permanent. Admissions and anecdotes, apologies and explanations, love and forgiveness. I'm not the feel-no-evil monkey. I'm not boxing anything away. I've filled in the gaps between the harsh lines of the index someone might make of my life so far. And somewhere along the way, I started thinking about the people in a dark room with a needle and a spoon, about a world full of people who have been sexually abused, who have had things done to them and who have done things that they regret. We are a huge community. I can't fix anyone else, but I can say, *I've been there. I get it. You're not alone. There's more, and there's reason to fight for it.*

The biggest reason I have is my son, Shane. I know Shane won't live with me forever. He came home for me, not for him, and soon he will leave to live his life. Shane and I laugh, wondering how many moms know every word to every Nine Inch Nails song, how many would go to a Slipknot concert and jump into the mosh pit with their sons. I'm glad that Shane and I can be idiots together, and my gratitude for the care and company he gives me without reservation is beyond words. But I am absolutely not just his friend. He has plenty of friends. And I don't want him to take care of me—at least not until I'm old and helpless. I am his mother and I want that to be our dynamic, even as he builds his own separate life.

Anything can happen, but at this writing Shane is twenty-two and the genetic proclivity for addiction seems to have skipped a generation. Besides, Shane tends to face things head-on. He doesn't hide from reality as I did. We are different, and I know he'll handle life's vicissitudes in his own way. I regret much of what he witnessed, but Shane does have a healthy fear of the monster that may sleep within him. Moreover, I have great faith in his strength and wisdom. I hope and believe he will steer clear of drugs forever.

My dear pug, Max, didn't have a long life. He was sick for years, and we finally had to put him down. I thought that Shane would be stoic about Max. He was so practical, saying, "The time is right. It needs to be done." I left the vet's office before they did the deed—I couldn't bear to watch Max go—and Shane stayed to be with him, along with Lee, my ex-boyfriend who remained a close friend, caring for Max and Freddie as if they were his own. When Shane came out of the vet's office his eyes were bright red. He was weeping. In a way I was glad to see it, only because it meant that he wasn't so busy trying to protect me that he didn't let himself be vulnerable.

Shane said, "Mom, you really need to come see him." So the two of us went back into the clinic. Shane and I sat with Max's body for a while. My son put his hand on Max's head and said, "I'm sorry, little boy. I didn't like you, but I really loved you."

I looked down at old Max. He wasn't in that broken body anymore. Maybe he was hanging out with my father somewhere. Maybe he'd bite old Dad on the shin for me.

After we said good-bye to Max, I told Shane a story about how when he was little, his hermit crabs died, and he had such a hard time letting go that he kept them in a Ziploc bag in the kitchen for three years. Shane laughed when I told that story. He put his arms around me and said, "Mom, we're going to be okay."

I grew up in a kind of dark fairy tale. I lived in a mansion. I was in movies and on television. My father was a rock star. I lived out other people's dreams. Maybe that's why it feels like it all happened to someone else, like there's a fog of unreality between what I lived and who I am. Or maybe that's the merciful lobotomy of years of drug use. Either way, only now do I feel like I'm a real person. There are psychological clichés that I've collected over the years: We're the product of our environment. We're the sum of our experiences. We need to live in the present. Those concepts accumulated in my head, but saying them and believing they should be true for me didn't make them a reality in my life. My description of my own healthy psyche has been around for years. At last I'm living the health and happiness that I always described but never experienced. I'm living my life instead of watching it happen. I'm free.

ACKNOWLEDGMENTS

As you can imagine, with a story like mine there are tons of people to thank. It hasn't been easy for any of us, but we made it through. I want to acknowledge the many people whose love and support over the years have helped make it possible for me to write this book.

I know this book reveals truths that any family would find difficult to have revealed publicly, and mine is no exception. I hope and pray for their tolerance, understanding, and willingness to support me as a sister, friend, mother, and daughter. Above all, I want to thank my amazing son, Shane Barakan. Son—you are the light of my life and I love you so much. I can't think of a better way to spend an evening than you playing your guitar and me chilling with a pug on my lap. To my brothers and sisters: Jeffrey—Bro, my childhood companion, growing up without you would have been hell and now that we're both adults and we're both still alive, we have so much to be grateful for. You are top of my list. Chynna—Chy, your sense of humor and music inspire me. You are such a great mom and a wonderful sister. Tamerlane—Tam, you're an amazing musician and a brilliant songwriter and I respect the man you've become. Bijou—Bij, don't be mad that you're not first. I did it in birth order. You are the baby after all. From changing your diapers to you changing my life, you mean so much to me I can barely stand it. My siblings—I love you all like a crazy person. My mom, Suzy January, who taught me how to be a lady. Mom—you are my little Shrimpie and I adore you. To my dad—I miss you Pops, and I'll always love you, regardless. Genevieve—you're an original, to say the least, and I love you. Michelle—you've always been a big part of my life and always will be. I love you. Mick Barakan a.k.a. Shane Fontayne—Papa, you helped save my life more than once and you're the best parenting partner I can imagine. You mean more to me than you'll ever know. Maria Villanueva—thank you for all your patience and kindness over the years.

I don't know what I'd do without my friends. They are the sounding board for all my decisions, and the source of most of my laughter: Owen Elliot Kugell—Squeaky, you're the best friend a girl could ask for. Susan Greenberg Minster—Snooz, you always make me laugh. Sue Sinenberg—Sue Sue my Blue Sue, we've been through so much and I'm sure there's more to come. Tom Barwick, Marissa and Connie, Josh, Lisa, Steven, Marion, Billy Baldwin, Danny Masterson and his family, and Jason.

Thank you to Shane's friends, Blaise, Jeff, Eric, Tim, and Jacob, who are also my friends. You loved me when I couldn't love myself and supported Shane through the difficult times. Katie Maria Mudd—now I know what it's like to have a daughter.

While I'm at it, this is an opportunity to thank the people who helped me get my start and guided my career: Patricia McQueeney, George Lucas, Norman Lear, Fred Roos, Patricia Fass Palmer, Alan Rafkin, Alan Horn. To my *One Day at a Time* family: Valerie, Bonnie, and Pat—it's been an amazing journey of love, loss, and redemption. I thank you all for your undying faith in me. It isn't misplaced. And Val, you look awesome in a bikini.

Endless thanks and love to my Mamas and Papas. Scott Mckenzie—you are my evil twin! Denny Doherty and his children, John, Emberly, and Jessica. Denny—you were the best Dutch-uncle a girl could want. I miss you. Spanky MacFarlane—boy, did we have fun. Mama Cass—thank you for your beautiful voice and the gift of your daughter, Owen, in my life.

I can't express enough gratitude to the people who keep the business motor (such as it is) running. Robert T. Tucker—Tuck, you've always been there and for that I'm forever grateful. Geneva Bray, Gwen Pepper, and Tony Martinez at GVA—you are dream agents in a town where that's hard to come by. Blair Berk—my miracle worker lawyer, thank you for keeping me out of jail and everything else. Arlene Dayton—my mother manager, I'll always love you. Dan Frattali—business manager extraordinaire at Frattali & Salem, heaps of gratitude.

Working on this book gave me a purpose when I came out of Narconon, and that purpose was realized by my friend and coauthor, Hilary Liftin. Not only do we work together like a house on fire, but I hope we remain friends long after the publication of this memoir. Hilary, you rock! Lee Allan—the funniest and most endearing friend, father of Max and Fred, and onetime boyfriend—I can't thank you enough for harnessing the vision of this book, putting it in the hands of the right people, and reading with sensitivity and insight, without asking for anything in return. Dan Strone—my amazing book agent at Trident Media Group, for your constant eye for detail and total commitment to helping me share my truth with readers. And for dealing with the *Celebrity Rehab* curveball. Jessica and Shea—for always helping with the important details. Many thanks to Neal Preston—photographer of some of the most important moments of the Phillips family public life, not to mention the greatest rock 'n' roll photographer of all time, and my friend and supporter for thirty years.

To my new and deeply respected colleagues at Simon Spotlight—thank you for recognizing the importance of telling this story in the most authentic way and never flinching at the gory details. Jen Bergstrom—my initial conversation with you gave me the courage to tell my story. Sarah Sper—you edited this book with a deliberate, sensitive touch, and great encouragement. Trish Boczkowski—you took over the reins and shepherded the book through publication with grace and dedication.

Cara Bedick—you never missed a beat in the changing of the guard. And last but not least, Michael Nagin—your involvement and excitement made the jacket come to life.

To the people who helped me get my life back more than once: Jeff Lukas, Cathy & Tom Steiner, Stacy Tregaskiss and everyone at Narconon Louisiana, Novus Medical Detox, LRH, Geraldine Owen Delaney a.k.a. G.O.D., Dr. Drew Pinsky, Bob Forest, Bill Wilson, and Bob Smith, and all my friends and family in recovery—I don't know what I'd do without you.

To Two Bunch Palms Resort and Spa—you are my sanctuary, my favorite place. To Palihouse—where most of this book was written, thanks for the fries and inspiration. To the LAPD—y'all saved my life and set in motion the miracle that is my recovery.

And, of course, love and gratitude to Freddie the Noble Pug, Max the King of All Pugs, and the newest addition to our family, Little Louie the timid Chihuahua, who has yet to reveal his special name.